DOING CHURCH

BUILDING FROM THE BOTTOM UP

By Alexander Venter

D1400733

VINEYARD INTERNATIONAL PUBLISHING
PO Box 53286
Kenilworth, 7745
Cape Town, South Africa
Email: vip@vineyardbi.org

First published 2000, Vineyard International Publishing, Cape Town, South Africa.
Second Impression 2003, Vineyard International Publishing, Cape Town, South Africa.

Cover by Vineyard International Publishing, Ladysmith
Reproduction by Castle Graphics, Cape Town.
Printed and bound by Paarl Print, Cape Town.

ISBN: 0-620-25634-6

FOREWORD

BY BOB FULTON

Have you ever read a book that caused you to say to yourself, 'I need to meditate on these ideas?' I cannot just read this book and put it back on the shelf. This is one of those books that you will refer to often as you attempt to plant or build your Church.

As Alexander acknowledges in his introduction, this book is based on some ideas that John Wimber was wrestling with in the late 1970s. John had been a consultant for Church growth at Fuller Seminary under the tutelage of Drs. Peter Wagner and Donald McGavren. He was introduced to the whole Church: ecumenical and evangelical, Church and parachurch; and to some new theological perspectives, one of which was George Ladd's view of the Kingdom of God. This experience deeply affected his concept of Church. I had known John and ministered with him since 1968 and his ecclesiological thinking definitely coalesced during this time.

Most of us who heard Wimber explicate his thinking about the way Church could be were dramatically impacted. Much of what we did resulted from reflecting on John's ideas on building a Church from the bottom up. Alexander was assigned by John to help him develop a training document called 'Building the Church from the Bottom Up.'

I have known Alexander for twenty years and he has demonstrated Christ-like character, devotion to holy living and is a reflective person. He has a keen mind and articulates his thoughts in a concise fashion.

This book needs to be read by pastors and key leaders in a local Church. It will help you to determine or discover vision, values, priorities and practical principles for developing a Church. The book is written in a style that helps one reflect instead of feeling coerced into thinking in a certain way. I have found Alexander's presentation and writing style very enjoyable.

Alexander wrote this book at my urging, and the result is much more than I anticipated. May you have a wonderful time reading and reflecting under the guidance of the Holy Spirit.

Bob Fulton
International Coordinator
Vineyard Missions and Church Planting

DEDICATION

TO THE MEMORY OF JOHN WIMBER AND THE LEGACY OF HIS LIFE

Embodied in the Association of Vineyard Churches as a gift
from God to all of us.

The following is the tribute that I wrote on the event of John's death.

16 November 1997

To Carol, Chris, Sean, Stephanie and Tim:

Our hearts go out to you at this time, and we are praying for you, as John is no longer with you 'in the flesh', but waiting for all of you at home with the Lord. We are sure that the mixture of sadness and joy is not easy—sadness for the absence of such a dear husband and companion, father and friend; but also joy for his going home into freedom from suffering, into peace and rest, having 'ceased from his labours'. May the God of all comfort be consciously close to you at this time.

We remember John as one who said repeatedly that he 'wanted to die in the saddle'. We salute him as a true disciple and soldier of the Kingdom who went about 'doin' the stuff' till he was 'taken up to glory'. John has been a father and friend to many, many people, but especially to us here in South Africa. We cannot thank God enough for bringing John and Carol across our paths—we were changed forever—with all the pain and joy that it has brought, which has been considerable!

What connected us with you from the beginning—and remained so throughout our journey while John was with us—was his easy, honest, real self, his sometimes embarrassing level of self-disclosure, his open heart and life, his inspiring vision of the Kingdom and the Church, and his passion to advance the Kingdom and plant churches. He would sit and talk and our hearts would 'burn within us', knowing that he was articulating what we all deeply and instinctively believed and felt. We were drawn to his radical commitment to Jesus and 'doin' the stuff'; his preparedness to trust and give ministry away; his heart and songs of worship (perhaps his greatest legacy); John's ability to be soft and show mercy, to repent and say 'I'm sorry'; his incredible generosity; his gentle authority and avoidance of all titles, ego-trips, etc.; his being in touch with his own human weakness; his honest struggles with his body, with his failures, with his sins; and his wise, winsome, bearded smile!

John, we deeply love and respect you and we're going to miss you—but only for a while! You're now doing what you said you would always like to do: to worship and bow down before the throne and cast your crown at His feet and then sit with Jesus (and maybe Paul and others) and pull out your 'back-burner' file and ask all the questions that you courageously and honestly left unanswered till this time—you did not lead us astray and pretend when you did not know, and for this we thank you. But now we envy you because you have the answers, at least some of them—no, in fact, you have the Answer that you have longed and looked for all your life: the heart of the Father and the Son in the fullness of the Spirit. Enjoy Him, John, it's been a long time coming, you're now home!

I will never forget when I had the privilege of working with you for eight months in 1982 in the Wagner house, how that one night you awoke with a physical and spiritual struggle. You thought that you were actually going to die and you went through to the lounge and wept and prayed and waited for Jesus to come and take you home, but it didn't happen—you got a song instead! And we only learnt of that experience the following Sunday when you tearfully sang and taught us the song. It instantly melted my heart and gripped me with such an overwhelming longing for God. This most beautiful and haunting song, with its simple words, captures the profound and pure yearning for God that I will always associate with you and your life and ministry, John Wimber:

NO ONE BUT YOU

No one but You, Oh Lord, no one but You, Oh Lord

There isn't anyone in this world like You

None on earth is there

Not one that could compare

There isn't anyone in this world like You

You are altogether lovely

And You're all I want to see

And when my life is through

I'm coming home to You

That's all I want to do, just come home to You

To Carol, we bless you for your love and support, for hanging in there with this man (which wasn't always easy—by his own admission!), and together with John, for being to us all an inspiration of worship, raw hunger for God and His purposes, and persistent intercession and ministry. We love and respect you and pray for your well-being as you face the immediate future. May the Father give you courage and strength as you journey on with your family, especially with your son Chris. And Chris, we continue to hold you and your family up to the nail-pierced hands of Jesus, trusting Him for His mercy, for His touch, for His plan for your life.

God be with you all. We honour you because we are not unmindful of the costly bittersweet price you have all had to pay for the path you've taken with John, the path that we too have chosen with you all.

With love and great appreciation,

Alexander and Gill Venter.

(on behalf of the team of pastors and Churches in the Gauteng Association of Vineyard Churches, South Africa)

POSTSCRIPT: Chris Wimber went to be with the Lord just short of three months after John's death.

THANKS AND ACKNOWLEDGEMENTS

To Carol Wimber, Penny and Bob Fulton,
for their invaluable input and endorsement.

To Gill, Zander and Misha-Joy,
for their understanding family support.

To the Gosling and Johnson families,
for so generously empowering my life and ministry.

To Costa Mitchell,
for his leadership and encouragement.

To Valley Vineyard, the leadership and the people,
for their prayers, love and support.

To the Vineyard International Publishing team—all of them—
for their encouragement, help and hard work.

To Sean Wimber,
for his permission and endorsement—all references and quotes
attributed to John Wimber, whether direct or indirect, are
done under licence to 'Doin-the-stuff'.
The website: doin-the-stuff.com and the
email: info@doin-the-stuff.com

CONTENTS

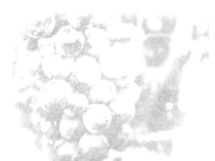

CHAPTER 1

INTRODUCTION AND
BACKGROUND STORY

Despite the impression that may be created by the dedication, this is not a book about John Wimber per se—yet another book about him would embarrass him. Carol Wimber has recently written the story of John's life 'The Way It Was' (see appendix 4). This is a book about a way of doing Church, the philosophy of ministry, which is associated with the Vineyard Churches. More particularly, it is a book about the roots, the ethos and thinking of the Vineyard, especially in the early days of its formation— between 1977 and 1983. Obviously John is intrinsically involved as the founder-leader of the Vineyard, and I will refer to him often.

The purpose of this book

My purpose is to record the understanding and approach to Church life that has made us who we are in the Association of Vineyard Churches. In doing so I will refer to some of the stories—it is crucial that we get a feel for the context, the happenings and the reasons behind the concepts and practice of Church life that we have come to call 'The Vineyard Philosophy of Ministry'.

The main source for this book is a document that I wrote in consultation with John when I worked with him for eight months in 1982. The document is called 'Building from the bottom up'. It systematically reflects John's philosophy of ministry. I shall not draw on other sources as such, except for some of the Vineyard resources listed in Appendix 4. Furthermore, I will not have foot- or endnotes—explanations will be in the text; and I will use inclusive language where grammar permits. So my intention is to relate as accurately as I can the basics of what John stood for—at least in the crucial formative years—and I have no reason to believe that he ever turned from any significant aspect of them. However, I must add that I take full responsibility for what I have written in this book. I have taken every care not to misrepresent John in any way. But obviously he has not seen this book to be able to comment on it or endorse it. Therefore, this is *my* understanding and written record of The Vineyard Philosophy of Ministry.

Who should read this book?

There are three categories of people that I have in mind as I write. Firstly, I am writing for all who are interested in and would like to learn about how people do Church, and in so doing, may learn something of the Vineyard history and approach to Church life. Secondly, friends of the Vineyard and others who are interested in our particular philosophy of ministry will hopefully derive real benefit from these pages. Primarily however, I am writing as a Vineyard pastor to the Vineyard family, both to its pastors, leaders and to our people. My prayer is that God will use this reflection on our roots to instruct, inspire and affirm us, and to help clarify the way forward in the post-John era. It can be used as reading and study material for leadership, for the average Vineyard member and for new people coming into the Vineyard—even as part of a membership course. It is also being included as a course in the Vineyard Bible Institute.

John used to say, 'When I'm gone, take the best and go.' This is my attempt, with the help of Carol Wimber, Bob Fulton and a few others, to put on record some of what we believe to have been 'the best'. The 'going' is what we, as the new generation of leaders, will do with it. We should certainly not cling ideologically to this philosophy of ministry as the be-all and end-all of everything. Rather, we should be so immersed in the spirit of 'the best' that we can confidently and creatively contextualize and develop it into relevant and workable ways of doing Church for this and the next generation, and for every new culture in which we plant Vineyards. We want responsible growth, not a clinging to the past.

An overview of the book

In this first chapter I give the brief background story, both of my own connection with the Vineyard, and of the development of the Vineyard Churches. The second chapter looks at what we mean by a philosophy of ministry. Chapter three begins to develop the Vineyard philosophy of ministry by examining the concepts involved in 'building from the bottom up'. In the remaining chapters we spell out, step by step, what it means to 'build from the bottom up'.

- Firstly, we have to decide on and define *the purpose* of the Church— the blueprint of the building (chapter 4).

- Then we clarify *the values* that undergird and determine all that the Church becomes and does—the foundation of the building (chapter 5).

- The next step is to establish *the priorities* in the life and ministry of the Church—the pillars around which everything else is built (chapter 6).

- What makes the building workable, like windows, doors, etc., are *the practices* that must be modelled and transferred to every believer in the Church (chapter 7).

- Knowing how to choose *the personnel*—both workers and leaders—is crucial in order to 'staff' the building (chapter 8).

- The logical conclusion is how to make the building fully functional in all its various departments—that is, implementing *the programmes* (chapter 9).

We conclude with a chapter that summarises the Vineyard approach to doing Church—the type of Church that John said he would like to join. In later years he reinterpreted this in terms of 'The Vineyard genetic code', which I have detailed in Appendix 1.

It is an enormous privilege to write this book. But why me? Let me explain.

CONNECTING WITH THE VINEYARD

Lonnie Frisbee

It began when I received a phone call from a colleague of mine. It was 1979 in Cape Town. I was pastoring an Assembly of God Church in Constantia. Derek Morphew said, 'I've got this guy from the States, Lonnie Frisbee. He will be coming to the pastors' meeting this morning and is free to speak at your Church at a mid-week meeting. I really recommend him. How about it?' (As pastors, how often are our lives and our Churches changed by such a phone call or such an invitation?) I had never heard of this man but I trusted Derek, so I cautiously agreed and hastily 'created' a mid-week meeting, inviting those whom I could—a smallish group turned up.

Lonnie was different. It was not only that he was a hippie from California, which was bad enough, but also that he had a radical sense of freedom that traumatized our religious culture. The pastor-part of me said, 'Oh God, Oh God ... what have I let myself and the Church into?' But another part of me, the non-religious me, felt a naughty sense of excitement! Lonnie spoke of our grieving the Holy Spirit, how we had neglected Him, and then he told us of what the Spirit would do if we repented, honoured and received Him fully as the One sent to us from the Father and the Son. He also spoke of his respect for his pastor, a certain John Wimber, who had dared to let God be God by taking his hands off and allowing the Holy Spirit to freely do what He does best. I could see where this was going and felt the eyes of some of the more daring members of my congregation on me. Being a good Pentecostal minister I prayed in tongues rather furiously under my breath as a precautionary measure—to reassure myself that I was still in control, I guess!

Praying to the Spirit

Then Lonnie prayed to the Holy Spirit, and my theological brain reacted, 'Where is this in the Word, brother?' He confessed the Church's sin of neg-lect and asked for mercy and forgiveness. Then he prayed, 'Come Holy Spirit.' All heaven broke loose! First slowly, then in growing waves of tears and tremblings, of joy and laughter, people began to move, shake and fall under the presence and power of the Spirit. As Lonnie verbally pointed out and identified people upon whom the Spirit rested there would be an immediate intensification of the power encounter. He said specific things to certain people that they and I knew could only have come from God. These 'words' had visible impact—some collapsed, others convulsed with weeping, others screamed. It was like being plugged into the electrical mains for some people. The place looked like a battlefield with bodies in every conceivable position—standing, sitting, draped over chairs, lying, leaning, bending, crawling, curled up. It was a holy mess!

As I watched, my tongues-speaking ceased and my, 'Oh God, Oh God ...' drowned in a complete meltdown of my own heart. I wept as I saw people that I knew very well, being touched and transformed by the Spirit of God. I knew this was God. What struck me was the total absence of hype, manipulation and religious jargon or atmosphere. It was raw, real and profoundly holy. In fact, it was fearfully beautiful, something my eyes had never seen before. I remember thinking that the only other thing I could compare this with was witnessing the physical birth of my own child—not that that had happened yet, but it had always been something that I had dreamt about as being one of the most awesome experiences this side of heaven.

This episode caused tension—talk about new wine and old wineskins! The fruit of changed lives far outweighed the concern of some. Personally, it set me on a course of opening up the Church to the renewal work of the Holy Spirit, and of wanting to find out more about the Church Lonnie was part of and how they allowed the Holy Spirit to run things.

John Wimber

Later, I was transferred to Johannesburg and through a friendship with Dave Owen, the pastor of the 'Invisible Church', I was brought into direct contact with John and Carol Wimber. They came to South Africa in 1981 on their second international ministry trip—they had come the year before at Dave Owen's invitation—with a team of 30 young people. We hosted the morning Pastors' Conference at the Northcliff Assembly of God, while the evening celebration-type meetings were held at a large conference centre. A few months later I travelled to California for a brief visit to John's Church—meeting at that time in Canyon High School, Yorba Linda.

I will never forget the first meeting I was in with John Wimber. It was the first morning of the Pastor's Conference in Johannesburg. When it was time to begin, John strolled up to the piano, sat down, and gently began to play and sing 'J-e-e-s-u-s what a wonder you are, you are so gentle, so pure and so kind ...' Slowly we all joined in, but I quickly found myself overcome by the simplicity of the words, the warmth, gentleness and intimacy of the experience, and I began to feel all tender and tearful. I held my emotions in check and looked around, only to see some of the US team on their knees, others standing with hands raised, others with tears streaming down their cheeks—that did it for me! Something in me broke, and I began to cry. Some deep part of me that I did not know or understand gave way. I found myself kneeling and weeping and worshipping. The songs, the worship, drew such longing, such love, and such desire for God from within me that I thought I would explode. Never before had I experienced the pleasure of God with such depth and intensity. It struck me that this must be the most natural way to worship—there was neither hype nor manipulation; just simple, honest, passionate adoration. It was profoundly healing.

Then John stood up and casually opened his Bible and began to talk to the pastors about the Kingdom of God. Again, there was no preacher's tone or loud voice, no religious jargon or sermonising; just an honesty, openness and clarity that was completely disarming. It just made such Biblical sense, it sounded so sane, so real to life, that I wondered why I had not seen it before! In the process we all got to know much more about John—his frankness and self-disclosure was unnerving, but very freeing.

Then he stopped and did the same as Lonnie had done: 'Come Holy Spirit!' Things began to happen all over in the meeting. The difference this time was that the ministry was not focused through one person, but all the Americans moved around and ministered to the pastors who were being touched by the Spirit. I was in awe when I overheard Debbie (she was a member of the American team and could not have been more than 20 years old) saying very detailed things to one of my elders in regard to his marriage. And all she said was true—he just collapsed in a heap crying out to God for mercy and help. I saw genuine power encounters time and time again around these people. But what was so compelling was the compassion and sensitivity with which they ministered to people. Their model of ministry was so accessible to me, to my people, to every ordinary believer in Jesus. We quickly joined in and were coached into the joyful adventure of being partners with God in Holy Spirit ministry.

The journey into Vineyard belonging

These experiences and other exposure made it clear to me, and other colleagues of mine, like Costa Mitchell and Derek Morphew, that John and Carol were doing Church in a way that embodied what we had been looking for. Not only that, but we also found that John seemed to continually articulate what we instinctively felt and believed—about Church, leadership, ministry, missions, etc. It was uncanny, exhilarating, affirming.

The question logically arose: what is God doing with this? How do I join up? John's reply was classic—only later did I understand the full implications—'You don't join Vineyard, you find out that you are Vineyard.' Who you really are and what is home for you is discovered in the relational mirror of like-minded people who share common values and are called to do similar things in the Kingdom together. This bonding is identified at the level of vision and values, but it is far deeper. It is profoundly spiritual and relational—as Paul says, God places people in His Body where it pleases Him (1Cor 12:18). The issue is the difference between family and friends, but more of this later. Finding your real home can take a long or short time, it can be painful or easy. For me it was a bit of both. It depends on your own inner journey, on what God is doing with you and your response to Him. However, I knew I was home.

The Assembly of God asked me if I did not want to be released with their blessing because they saw what was happening in me. I accepted this grace on their part as an act of God's leading. John then invited me to go to

California (early 1982) to work with him for an eight-month period. The idea was to be exposed to the model of Church life and ministry, to learn from John and then to come back with him and a large team to plant a Vineyard in Johannesburg. This would be the first international Church plant.

The Vineyard plant in South Africa

Dave and Costa had already started the core group and prepared for the invasion. It was great—a team of 72 came from various Vineyards in California, each person taking their vacation and paying their own way. They did street evangelism and big meetings with many conversions, healings and power-encounters. After two weeks we baptised 65 new believers and started a number of small groups. Together with the rather large core group, we were left with a sizeable baby!

As an aside, it was unfortunate that the tremendous potential of this large ministry team doing an international Church plant was not fully developed. The sending Churches were greatly impacted with new energy, vision and joy by the returning teams. Individuals were forever changed by the experience. The new Church started the right way—mostly with new believers. I remember when John phoned Dave after God clearly spoke to him to go and plant a Vineyard in Johannesburg. But this decision to plant was later questioned by John and his team due to certain difficulties that arose in the Vineyard in South Africa and because of the sensitivities with other denominations around the issue of Vineyard plants. John said from the beginning that the Vineyard had a twofold calling: to bring renewal to the broader Church and to plant Vineyard Churches. So as not to allow the latter to benefit from the former—to keep integrity with the broader Church—John exclusively pursued international renewal conferences for the benefit of the broader Body of Christ throughout the 1980s and refrained from planting Vineyards in certain countries. God will and has begun to honour John's obedience and respect for the broader Church, but strategically speaking we lost something valuable by not making the South African type plant our regular practice. And with reference to the difficulties in the South African Vineyard, the investment has more than begun to pay off—for us, for Africa and further afield.

However, I need to return to the story behind the writing of this book. While I worked with John he used me and one or two other researchers to prepare materials for the Fuller Seminary courses which he presented (e.g. 'Signs and Wonders and Church Growth', MC510) and for teaching various Vineyard seminars (e.g. the Healing Tape Series—four volumes). The last project that I researched and wrote with and for John, before I returned to South Africa, was 'Building the Church from the bottom up', a forty-five typed page document which systematically articulated for the first time the Vineyard philosophy of ministry. As far as I know John taught it once and then certain sections were converted into the present 'Five Year Plan' course. Ever since John's death I have felt an inclination to rewrite the original document in book form. As a result of a more recent quickening from the Lord (February 1999), and the enthusiastic endorsement from Bob Fulton, I began to put fingers to keyboard.

SUMMARISING THE VINEYARD STORY

My intention here is to give only a sketchy overview of the Vineyard story, especially of the early development (a comprehensive history of the Vineyard is now available—see appendix 4). This will give a context for the Vineyard approach to doing Church, and secondly, it will give a picture of the Vineyard to those who have not heard it before—albeit a very brief one. Many seeds that took root and have made us who we are today, were planted in John and Carol's early experiences of Church and the subsequent development of the Vineyard.

Salvation and early experiences (1962 to 1974)

John and Carol were already married and had three children when they both came to faith in Jesus in a home Bible study group in 1962. John had been a successful professional jazz musician and songwriter for many years. The idea of Christianity had not appealed to him much, but through a series of personal and marriage struggles they were brought into contact with a Church in Anaheim, Southern California. John tells the story of his conversion and experience of Church as only he can tell it in an unforgettable talk entitled 'A Fool for Jesus' (see appendix 4).

John saw Church through the eyes of a raw unbeliever. A deacon asked him, when he first came to Church, 'Are you washed in the blood of the Lamb, brother?' and John recoiled with disgust, 'Oh no, do you really do that here?' He wondered why the voice of 'the guy' who met him at the door changed when he got behind the wooden box up front in the Church. Even more perplexing was the further change of language and tone of voice when 'the guy' prayed. John couldn't relate to it—it was all so religious. This has deeply influenced the way Vineyard avoids religious talk, dress and behaviour, and places high value on honesty, reality, being relevant to where people are at and accepting them for who they are.

The music and the songs really switched him off—after all, he was a songwriter and musician of note! It was all so sad and slow and discordant. When a woman got up to 'give her voice to God' through 'rendering an item in song' John thought he saw God waving His hands in protest: 'Oh no, Oh no, don't give it to Me!' With his background in music and songwriting John was uniquely equipped to pioneer a style of worship that is now synonymous with Vineyard—music and worship that is alive, contemporary, personal, fresh, warm, intimate.

Understanding 'the deal' of the gospel

What really got hold of John, when he understood the gospel of Jesus Christ, was 'the deal' that was being offered him: Jesus gave up His all in taking John's messed-up life on Himself. He offered John His life of adventure, healing the sick, casting our demons and raising the dead. All John had to do was to give up his life and live Jesus' life 'doin' the stuff'. John knew himself and his life—he was sick to death with it—so he had no hesitation. What a deal! He signed up. But he quickly found that in the eyes of his friends he was a fool. His constant refrain became, 'I'm a fool for

Jesus, but whose fool are you?'

This revelation of the Kingdom of God, of this man Jesus, and His invitation to us to 'do the stuff' with Him, was what John lived and died for. Soon after his conversion John read the gospels and then came to Church asking 'When do we get to do the stuff?'

'What stuff?'

'You know, the stuff in this Book—healing the sick, driving out devils, feeding the poor, helping the broken-hearted, raising the dead and all that.'

'Well, we don't really ... you know ...'

John was indignant, 'You're trying to tell me that I gave up my life and signed up just to do this Church thing every Sunday. The deal was that I could get to do the stuff—when do I get to do it?'

'Doin' the stuff' of the Kingdom

John did get to do the stuff of the Kingdom, but initially not in the way he expected. Sean, their three-year-old son, was one day in 1964 stung by a swarm of bees. Despite the extreme emergency, John and Carol laid hands on him and prayed and prayed for God to heal Sean. John found himself praying so fervently that he was speaking in what sounded like a Chinese language he had never heard or learnt before! A miraculous healing took place before their very eyes. This was one of a number of supernatural Spirit-phenomena that happened in their early years. They did not really understand much of it and Carol and the local elders discouraged John from going any further with any of it. But God had in mind that the Vineyard would receive this heritage of 'doin' the stuff'—the words, works and wonders of the Kingdom of God—and it has become part of the heart of what the Vineyard is all about.

The natural outflow of John's experience of salvation and vision of the Kingdom was a lifestyle of evangelism. John was so excited with 'the deal' he had bought into that he could not keep quiet. In fact, he had a passion to bring people into the Kingdom, to 'win the lost at any cost', as he used to say. He and Carol led several hundred people to Christ and discipled them in the basics of the faith between 1963 and 1970.

He became a leader, assistant pastor and eventually the co-pastor of the Society of Friends (the Quaker Church) in Yorba Linda, Anaheim. It was not long before he found himself becoming tied up in the institutionalism of the Church. Although the Church grew and was successful, John lost relational contact with unbelievers, personal evangelism dried up, his ministry became cold and professional and he recognised a growing disillusionment within himself. As a way of dealing with his problems John resigned the pastorate in 1974 and accepted a position as director in the Department of Church Growth at the Charles E. Fuller Institute of Evangelism and Church Growth at Fuller Seminary, Pasadena. However, the Wimber family did continue as members of the Friends Church.

Church Growth, disillusionment and new beginnings (1974 to 1977)

Over a four year period he travelled across the USA from corner to corner, working with over 2000 different Churches representing twenty-seven different denominations, consulting with pastors and Church Boards, researching, teaching, doing conferences, etc. John was privileged to get a unique overview and a reasonably accurate analysis of where the Church in America was at—and what he saw did not help him! However, the experience gained in these years was absolutely invaluable in the formation of the Vineyard.

Ironically, during these years John's disillusionment deepened. He kept crying out, 'Oh God, what's wrong with me?' He was at his lowest—angry, frustrated and desperate—when God spoke to him one night in a hotel room in Detroit: 'John, I've seen your ministry, and now I'm going to show you mine.' This gave him hope and soon afterwards he sensed the Lord telling him to go home and pastor the group that had formed there a year before. God used Peter Wagner, and a few others who did not know John, to say to him, 'Go home and plant a Church in Yorba Linda.'

Carol had come into a charismatic experience of the Spirit with speaking in other tongues—much to John's conservative evangelical consternation! It led her into deep repentance in regard to her attitude and beliefs about the Holy Spirit and His gifts, and she sought restitution with people who had been hurt. It also led her to believe God was doing something beyond their local Church experience. Carol and some others joined a home group in August 1976 which Bob Fulton had started. When they gathered they just sang in worship, read Scripture and prayed. Many broken and disillusioned people came. They would regularly dissolve in tears and cry out for mercy as they sang love songs to Jesus. There was a deep experience of confession and repentance. Slowly they got healed up. By this time most of them were seeing the group as their Church. The Friends Church asked the group to leave the denomination, but not without first giving them their full blessing (in response to the group's request). Carol has often spoken of the Vineyard being born out of a raw and desperate hunger for God in worship—the Father's presence being the most authentic and original place of repentance and healing. She also speaks of the 'Quaker heritage' in the Vineyard because of the blessing they received.

The group grows into a viable Church

John managed to avoid this group for a while, but they all knew that God had appointed him as their leader/pastor. They were praying for him to see the light! When John first saw the group of about fifty people, he felt quite disdainful, saying, 'This group will go nowhere, it has no leader.' But deep in his heart he knew God had called him to lead it. As was so characteristic of John, he repented and humbled himself, and then he too sat and worshipped and wept and got healed up.

By mid 1977 the group was a growing viable Church—with a pastor! They had their first formal Church service, where John preached his first official sermon to his flock, on Mother's day, 8 May 1977. They called the Church Calvary Chapel, Yorba Linda—John linked up with Chuck Smith's Calvary Chapel movement believing it to be a contemporary and relevant evangelical movement he could work with. Drawing on his experience in Church

Growth and relying on the Holy Spirit, John set about forming a Church that he believed in. He sought to create a worshipful, relational, healing, training and evangelising environment. He modelled and led worship, small groups were started, and he taught through Luke's gospel with a view to training the Church in the healing ministry. For months they prayed for the sick without anyone getting healed. Instead, those who did the praying seemed to get sick! However, through the perseverance of faith, eventually the breakthrough came and people began to be healed as they ministered to the sick and needy. John said, 'We got one!' His initial practice of doing most of the prayer-ministry himself changed one Sunday night when he decided to anoint the people with oil to do the ministry. This was a crucial step for the future Vineyard model of ministry—'equipping the saints' to do the ministry of the Spirit.

Pastoring an exploding Church (1979 to 1983)

At this time, after a particular Sunday morning service, God clearly spoke to John about a certain young man who was walking out of the meeting ahead of him. 'Ask him to give his testimony tonight.' Although John had not met him, he had heard of how God had used him in the revival among the hippies, the 'Jesus People', on the beaches of Southern California. It was Lonnie Frisbee. And it was Mother's day, 1980. John had also heard that Lonnie was rather unpredictable. Nevertheless, he obeyed God and invited Lonnie to speak, but he was not prepared for what God had in store for them! After Lonnie spoke, he asked the Holy Spirit for forgiveness for the way the Church had grieved Him, and then he said, 'Come Holy Spirit.' And He came!

There was an outpouring of power that none of them had ever witnessed or experienced before. All sorts of spiritual phenomena took place, weeping, wailing, shaking, falling, speaking in tongues, etc. It was a controversial happening that deeply disturbed John and certain staff and Church members. He did not sleep that night! But early the next morning God super-naturally confirmed, through a friend of John's, that it was His doing. From examining the Scriptures and evaluating the good fruit that emerged, John endorsed it as a mighty work of God. It had been like a second Pentecost. This raises the issue of identity—John was clear in his mind and in the subsequent development of the Vineyard that we are not Pentecostals or Charismatics. We are Evangelicals, but of a different sort! Peter Wagner called it 'Third Wave', meaning evangelical in doctrine but pentecostal and charismatic in practice—albeit with a different style or ethos in the way things are done (see Power Encounters, appendix 4).

The young people were so energised by this event that they roved around the neighbourhood, almost daily, like packs of wolves wreaking havoc in the Kingdom of Darkness. They would knock on doors and ask if there were any sick people in the home and then pray for them and lead them to Christ. They did the same in the streets, on school campuses and in the shopping malls. About 1 700 people were converted and 700 of them were baptised in water over a period of about a year. Power encounters and spiritual phenomena continued to happen in the Church meetings—John found reassurance and instruction from similar happenings in meetings held by John Wesley, Charles Finney, George Whitefield and Jonathan Edwards. This story is described in Power Evangelism, pp. 36-38.

Vineyard becomes a movement

By this time a number of pastors had gathered around John wanting to learn about doing Church in a similar way. They had become good friends during the previous few years, and unbeknown to them, they formed the foundation of the Vineyard movement. God used John to give leadership to this growing group of pastors—they began to buy into John's vision and values of Church life. One of them, Ken Gulliksen, was pastoring a Church in West Los Angeles, Hollywood, which he had started in 1975. God had shown him, from Isaiah 27:3, that he should call it 'The Vineyard' and that it would include many other Churches and Church plants. In fact Ken had planted five Vineyards from the one that he was pastoring by the time it became clear that God had destined John to be the overall leader—as Bob Fulton says, 'Ken gave the name, but John gave the game.'

At the same time, the direction that John and the Church were going in caused increasing tension for Chuck Smith and the Calvary Chapel movement (their theological framework and practice was closer to evangelical dispensationalism—John had moved from this to a Kingdom paradigm). Chuck agreed to release John with his blessing, so that John could lead the Church and the group of pastors in the way he believed God had shown him. Thus the Church changed its name in May 1982 to the Vineyard Christian Fellowship, Yorba Linda. Most of the pastors associated with John then changed the name of their Churches to Vineyard Christian Fellowship. This was born out of a conviction from the Lord that they were committed to one another as family, and called to work together in the advancement of the Kingdom of God. As they say, the rest is history!

But the picture would not be complete without some comments on the further development of the Vineyard as a family of Churches.

The development of the Vineyard Christian Fellowship (1984 to 1999)

It needs to be stated that there was no predetermined or coordinated plan to plant new Churches and grow the movement (despite the one-off South African venture). In fact, during the first few years there was much uncertainty and debate around the question of whether the Vineyard should become a fully-fledged movement, or more honestly speaking, a new denomination. The infernal debate over a constitution was part of it and threatened to derail all the relationships—true to form! The question was finally settled in 1988 by intentionally acknowledging that Vineyard had become a 'denomination', but in the sense of a structured movement without an overarching and detailed constitution!

The guiding idea was to leave it all with God, to be relational, to be open and vulnerable, but to have a clear commitment to one another as family by carrying the common name 'Vineyard Christian Fellowship'. The name would embody a certain way of doing Church expressed in a shared vision and common values. The 'power' Vineyard has over pastors and Churches is twofold. Firstly, in real terms, the quality of the relationship with those concerned will determine the level of influence and the responding submission. Secondly, if that breaks down, as a last resort, the use of the Vineyard name can be withdrawn. Even then, the only recourse both parties have is to go to the Body of Christ for arbitration as Paul instructed in 1Cor 6:1-8—and no legal proceedings!

However, most of the expansion was spontaneous and Spirit-directed—although John did have a calling and vision which he had carried in his heart for many years. He often spoke of a map of North America that he had seen in his mind's eye. It had a dark background with strong shining lights representing all the main cities, especially up and down both the West and East Coasts of America. The lesser cities had lesser lights. There was a complementing vision that John had, of a ballistic-type-missile going from the US and exploding in the United Kingdom with the 'fallout' going all over Europe and by implication around the globe. John believed these visions referred to planting Vineyards in the cities of the USA and doing renewal ministry in Europe and beyond. But as time went on John believed that the end result would be Vineyard plants in all the major English-speaking cities of the world. He said God had given him faith for ten thousand Churches—the first thousand would be 'the hard work' and then the rest would flow from that. What is of interest is that John did not really anticipate the extent to which Vineyards would be and are being planted into other cultures.

Renewal and Church planting

Back to the story. In the early 1980s many new Vineyards were planted, primarily in the USA. Those were heady days. Young people with relatively little training went out and saw God do great things through evangelism, signs and wonders, and Church planting. But there was also real warfare. I remember when John stood up in Church and announced the death of Keith Green together with the Smalley family who had been sent out to help in a Vineyard Church plant. They interrupted their journey to visit with the Green family for a weekend and were killed when Keith took them up for a flight in his light airplane. I can still hear John saying, 'This is real war ... we've lost some of our best soldiers ...' as he was overcome with emotion. There were similarly inexplicable things that happened to others who were pioneering. Yet the call to plant Churches went ahead in the USA almost unrestricted. They have grown to just on 500 at the time of writing.

The calling to help bring renewal to the broader Church was pursued in the USA, and then increasingly overseas, through conferences and translocal ministry teams. There were many, many requests for the Vineyard to come and share what God had given them, especially in terms of worship e.g. 'Why We Worship' conferences and ministry in the power of the Spirit e.g. 'Equipping the Saints' conferences. There were other themes and types of events, both small and large, led by John and many other pastors and teams from different Vineyards around the world. I know here in South Africa we have been very busy ministering in other Churches, many times having to turn down requests because we could hardly attend to our own vineyard! Although it was exceptionally prominent in the '80s and early '90s, this renewal ministry continues strongly to this day.

There was a shift at the beginning of the '90s from renewal to Church planting, especially outside America. During the '80s John had honoured a 'gentleman's agreement' that he had entered into with a number of Church leaders, informally represented by David Watson (largely mainline Churches who were receiving renewal ministry in various nations). John had agreed that he would not plant Vineyards in these Western countries for a number of years while renewal conferences were impacting the Churches. As I stated earlier, it was to keep integrity with the broader Church and not draw away members into new Vineyard plants, but from 1990 a new wave of Vineyard plants began. In 1989 there were 22 Vineyards in 3 countries. To date there are just over 1,200 Vineyards in 60 countries, in addition to the USA. It is interesting to note that according to Bob Fulton, the International Co-ordinator, 88% of these Churches are plants with only 12% being 'adoptions' into the Vineyard (I will discuss adoptions in the next chapter).

Structural developments

In terms of the structural development, John was very sensitive to American imperialism. Within the USA, a National Board with a National

Director was created in order to lead the USA Association of Vineyard Churches (AVC). John Wimber became the International Director and Bob Fulton the International Co-ordinator. Outside the USA, John recognised and released each new national AVC with a clear national leader, into a viable Vineyard population (the guideline is about twenty Vineyard Churches) as the particular nation grew. They then constitute their own National Board with the leader becoming the National Director—there are presently eight autonomous national AVC's. Once a year all the National Directors meet in a structure called Vineyard International Consortium (VIC). This is not a governmental body per se, but rather a fellowship of national leaders, for mutual accountability, sharing what God is doing and together discerning the way forward.

Since John's death, Bob and the VIC team recognise and release new national AVC's. It was agreed that John would not be replaced as International Director—he had put things in place so that business should continue as usual after his death, which is precisely what has happened. Since John's death, four new national AVC's have been recognised and released and Vineyard plants have penetrated fifteen new countries.

Some final reflections

This brief sketch of the Vineyard would be incomplete if we did not mention the fact that things have been far from perfect. In the midst of all the growth, there have been problems, mistakes, broken relationships, pain, controversy, and different periods with different stresses. In the mid-'80s God disciplined the Vineyard in Anaheim in a number of ways and John preached on repentance and the sins of the Church for an extended period. This was a difficult time—some people could not handle it and left. The period of the prophetic ministries that came into the Vineyard—the late '80s—produced a mixed bag of reactions. Many benefited from the input while others left the movement. John's correction and adjustment of 'the prophetic' came too late for some. The early to mid-'90s, with the start of the so-called Toronto Blessing, also resulted in a mixed blessing. This fresh wave of renewal swept through the Churches—Vineyard and many others—but also led to controversy as to how to pastor it and what to make of it (theologically, that is!). Again, John took a pastoral stance that secured some but upset others. There was enormous blessing, definitely some 'casualties', as well as strong reaction from a number of conservative evangelical groupings (see appendix 4 with a list of articles, apologetic in nature, responding to a number of issues for which John and the Vineyard were criticised).

Although John and the leaders with him sought to do their best, they would be the first to admit that the values that formed Vineyard were not always upheld and implemented. John was not always an easy man to work with, but he was honest, able to repent, and in touch with his own weaknesses. 'I'm just a fat man on my way to heaven,' he would say, but at other times he said, 'I'm an angry man trying to get to heaven.' He was often dismayed at his own depth of sinfulness and brokenness. His closest friends report that if John could have his time over again there would be things he would change and do differently. But on the whole, and without doubt, he would pursue the same life-mission of seeking to advance the Kingdom of God to the ends of the earth. The post-John era will see to what extent the Vineyard fulfils this mission—which is still the mandate for the whole Church according to Jesus' Great Commission (Matt 28:18-20).

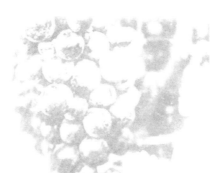

CHAPTER 2

PHILOSOPHY OF MINISTRY

This chapter looks at the background to John's meaning and usage of the phrase 'philosophy of ministry' and especially its early development in the late 1970s and early 1980s. The theological assumptions underlying John's philosophy of ministry will also be discussed. These have to do with the Church, in its nature and purpose, being understood in terms of the Kingdom of God—which was at the heart of John's thinking and practice of Church life in the Vineyard. Some of the implications will be spelt out, leading to an understanding of what John called Vineyard 'family' as opposed to 'friends' of the Vineyard, and the difference between adoptions and Church plants.

We will also examine three sociological models of community that John applied to Church life. Over the years it has been an effective way of communicating how Vineyard seeks to 'do Church'. Lastly, we will apply these models to the issue of Church membership and commitment.

BACKGROUND AND MEANING

For some of the time while John worked as a Church Growth consultant, he had an assistant by the name of Jack Sims. Jack was trained in sociology and market research. Together with John's theological and Church Growth training, John and Jack worked out concepts and language to explain how John conceived of doing Church.

Repackaging Church for Baby-Boomers

One of the factors that strongly influenced this development was John's commitment to be relevant and contemporary by building a Church for the Baby-Boomers (the 'postwar generation'—those born between 1945 and 1965). The boomers grew up in the shadow of post-Second World War life. They rejected authoritarian leadership and formalism—often seeing it as hypocritical and plastic. They sought meaning and would not just accept everything as truth. They wanted reality and not pretence, and they experimented with new music forms and ways of living (e.g. rock music and the hippie movement). So the language, dress, style of music and ethos had to be in touch with where the boomers were, while at the same time not in any way compromising the integrity of the gospel. It was the age-old challenge of repackaging Church for a new generation without losing any of the God-given non-negotiables.

Through his experience as a Church Growth consultant, John came up with about fourteen models that described the Churches he had seen in the USA. None of them really satisfied him, so he developed a model that he could believe in and give his life to. He called it 'The Church for the unchurched'. I remember meeting Jack Sims when I visited Yorba Linda in 1981. He spoke of a pamphlet that he and John had in mind. It would have all sorts of happy smiling faces in a circle on the front page, with a question in the middle, 'Why are these people so happy?' On turning the cover-page the answer would be: 'Because they are going to heaven without having to go to Church!' So many people have found Church to be boring, out of touch, unrealistic and irrelevant. If they got involved, they seemed to get messed up! The idea was to aim the pamphlet at these people—the non-believers, the irreligious, the fearful, the hurting, the disillusioned—and create an environment that they could relate to and be at home in.

The language of 'philosophy of ministry'

This is where the language of 'philosophy of ministry', with its categories of purpose, values, priorities, practices, personnel and programme, came from. It is language from sociology, and expresses the way a group of people or a community organises itself: the values, the dynamics and the structures that determine their common life and experience. Applied to the Church it basically means an approach to ministry, the way of doing Church. The above-mentioned categories systematically develop and clarify the various aspects of the philosophy of ministry—the subject of the following chapters.

Whatever one's philosophy of ministry, hopefully it is well worked out. Whether one is conscious of it or not, every pastor and every Church has a philosophy of ministry—for better or for worse, either intentional or unintentional, either inherited or newly grown, either static or dynamic, either thought-through or not. If one is in any Church for any meaningful length of time one will pick up the approach to Church life and ministry. Often it is stated in point form on the 'welcome brochure.' But do not be deceived! What is stated is not always what is experienced. Often, what you first see is not what is really going on. It is not what people say, it is what they live that tells you who they are. The same applies to Church.

What are the assumptions behind a particular philosophy of ministry? Some people have stumbled over this use of sociological language because it is not theological. John was careful to always clarify the underlying assumptions when he consciously used language, concepts, tools or categories from other disciplines. He would put his own (Biblical) meaning into words or concepts that were in common usage. In other words, because of his 'philosophy', to be relevant he sought to use words in current usage, but was careful that they communicated what he intended to communicate—in terms of God's truth.

The Early Church did the same—think of *ekklesia*, the common Greek word for the gathered people in any town or city who exercised governmental powers for the well-being of the city. The early believers took that word to describe the Christians: the ones called out by Jesus to gather in His name for the purpose of exercising His governmental powers for the well-being of the city. Just think of it! That is what they understood by 'Church', the common English word translated from the Greek *ekklesia*. That was not the only 'secular' word that they used and reinterpreted in order to communicate the gospel more effectively in their world (for example, see Leon Morris, The Apostolic Preaching of the Cross).

What were John's underlying theological assumptions that gave content to his philosophy of ministry, that determined his concept and practice of Church?

 # UNDERLYING THEOLOGICAL ASSUMPTIONS

The approach to the Bible

The assumptions underlying the thinking and practice of Vineyard Church life are formed by, if not derived from, the Bible. At this point I will merely introduce John's approach to Scripture, because I will deal with it in more detail when discussing values in chapter five.

John's understanding of scripture was basically conservative evangelical—which does not mean being fundamentalist or politically conservative! What it means is that we believe the Bible is the inspired Word of God, our authority for life and faith, but at the same time, we take into account historical doctrine and responsible Biblical scholarship and the accepted rules of Biblical interpretation (Orthodox Evangelical hermeneutics).

This means that we experience what the Bible really teaches when we try to lay aside, or at least acknowledge, our doctrinal, denominational, cultural and philosophical presuppositions, and read the Bible, with the Spirit's help, in its historical setting, in its own terms, categories and thought forms. We do this with the assumption that it describes people's experience of God and teaches us how to live life as God wants us to live it. Thus, we endeavour to let the Bible speak for itself, to hear God through its pages, to be both informed and formed by its truth.

John was always careful to say that the purpose of Scripture was not that we should be knowledgeable in it, rather that we should practise it, that we should encounter God in and through it, and that we should be transformed by it. There is therefore a particular emphasis on life-related and life-applicable Biblical understanding and teaching.

However, in terms of a guiding 'theology' or system of meaning and understanding, John found in the Biblical theology of the Kingdom of God a key that unlocked not only the Bible itself, but also an approach to Church, the world, life, people and history. This is what was behind the assumptions that determined John's worldview, the way he saw reality and the way he understood truth. The Biblical theology of the Kingdom of God has almost become synonymous with Vineyard because it has become so much a part of our underlying assumptions of life, Church and the world.

The theology of the Kingdom

One of the main influences in John's life, if not the major influence, was the theology of the Kingdom of God as understood and communicated by George E. Ladd. A further complementary influence was James Kallas' theology of the Kingdom. This is not the time nor place to go into these theologies (see the resource list in appendix 4) except to explain their connection with the nature and purpose of the Church. The key issue here is that John saw the Church and the world through the lens or prism of the Kingdom of God. And what did he see?

The picture goes like this: God made everything and therefore He rules over it all. But there was a rebellion in His Kingdom—Satan deceived Adam and Eve and became 'the god of this world' (2Cor 4:4). Satan implemented his policy and practice of sin, sickness, demons and death. So our world has become 'this present evil age' in which we all live (Gal 1:4). However, God promised, in the Old Testament, that He would put an end to this present evil age by sending His Messiah to defeat wickedness in all its forms, save His people, and bring salvation to all the earth. God promises war—'You want war Satan, you've got it!' God will establish His Kingdom by destroying the Kingdom of Darkness, heaven will come to earth, and evil will go to hell!

This future promise of God was fulfilled when Jesus came forgiving sins, healing sicknesses, driving out demons and raising the dead. Not only in His life, but even more so in Jesus' death, resurrection and ascension, was Satan and his rule decisively defeated. 'For this purpose the Son of God appeared, that He might destroy the works of the evil one' (1Jn 3:8). Therefore, the phrase 'Kingdom of God' in Scripture is a dynamic concept—it means the action of God's rule, more than the realm or place of God's rule. Jesus said, 'If I drive out demons by the Spirit of God, then the Kingdom of God *has come* upon you' (Matt 12:28—italics added).

But, and this is a big BUT, there is an apparent contradiction here. What is 'wrong' with the above picture? As they say, can you 'spot the error'?

Evil is still rampant, people still sin, get sick and die! Why?

This is what Jesus called 'the mystery' or 'the secret' of the Kingdom of God (Matt 13:11f—explained in the parables). It means that the future age of God's rule has become present, has been fulfilled in the (first) coming of Christ, BUT without being consummated, without putting an end to this age and without taking over completely. This will happen at the Second Coming of Christ. In other words there is a tension between fulfilment and consummation, between the 'already' and the 'not yet' of the Kingdom of God (the apostle John actually uses these words in 1Jn 3:2). The consummation of the Kingdom will see the literal and full experience of Rev 21:3-4: 'Now the dwelling of God is with people, and He will live with them ... He will wipe away every tear from their eyes, there will be no more death or mourning or crying or pain (or sin, or sickness, or demons, or poverty, or injustice, etc) for the old order has passed away.'

The diagram below summarises this picture of history and reality—the Biblical view of the Kingdom of God. This diagram, drawn and adapted from George Ladd, has over the years become a classic Vineyard means to explain the heart of our theological understanding.

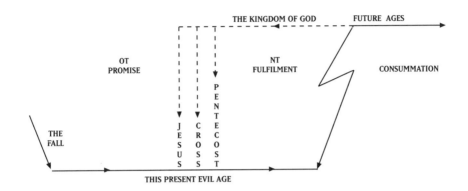

IMPLICATIONS

The implications of this theology of Kingdom, especially the mystery or 'tension' of the Kingdom, are very important. I will discuss only four as applied to the Vineyard.

Firstly, it defines the true nature and purpose of the Church

Those who are 'born again' (more accurately 'born from above', Jn 3:3-7) have already entered the Kingdom of God. In other words the Church lives between two ages—the future age of the Kingdom and this present evil age. We live the eternal life of the future right here in the present, bringing heaven to earth. Just think of it! It means war! We are in the thick of it, whether we like it or not, whether we know it or not. We are the instruments of God's rule confronting and destroying evil in all its forms—we are indeed the *ekklesia* of God, enforcing and advancing, for the sake of this world, the victory that Jesus has already accomplished.

In Vineyard language we 'speak the words, and do the works, and see the wonders of the Kingdom'. Signs and wonders are part and parcel of the essence of the gospel. Jesus has been given all the authority in the heavens and in the earth. The Church, the community of the Kingdom, is commissioned with that authority to advance God's Kingdom to the ends of the earth (Matt 28:18-20). Only then will the Kingdom be consummated. Jesus Himself placed this condition on His Second Coming (see Matt 24:14). What a mix of fearful responsibility and awesome privilege! John understood Church in these terms and faithfully and sacrificially gave himself and the Vineyard to do our part in this war of the Lamb.

As an aside, theologically speaking, the implication of what we are saying means an end to all dispensational and cessationist thinking (the belief that God deals with humans in various dispensations—that miracles and healings were valid in the time of Jesus and the early apostles because they authenticated His Messianic ministry, but since the formation of the New Testament canon miracles and healings have passed away). John abandoned this theology the first time he read George Ladd's exposition of the Kingdom of God.

Secondly, the history of the Church, and especially the history of revivals, is understood in terms of Kingdom breakthrough.

The Kingdom of God in Scripture is not an idea; it is an event, an intervention of God in human history. *Renewals* are Kingdom breakthroughs within the Church. They refresh, reform and renew the Church. *Revivals* are Kingdom breakthroughs in and through the Church into the world, in terms of multitudes coming to faith. Lastly, *awakenings* are Kingdom breakthroughs that affect a whole nation, in terms of its moral fibre and conscience, resulting in reform in the socio-political structures and generally a change of destiny. Each is a work of the Kingdom, different in time, degree, power, influence and purpose. The outpouring of spiritual power, with all the phenomena of the Spirit, is understood as a manifestation of the Kingdom's presence among us. To be more accurate, it is a foretaste, sometimes overwhelmingly so, of the life and power of the resurrection being manifested in our bodies—seen in the crying, shaking, falling and other similar phenomena. We taste 'the powers of the coming ages' (Heb 6:5). Divine healing and the healing ministry is understood in the same way—as an event of the Kingdom, a manifestation of the Spirit's work, a foretaste of the resurrection.

The 'tension' of the Kingdom reminds us that sometimes people are healed (the 'already') and sometimes people are not healed (the 'not yet'). We do not have an extreme 'faith view' or 'Kingdom now view', that says everyone we pray for must be healed now, and if not, it is a lack of faith, or a result of sin in one's life. Likewise, the phenomena of the Spirit are part God and part human and therefore must be discerned and pastored. John was very clear on this. He sought to be responsible in his pastoral practice, especially with regard to the renewals of the Spirit, even though it cost him friendships both within and outside the Vineyard.

God is truly more sovereign than we would ever realise. Revivals and spiritual phenomena are all part of the 'already' and 'not yet' of the Kingdom. This should keep us humbly dependent on God, not claiming too much for ourselves. It should keep us from triumphalism and elitism, which is an overemphasis of the 'already' of the Kingdom, manifested in 'this is the last great move of God ushering in the Second Coming' or 'we are the end-time army' or 'those not in the flow will be left out', etc. On the other hand it should keep us from defeatism, an overemphasis on the 'not yet' of the Kingdom, a kind of negative conservatism, a paranoia and protectionism, that is manifested in certain parts of the Church. In this regard, John's sense of historical perspective kept him balanced and humble, and hopefully will be an enduring characteristic of the Vineyard.

Thirdly, the Church is the community of the Kingdom.

The Church is one community—the same in nature and purpose, no matter what structures or approaches to Church we may have. John caught this well. He was truly ecumenical and catholic—embracing the whole, universal Body of Christ as expressions of the community of the Kingdom. Frequently he would say, 'We must love what God loves, the whole Church.' He rebuked any sign of sectarianism. We need to work with, learn from, and honour the broader Church. There has been, and presently is, so much mutual attacking in the Body of Christ. With family like this who needs enemies! John and the Vineyard did, and still do, have their fair share of ... shall we say, critics? But that does not mean that we love without discernment, that we endorse everything without testing what is going on. We can agree to disagree on many aspects of life and ministry, and still respect one another and work well together. The exception to this is the basis of our Christian fellowship, the non-negotiables of orthodox evangelical faith—basically that which is embodied in the Apostolic and Nicene Creeds—which the Vineyard holds to (see the Vineyard Statement of Faith, appendix 2).

Fourthly, the Church is not the Kingdom of God.

The Kingdom is the rule of God, the Church is the community that receives and expresses that rule of God. Because of the tension between the 'already' and 'not yet' of the Kingdom, the way in which the Church structures itself to best express the Kingdom will always be penultimate, never 'the real thing'. The new wine is contained in and communicated through the wineskin—Jesus used this to illustrate the coming of the Kingdom and the structures through which it flows (Lk 5:33-39). Whether the wineskin is new or old, flexible or tearing (because of the presence of the Kingdom), it is still man-made and therefore it will always be penultimate. Only the wine itself is ultimate. God does not allow anyone to own the wine, although many may think they do.

We must not and cannot worship our philosophy of ministry, thinking it is the Kingdom. Of course, the best-kept secret is that the Vineyard has the best approach to doing Church—that is why I am writing this book! (A little facetious provocation is a godly thing, it keeps us humble!) Denominationalism comes easily when we take ourselves too seriously— G. K. Chesterton is reported to have said, 'Angels can fly because they take themselves lightly.' Denominationalism is to confuse our Church, our approach, our structures, even our beliefs, with the Kingdom. Many fall into this trap. Human nature is such that it is easier to follow rules or a system than to live in a relationship of trust with a person. It is easier to serve a visible king or structure than to live under invisible government. We must watch our hearts as they are so easily seduced and then deceived.

However, the opposite reaction is equally wrong. Some idealists say that there should be no denominations, no different or particular families of Churches—just belong to all by belonging to none! 'We are all one, so let us be one' often means in practice 'you in your way and I in His', or 'you join me', etc. This type of 'no denominations, let us become one' thinking is not concrete. No one takes responsibility; it amounts to a nebulous nothing. Maybe one day, before Jesus comes, all denominational identities and philosophies of ministry will fall away. I doubt it—but I would be so happy for Jesus to prove me wrong! My understanding is that this type of idealism assumes that the Church is the Kingdom. Only when Jesus comes will the Church lose its identity fully and experientially in the Kingdom—then there will be no need for a wineskin, the King Himself will rule visibly, politically, economically and spiritually. In the meantime, the Church is still penultimate, because it is in a certain sense a human creation, a 'this age' phenomenon. This is the mystery of the Kingdom, the 'already' but the 'not yet'. Therefore, honesty says that to belong to the universal Church I need to belong to the local Church, and to belong to the local Church I need to be at home. There are many different expressions of the Kingdom for many different types of people, meeting many different types of needs. No one is better than another, just different from each other, and still fully and equally part of the same Kingdom.

John Wimber's view of Vineyard and Denominations

John was realistic in this regard. He was unapologetic, yet sensitive, about the Vineyard and about his calling to do Church in a way that would be a home for those who identified with it. He called for clear commitment, on the basis of clear understanding—where is home for you? All the post-charismatic independent Church movements or 'flows' or 'streams' (as they are charismatically called!) which have exploded into existence over the past two or three decades, are actually denominations, whether they acknowledge it or not. They are all spiritual homes with a particular philosophy of ministry. Some say, rather presumptuously, that they are the new wineskins for the new wine of the Kingdom that is being poured out in the world 'in these end times'. Despite the presumption, Church Growth researchers and statisticians agree that by far the major growth in Church and missions across the world is from the Pentecostal and Charismatic groupings. They are the truly practising evangelicals—and do not tell the Evangelicals, it is another of God's best-kept secrets!

The point is that we must not become denominationalistic. We must live and work well together, with mutual respect, like mature families in a community. We must genuinely advance the Kingdom and grow the Church, and not do things in order to reshuffle the pack of cards to make us look good, i.e. to grow our Churches and build our Kingdoms at the expense of others. 'Transfer growth' is so common in the Church today. The Kingdom is not extended one bit. It promotes consumer Christianity—'What is the flavour of the month? Let's go there.' The Vineyard should have no part in it! John's attitude was that we should be as humble, honest and realistic about our Church and the Church as we are about the Kingdom of God.

To summarise—the Vineyard identity

The above discussion leads to the issue of how we see ourselves: our identity as Vineyard (which was alluded to in Chapter one).

If we talk about identity in terms of theological and Church traditions, then Vineyard is basically conservative Evangelical; not Pentecostal, nor Charismatic. But we are Evangelicals with a difference—our experience and practice is Pentecostal and Charismatic, although our practice has a different style. Further, we do not theologize in the same way as the Pentecostals do. Our framework is the Kingdom of God—for example, we teach healing, among other things, from a Kingdom viewpoint, rather than from the atonement of Christ. Although this is not a major issue, John always felt theologically more at home in a conservative Evangelical framework. (I have already said that this does not refer to a Biblicist or Fundamentalist or Dispensationalist or Cessationist framework—if you understand what these creatures mean!)

What deeply impressed John is the practice of the Pentecostals in their evangelism and Church planting—their healing the sick, driving out devils and 'doing the stuff of the Kingdom'. The basic difference in John's mind was between proclamation and demonstration. The conservative Evangelicals do proclamation (a rational framework), but the Pentecostals do demonstration together with proclamation (an experiential framework). Whenever they preach they pray for the sick, cast out evil spirits and practise 'power encounter'. David Barrett and other Church Growth statisticians all point to the phenomenal growth of this wing of the Church since the 1900s—it is estimated that there are over 600 million such believers at present. The Vineyard is fully in this movement, although as part of the 'Third Wave' (as Peter Wagner calls it—first the Pentecostals, then the Charismatics, then the 'renewed' Evangelicals).

In short, the Vineyard has an identity that embraces Evangelical theology and Pentecostal experience, and in so doing it cuts across Evangelical experience and Pentecostal theology. John developed the diagram below in order to explain how we see ourselves.

Vineyard—Church identity

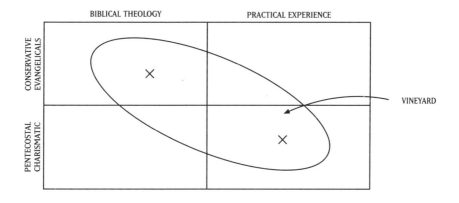

A number of John's leadership letters to the Vineyard pastors deal with the above issues, explaining his stance on the identity of the Vineyard, denominations, philosophy of ministry, loving and accepting the whole Church, sectarianism, tolerance, working together, pastoring the renewal, the phenomena of the Spirit, etc. For those who want to pursue these more detailed discussions, the materials are available through the USA AVC (see appendix 4, Vineyard Reflections).

Applying the above discussion means understanding the difference between 'family' and 'friends' and between 'adoptions' and Church plants.

FAMILY, FRIENDS, ADOPTIONS AND PLANTS

Although there is an awareness of belonging and commitment to the whole family of God, John used the terminology of being 'in the family' or being 'friends of the family'. This was to distinguish between those who are committed to and belong in the Vineyard and those who like the Vineyard and draw from it in various ways.

Being part of the family

To be part of the family is to know that God has placed you in this particular part of the Body. How do you know that? God must speak to you in one way or another, and it should be confirmed by a similar sense from the leadership of the particular Church. It cannot be unilateral either way. From a human point of view it comes down to knowing inside that this is your home, through an identification with the vision and values being lived out in this particular Church. How do you discover this? Through relationships. Sometimes you know instinctively that you are home. That does not do away with the need to connect meaningfully with some of the leaders and the people, and to discover what they are about, so that you can make an intelligent and responsible commitment.

Some Vineyards facilitate this process through an 'exploring membership' course. The bottom line, however, is bonding through relationships. Becoming and being family means taking on the family name—which symbolizes your commitment to take on the responsibilities and the privileges, the liabilities and the assets, the blessings and the disciplines, of the family. This applies both to individuals committing to local Vineyard Churches and to Pastors and/or Churches becoming part of the Vineyard Movement. (When an existing Church 'joins' Vineyard we call it an 'adoption'—explained below.)

Before we discuss being a friend of the Vineyard, we must restate that Biblically speaking no one can say they belong to the universal Church without concretely belonging to a local Church. It is non-negotiable that every last disciple of Jesus be committed fully and responsibly to a local family of believers. God is a family-person, that is why He is Father—He is a father to the fatherless and He places the lonely in families, but the rebellious live outside in a dry place (Ps 68:5,6). The lonely, it is assumed, must respond to God's placing them in the family or they too might be deemed rebellious. I am reminded of demons who lose their 'home' and roam restlessly in dry places (Lk 11:24). This ironically can describe a relatively large group of hurt, disillusioned and homeless Christians—a product of modern consumer Christianity. How sad! What applies to the individual Christian also applies to the local Church. Independent Churches should belong in a family of Churches for their own sake, to be accountable and to receive care.

The characteristics of an authentic Church

Some seek a 'phantom' Church existence because of the fear of being controlled and hurt again, whether by a local Church or a denomination. A 'phantom-type Church' (see sociological models below) is not a real Church. We need to keep in mind what the Reformers agreed was the Biblical measure of what and when 'a Church' is really Church. Their five marks or characteristics of an authentic Church of Jesus Christ have been accepted right across the board:

- Where born-again believers gather regularly in the Name of Jesus Christ for fellowship, worship, prayer, ministry and mission.

- Where the Word of God is faithfully preached.

- Where oversight and discipline are properly constituted and administered.

- Where the ordinances (sacraments) of Christ are properly administered (baptism and communion).

- Where recognition and respect is given by the broader Church.

Being a friend of the Vineyard

Being a friend of the Vineyard means identifying with and learning from our philosophy of ministry, but for whatever reason, not carrying the same name. Friends do things together. They share and laugh and hang out together. Much of that has taken place over the years through conferences and other events with many other Churches and denominations. This has largely happened through the renewal ministry of the Vineyard in the broader Church. John certainly did make many friends! Clarifying the difference between family and friends makes for good relationships all round. It sorts out expectations and frees people to relate accordingly. There is no reason for any pressure whatsoever for anyone to 'join' the Vineyard.

In fact, John would say, 'Why join—you can get all the benefits anyway.' He would add, 'Don't commit to us unless God really tells you—you don't know what you're letting yourself in for!' This applies both to individuals who are friends of the Vineyard but keep their own Church membership, and to pastors and Churches who seek a close relationship for the benefit they can derive. Whatever God has given Vineyard—just as He has given other Kingdom deposits in every other Church family—is actually His and is available to the whole Body. Those in the know will agree that John has been ultra-generous over the years. He has not only made all the Vineyard materials available to those interested, but he has also given much of it away.

Being adopted into the family

An adoption takes place when an existing Church senses, through its leadership, that Vineyard is their spiritual home. This happens and will continue to happen. However, we need to be very clear on our calling to be a Church planting movement and not to grow by adoption. The latter should be the exception to the rule, or else we could find ourselves spending most of our time and energy on integrating other Churches. John always said that we must give birth to our own, because frankly, it can take enormous effort to turn a community with its established culture and value system into something different. In any case, why would we want to change them? That is why John said, 'You don't join Vineyard, you discover that you are Vineyard.' Then the process is not so taxing, nor distracting from our real calling—we just need to give time for relationship and bonding to take place, to confirm common values that have already taken root and then, together, get on with God's primary calling.

If God has provided a home in the Vineyard for certain Churches, then we go through an adoption process. John put it simply: courtship, engagement, and marriage! It is getting to know the pastor and leadership, hanging out and sharing ministry, so that they can be exposed to who we are and what we do. This normally happens through relationship with the closest local Vineyard pastor and/or a senior Vineyard pastor in the area. If they are from an existing denomination or family of Churches, everyone must walk in the light with everyone else. Intentions must be put on the table from the beginning and the process must have the blessing of all concerned— otherwise it becomes an ungodly process. At the appropriate time, release and blessing is received from the sending denomination (if applicable) and commitments are then entered into. Later, the change of name and the actual adoption takes place.

Having clarified the theological assumptions of the Kingdom and the Church, and having explained some Vineyard terminology and perceptions, we are now in a position to look more specifically at the Vineyard philosophy of ministry, as John presented it in 1982. This is where I begin to draw on and expand the forty-five page document, called 'Building from the bottom up', that I referred to in chapter one. Firstly we will compare three models of how communities operate, and identify one as our approach in the Vineyard. Then we will apply these sociological models to the issue of Church membership and commitment, and look at how the Vineyard applies them.

THREE SOCIOLOGICAL MODELS OF COMMUNITY

John 'borrowed' these models from sociological studies. They are called Social Set Theory, and are aimed at describing aspects of group dynamics and how individuals see themselves in relation to the group. It also explains how people relate to others outside their group. Applying it to the Church gives us a different view of things and helps us to clarify dynamics that we have not understood before. We experience things, but we do not know how to understand or explain them. Hopefully these models will give us a clear view, an explanation of both our past and present experience of Church life. As in all models, there are limits and weaknesses—they generalise and use stereotypes because they are designed to communicate through pictorial understanding. Nevertheless, they do communicate various approaches to social organisation and Church life powerfully.

Fuzzy-set

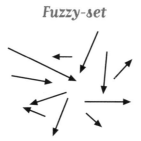

This approach to 'being and doing' community represents at best a completely 'laid back' environment, at worst it is anarchic, out of control. It is a formless anti-authority driven society—a free-for-all, everyone pulling in his own direction, each one doing his own thing. As an approach to social organisation this is technically called *laissez-faire* (French— literally means, 'left to do'), which refers to no government interference in any individual actions.

In terms of Church life it means no leadership, or very weak and non-functional leadership—a giving away of responsibility. Therefore there is no direction, no cohesion, no structure. It is like the description of Israel in the book of Judges: 'in those days Israel had no king and everyone did what was right in their own eyes' (17:6). There is a concept of Church that is practised in some circles that can be described as a 'phantom' Church. They put radical emphasis on just 'being', wanting to be completely relational, with no meetings or structures or leadership. Often this concept arises out of a 'super-spiritual' worldview in which any man-made structure or intervention is despised. It amounts to being 'invisible'. This 'phantom' Church is not so widespread within the contemporary Church. However, what is much more common, and in fact what seems to be the norm, is the next model.

Bounded-set

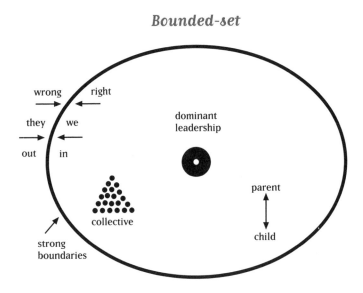

Sociologically speaking, this approach represents the opposite of the Fuzzy-set model—it is a strongly ordered, structured and directed form of community organisation. It is a rigid, control-driven society. Because this model describes a common phenomenon in the way many Churches are 'run', I will list the characteristics in some detail. I use the word 'run' intentionally because it is frequently used by pastors—'the way I run my Church ... how do you run your Church ...?' It reveals a certain mindset that has to do with ownership, management and technology as opposed to family, teamwork and servanthood.

1. **Leadership** is centred on the leader, whose style is usually dominant,

directive and autocratic. It is normally singular leadership, which often results in a superstar syndrome with a serious lack of accountability.

2. **Boundaries** are constantly being defined and reinforced to keep order and discipline. It leads to a we/they and in/out mentality, an exclusivist and exclusionist approach. Everything is seen from a moral perspective in terms of right and wrong, with a low level of tolerance. The result is a performance orientated and guilt-inducing environment.

3. **View of people** is that they are there to achieve the pastor's vision. The leader sees them as a collective whole, not as individuals with unique needs, dreams and gifts.

4. **Identity and recognition** comes from being 'in' and from being 'right'. The person's sense of worth and value comes from being a good member, a hard worker, or an obedient leader.

5. **Structure** is hierarchical, based on strong principles of organisation, management, ideology and institution.

6. **Relationships** are characterized by a parent-child mode of interaction.

7. **Evangelism** becomes the primary aim for existence because without new people it dies. The idea is 'to get more, bring them "in", make them like us'. In practice it often means proselytizing people from other Churches. Once they are in, the secondary aim is to keep them in at all costs. Leaving is a major issue—often things are personalised, involving hurt and acrimony.

Summarising the values: what undergirds this way of doing Church has to do with placing high value on numbers, budgets, programmes, promotion, visibility, success, performance, attendance, indoctrination and conformity.

The Centred-set model

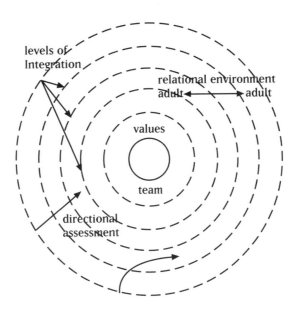

This approach to community organisation is completely different from the other two—it is not a 'middle-of-the-road' position. The Centred-set is a paradigm or frame of reference that is responsibly liberating. It is a flexible, value-driven society. The idea is that people are drawn to a set of values with which they identify, represented by the centre. They are drawn through various levels of integration by the team of leaders who are living out these central values. In other words, who the leaders are, and what they represent, attracts others, who see in them the kind of life that they would like to live. This way of doing Church is not commonly and actually practised, despite the fact that most leaders would like to think that this paradigm governs their operation. There are a number of implications and characteristics that flow from this model (which introduces, in principle, the Vineyard philosophy of ministry).

I. **Vision and values** point to a common focus and commitment to the centre—representing a vision of the Kingdom with its basic set of values. The values can differ from group to group, as each understands and interprets the Kingdom and what that group is called to. The point is that the group is centred on values that are being lived out and not only spoken about.

2. **Leadership** is a team effort, not an individualistic approach. Leaders lead by example, reinforcing and instilling the basic values by modelling and facilitating life and ministry in its various aspects.

3. **Assessment and integration** take place on the basis of people's direction, i.e. are they journeying toward the values that the group is committed to? This makes for an inclusive and integrating approach. It frees people to integrate toward the centre at their own pace of commitment and growth; or they can change direction if they discover that this group is not for them, and seek another environment with values similar to their own.

4. **View of people** is that they are treated as individuals—not as a collective whole—each having unique gifts and callings that must be developed. They are not objects of ministry, or resources to be used for the purpose of the group.

5. **Identity and worth** comes from within the person, from his relationship with the Lord, as growth in personal life and calling takes place. It frees people to function in the Body without having to seek recognition from others, especially those in authority.

6. **Relationships** are conducted on an adult-to-adult basis. It accepts people for who they are and where they are, and motivates them to take responsibility for their own lives and to grow into maturity.

7. **Structure** is a relational environment practising lateral teamwork, avoiding hierarchical thinking and structures—structures should be flexible and functional.

8. **Evangelism** takes place primarily through friendship and relationship. We do not need to evangelise in order to survive, or to grow big. We do it because we love people and want to help them live (God's kind of) life.

Summarising the values: what undergirds this model and makes it work is the emphasis on acceptance, relationship, process, nurture, equipping, teamwork and real life, as opposed to getting, keeping and controlling.

The issue of membership and commitment

In the Fuzzy-set model there is no meaningful concept of membership and commitment, and if there is, it will probably not be measurable. In the Bounded-set model there is a clear and sure method of making members and of measuring commitment. What would be the criteria for membership and for measuring commitment? Think about it. What have you experienced in Church? What have they expected of you? Generally it goes something like this: if you go through the membership course (and in some cases, sign on the dotted line), obey the leadership, believe what they teach, attend regularly, tithe faithfully, and do nothing immoral, then you are 'in'. If, however, you break any of these along the way you are 'out'. Neat and tidy!

How do we understand membership and measure commitment in the Centred-set approach? Here we have a relational and dynamic, rather than a structural and static, view of membership. You are a member to the extent that you connect with others on the same journey towards the centre, seeking to live out a common set of values together. Your commitment is measured by the direction in which you are travelling—are you moving toward the centre with us? If you are, then commitment means loving and sharing, through taking responsibility within relationships and continuing the journey together. This matches the Biblical concept of functional and relational membership—if you are not connected and functioning in the Body then you are not part of the Body. Disconnected means dead (Paul's teaching in 1Cor 12). Can you conceive of a floating finger visiting many other bodies? If it does not belong somewhere it belongs nowhere! Connected means committed: discovering your gift and beginning to function by taking responsibility for the well-being of those you are in relationship with, and pursuing the centring vision together.

The dynamic and integrating view of membership

Each level of integration, each dotted line of the concentric circles in the Centred-set model, represents a deeper level of joining, of journeying, of relating, of taking responsibility.

I developed the following diagram for our Valley VCF 'Exploring Membership' course to communicate this dynamic process of belonging and commitment.

Centred-set view of Belonging

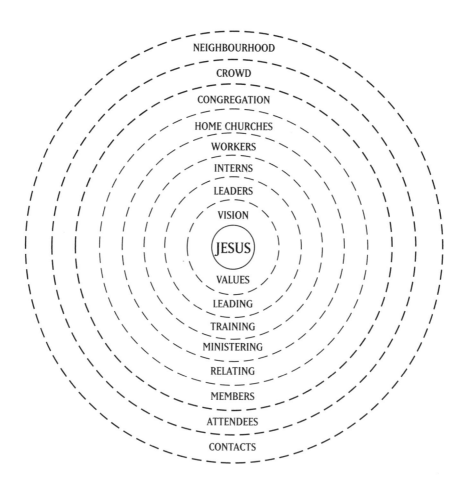

Contacts are people who attend Church periodically—as represented by the outer circle. Are they then in or out? No, the question is: in which direction are they moving? It will be too early to tell. Because we do not think in terms of being 'in' or 'out', we love everyone who comes into our orbit equally (hopefully!). These contacts also represent the neighbourhood or city in which the Church ministers.

The crowd is the next line inwards, representing those who attend regularly—they are enjoying what we do and want to hang out with us! We can see them as the crowds who follow from a distance, but are not yet committed.

The congregation are those who have integrated further—into active worship. When people not only attend, but really enter into worship, you know a connection has begun. God can speak to them. It takes time and trust—some go faster and others slower. There must be no pressure. They come at their own pace as they experience love, acceptance and forgiveness. Active worshippers generally consider themselves as members—whether they have been through a membership course or not—because they have found a home in which they experience God.

Home groups represent the next level of integration. They are now connecting with some individuals and families through relationships. This happens best through small groups (kinships) and brings about a certain belonging and commitment in functional terms. At this level of involvement (and often before) people become members more formally by going through an orientation or membership class (some Vineyards call it a 'corridor group'). The vision, values and priorities of the Church are explained so that they make an informed and responsible commitment to membership. Ideally speaking, the course should just complement and confirm what they have discovered and already know in their hearts, both from God and through their relationships; that this is home for them. They identify with the centre. But it does not stop here as though they 'have arrived'.

Workers are those who, through regular home group belonging, begin to minister to others. As people get healed through relationships and ministry, they too begin to love others by discovering their gifts and callings in doing the works of the Kingdom, first in the home group, then in the Church and beyond. These are the workers who carry responsibility for the Church's well-being.

Interns are those who go further by committing to both formal and informal training—so as to be more effective in ministry in and beyond the Church.

Leaders are those who are relating, ministering and in training, but who also lead and organise others in ministry, and train them to be more effective. They lead functionally, forming the Church by instilling the vision and values that are at its core. They are the mature people (the Hebrew understanding of elders) who live, and draw others into living, more and more like Jesus—He is the centre.

Further clarification of the Vineyard approach

In the early days John and the Vineyard were criticised at times for not having a clear concept and practice of membership. At first glance, many Vineyards using the Centred-set approach might appear to be purely process and relationship—easy come, easy go—similar to the Fuzzy-set. Is this necessarily true?

John used to say, 'We have a wide open front door and an even wider open back door!' For some that has meant a lack of care and accountability, too much of a 'laid back' approach. (Some Vineyard people have been so 'laid back' that they have been horizontal for a long time! It has been an excuse for not wanting to take responsibility for growing up.) However, what John meant was that we must make it easy for people to come and explore our environment and if they do not connect, it must be easy for them to leave. We are looking for people who, almost instinctively, identify with our values. When we find them we must help them to connect and come to a clear commitment of membership, no matter how it is formalised or expressed. If this does not happen, leaders will not know how to account for those whom God has given into their care. The shepherd knows the sheep and the sheep know the shepherd (Jn 10 cf. Heb 13:17).

The rest must be free to come and go, without our feeling insecure or making an issue out of it. In some cases we can help people to move on, by recommending a place for them where they will be more at home. It is not a matter of a right or wrong, or better or worse Church. It is just that each Church is different. Not all people accept Vineyard values. Some of these people can be seen a mile away! It is better for them, and us, that they move on. Sometimes the quicker the better!

Processing those who come to us: a people flow chart

John had another saying that has been misinterpreted: 'We are not in the people-keeping business, but in the people-processing business.' This does not mean that we have low expectations of commitment; that people who consider themselves as members, can 'hang out' with us for a while and then move on as and when they choose. John's phrase could convey the impression of a very informal membership that basically accommodates western independence and individualism. No!

On the one hand, John was countering the mindset of ownership and power-base building, which is protective and controlling. On the other hand, and more specifically, he was referring to the mobility and transience in our modern suburban society. On average, families move home every three to five years, and they change jobs frequently (mostly economically driven). We must be realistic about our constituencies, and diligently heal and grow people while we have them, so that when they are moved on they are better equipped to follow Jesus and do the work of the Kingdom. In fact, while they are with us, they must drink so deeply from our fountain that they are spoilt for anything less than a life of full discipleship to Jesus in a similar family of faith—even to the point that future decisions on possible moves are based not on economics, but on more genuine spiritual considerations.

There was also an element of mission-mindedness in John's statement.

Everyone that God gives us from the world, needs to 'go through the family process' and eventually be sent back out into the world in one or other form of mission. It is a type of 'people-flow'. Not that they necessarily leave the Church, but that they 'grow up, before they grow old' (John's phrase). Growing up means deeper involvement in the world, wherever they are, as an effective agent of change; as people who win others for the Kingdom by drawing them into the family.

The diagram below, which I developed for the Valley VCF 'Exploring Membership' course, gives a picture of this 'people-flow'. The three main aspects are *gathering* from the world, *growing* through the family and *sending* into the world. I use the word 'growing' rather than 'processing' because the latter can appear to contradict our value of not using people or treating them as objects of ministry. There is a clear point of commitment and a clear point of sending out again—we commission members to the next place God has called them, whether another Church, or mission or Church plant. We do not believe in members being dislocated between Churches and not being committed in either place. Worse still is when members just slip out of the family, unnoticed, for one or other reason. It is often because of some unresolved issue—this is 'growing old without growing up'! If one joins properly, then one must leave properly; it is all part of adult relationships.

The process of growth follows similar lines as the process of integration in the Centred-set model: from contact, to integration, into relationships, being 'healed up', beginning to minister, being involved in training, exercising leadership, and then being sent out. These processes happen in and through the ministry structures in the Church, such as Sunday meetings, home groups, various kinds of ministry and mission groups and other programmes in the life of the Church.

A People Flow Chart

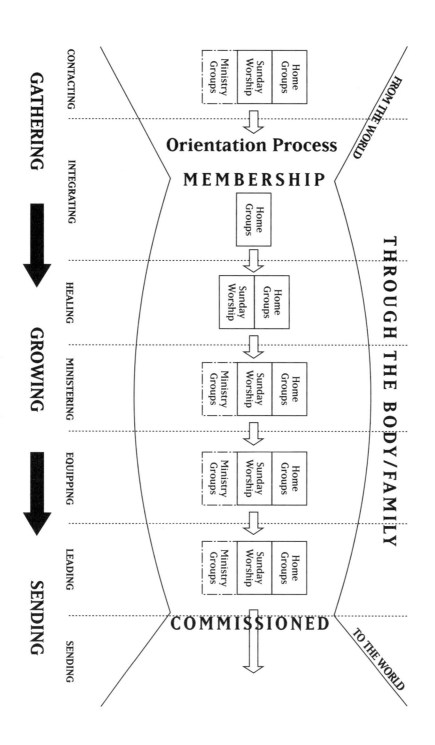

GATHERING

CONTACTING

FROM THE WORLD

Home Groups
Sunday Worship
Ministry Groups

Orientation Process

INTEGRATING

MEMBERSHIP

Home Groups

HEALING

Sunday Worship
Home Groups

THROUGH THE BODY/FAMILY

GROWING

MINISTERING

Ministry Groups
Sunday Worship
Home Groups

EQUIPPING

Ministry Groups
Sunday Worship
Home Groups

LEADING

Ministry Groups
Sunday Worship
Home Groups

SENDING

COMMISSIONED

SENDING

TO THE WORLD

CHAPTER 3

'BUILDING FROM THE BOTTOM UP'

Having gained a background understanding to 'philosophy of ministry', and in particular the Vineyard theological and sociological assumptions and their implications, we now look at how we approach building the local Church. The 'building' metaphor was common to Jesus and to Paul. We will briefly comment on some aspects of how they used and understood this metaphor. This will be followed by a discussion on the importance and value of having a philosophy of ministry and a plan on how to implement it. Then we will get to the heart of what John meant by 'building the Church from the bottom up'—the overall framework of purpose, values, priorities, practices, personnel and programmes.

When I prepared the original manual in 1982 (Building the Church from the bottom up), John wanted the introduction to start with the building image from Jesus and Paul, but not to present it necessarily as an explanation, rather as a sobering challenge.

'I WILL BUILD MY CHURCH'—JESUS

Jesus emphatically stated, 'I will build my Church.' This must rank as one of the most powerful and positive statements about the Church ever made.

It continues, '... I will build my Church and the gates of hell will not prevail against it ...' (Matt 16:18)—this is the 'old' language. At first it may sound as if Jesus is saying that He will build the Church in such a way that, although it will be on the defensive, holding out against the onslaught from 'hell', it will nevertheless not be overrun. Wrong! It means the exact opposite! Jesus will build His community (Greek *ekklesia*) as the instrument of His heavenly rule destroying evil in all its forms here on earth, and the very government of hell itself will not be able to withstand the onslaught of God's Kingdom through the Church. If you think of what this really means, it is mind-boggling!

This picture and understanding of the Church is confirmed in Jesus' next phrase, '... I will give you the keys of the Kingdom of Heaven; whatever you bind on earth will be bound in heaven, and whatever you loose on earth will be loosed in heaven.' Peter, in a unique pioneering way, and the Church in an ongoing way, have been given the authority of the Kingdom of the Heavens to defeat evil power in the unseen world by defeating it in our seen world. We do this by opening God's life and rule to people and locking out evil, by loosing people from their sin or by binding their sin to them—depending on their response to the Kingdom.

Jesus wants to build His *ekklesia* as His governing body in every city, town and village, at war with evil, enforcing Satan's defeat. The exciting thing is that He really meant it and He is doing it. How can we be part of His glorious enterprise?

Being part of His building process

We need to realise that it is His Church, not ours. We need to know who owns what and who is the Boss! We need to give the Church back to its rightful Owner so that, in all things, the initiative lies with Him. This is implied by the confession which we must all live out: 'You are the King (Messiah), the Son of the living God.' Jesus started it all, and wants to bring it to completion. Given half the chance, I am sure He will do a great job. Have you ever doubted Him? Furthermore, have you ever dreamt of Church as Jesus intended Church to be? We are to be Jesus to this world—nothing more, nothing less.

The Bible has some glorious pictures of what the Church will end up looking like. But I believe that Jesus is presently disentangling Himself and His people from the web of our own constructions of committees, doctrines, rules, systems and institutions. Many people are tired and disillusioned and do not want to be 'crunched' in the systems we have made. Some opt out of Church life completely, while others seek a fuzzy phantom Church believing that there they will experience 'the real thing', without being hurt again.

The balanced approach, as the 'tension' of the Kingdom teaches us, is that we must, paradoxically, be both hands-off and hands-on at the same time. We have to be involved whether we like it or not because Jesus builds His Church with 'saved-sinners', like you and me. We are all 'living stones' being built together as a home for God to live in. Thus we need to learn from Him, be led by Him and work with Him in the building of His Church. For too long we have either frustrated, or resisted, or interfered with His building programme. For too long we have made monuments of His movements. Sometimes we have built Church, thinking it was His or He was building with us, only to find out that we were actually doing our own thing—building our own kingdoms. 'Unless the Lord builds the house, the labourers labour in vain' (Ps 127:1). If He is not the author, He will not be the finisher—in that case, we carry the can.

God is increasingly shaking all things so that what cannot be shaken may emerge. We know that this applies not only to the world with all its political and economic systems, but more importantly, to the Church, because judgement begins first at the house of God (Heb 12:25-29 cf. 1Pet 4:17). Only that which is a true manifestation of the Kingdom—what is built on the rock of Jesus and our lived confession of His Kingship—will be revealed as unshakable. All other things will collapse like a house of cards.

'Since we are receiving a Kingdom that cannot be shaken, we must be thankful, and worship God with fear and awe, because He is indeed a consuming fire.' God is a jealous God. Idolatry—the stuff of our own making—will be judged by fire (Deut 4:24)!

'BE CAREFUL HOW YOU BUILD'—PAUL

Paul uses many different metaphors, pictures and symbols to convey his understanding of the Church—largely because the Church is so dynamic and glorious that one metaphor would not explain what God intended when He made the Church. However, we will make only a few points, largely reinforcing the above discussion, on Paul's building metaphor of the Church (from 1Cor 3:9-17).

Firstly, it is an enormous privilege and an awesome responsibility.

It is serious business to be involved with Jesus in building His Church—even more so if you are a leader or pastor. Paul rebukes any divisions or partisan-spirit, both among leaders and among the people in the Church. His overriding thrust is that we are all just servants of Christ, enjoying the amazing privilege of employing whatever gifts God has given us for the building up of the Church. This privilege must not be abused. How? By taking the responsibility that comes with it very seriously.

Secondly, the foundation is all-important.

Paul says that Jesus Christ is the foundation—His person, life, death, resurrection and ascension—that is our faith, knowledge and lived confession of Him. The foundation must be laid correctly because its integrity will determine the strength, stability and size of the building.

Thirdly, the quality of the building work is crucial.

We can build either with 'gold, silver and precious stones' or with 'wood, hay and stubble'. In other words, our heart attitude, diligence in labour, usage of gifts, relational teamwork and beliefs, will all determine the quality of what we build.

Fourthly, there is diversity of work within an overall unity of identity.

Paul says that we all work together for the same Head of the Church, from the same Cornerstone, but our gifts, personalities, cultures and contexts will determine the diverse and different ways in which we build. Unity is not uniformity. Each local Church, and the way it is built, has its own personality—even within a particular family of Churches. If they all look the same, smell the same, dress the same and speak the same, there is something drastically wrong. Paul said that division was caused, not by personality clashes or theological differences, but by the carnal or lower nature (1Cor 3:1f). When ungodly ambition or pride is left unchecked and unchallenged, either in leaders or people, it becomes divisive. Diversity is often used in this way to break the unity.

Fifthly, we will be held accountable by a 'quality-control' testing process!

Jesus is most interested in how His Church is built, because it reflects directly on Him. So He does the quality testing Himself—by sending the fire or the storm. Remember the house built on the sand of just hearing God's Word, in contrast to the other built on the rock of doing God's Word (Matt 7:24-27)? The true nature and quality of what we have built is only really revealed when difficulties and problems come along. No matter how 'successful' a Church may appear to be, what it is really made of will only be seen when it is tested by the storms of life or the fires of opposition and persecution. We ultimately see what is built on His Kingdom—as opposed to our 'kingdoms'—when a great shake-up touches the Church. Then Church leaders will see the quality, not only of their ministries and work, but also of their very lives.

Although it may appear that many leaders are not called to account here on earth, be assured of the fact that Jesus takes a personal interest in this matter! James, Jesus' younger brother and leader of the Church in Jerusalem, assures us—or warns us—that leaders, teachers and pastors will incur a stricter judgement (Js 3:1). If our lives and our work do not appear to be tested too much here on earth, they certainly will be tested when we stand before the risen Lord. On that day, who we really are and what has been of eternal consequence in our work, will 'be made manifest' for all to see. This is the meaning of the Greek word for 'appear' in 2Cor 5:10. Paul says that 'we must all appear before the judgement seat of Christ that each one may receive what is due to him for the things done while in the body, whether good or bad'. I fear that many of us will suffer loss and just get through, smelling of smoke and fire. Lord, have mercy!

To follow up on this challenge, we are going to examine the importance of having a clear philosophy of building the Church and a plan to implement it.

THE VALUE OF HAVING A PHILOSOPHY AND PLAN OF BUILDING

Some people do not place much importance on working out and defining their approach to doing Church, and then creating a plan to implement it. The idea is to just pray and trust the Lord. This 'spiritualistic' paradigm (as Christian Schwarz calls it, see Appendix 4) is based on an overly spiritual worldview where any human effort is despised. It can actually be an excuse for laziness. There is no need to go over the well-worn ground of justifying why we must do planning—such as, 'If you aim at nothing, you will surely hit it!' The Vineyard Five-Year Plan (see appendix 4) has a list of Scriptures from Proverbs that are quite enlightening and challenging in regard to planning. The idea is that we need to be diligent and plan, but to do it before God, trusting Him for guidance.

The other extreme is to so define, plan and promote things, as if all depends on our effort—almost like running a business. It is based on the assumption that if we simply do the right things in the right way, then the Church will grow big. The idea is reflected in the extent to which Churches have turned to business in the past few decades to learn how to do things. Schwarz calls this the technocratic paradigm of doing Church—the belief that we can make it all happen. I remember how John used to emphatically say, and more so in his later years, 'We do not grow Churches, only God grows Churches.'

Both extremes must be avoided. However, it requires real effort to reflect on what we are doing and why we are doing it, where we are going and how we will get there. Socrates' famous dictum, 'the unexamined life is not worth living' can be applied to the Church; 'the unexamined Church is not worth doing'. If there is no decided purpose, no real foundation and no planned building process, what on earth are we doing?

The profound homelessness of the contemporary Church

If this is not resolved, human nature will take the line of least resistance and will fall into accommodating, pleasing and appeasing, instead of leading. A number of other determinants then influence, form and lead both the pastor and the Church. The result is Paul's picture (Eph 4:14) of being blown back and forth by every wave and wind of new doctrine, new method, new book, the latest conference, the latest way of doing Church—be it 'Vineyard-style', or 'Restoration', or 'Word of Faith', or 'Purpose-Driven', or 'Seeker-Sensitive', or 'Cell Church', or 'Prophetic Renewal', or 'Apostolic-team', etc. The wind or wave can also be the latest evangelist or teacher to hit town, the most recent circumstance to affect the Church, a controlling elder, a primary group that wields power, or some intercessory/prophetic people who intimidate the pastor. The list can go on and on.

The way many Christians and pastors have become conference and seminar junkies, reinforcing Church consumerism, is a sad commentary on the profound homelessness, lack of identity and shaky foundation in the contemporary Church. Many pastors are so insecure and so desperate to get their Churches to grow, that they will do almost anything to be successful. At worst, it is a form of spiritual prostitution, running after every other thing that comes across our path. At best it is like the quote from Gandhi, 'There go my people, I had better run after them, because I am their leader.' Does any of this sound familiar?

Of course, this does not mean that one is closed to new methods, new people, new paradigms or the latest conference. We must always be learning and growing. We cannot worship our particular philosophy of ministry—it is always penultimate and needing to be reflected on.

A philosophy of ministry roots you in what you believe

The real issue is knowing what you believe and what you are building, and then from a place of identity and security, integrating what is needed from other sources. It takes time for young believers and young pastors to really know what they believe and what they want. One may change quite radically in the early years, but once one has found a real home, where one can identify with the basic vision and values, then one should lay that foundation and build on it, making adjustments, additions or beautification as one learns along the way. Once the foundation is set, one cannot change it without undergoing fundamental disruption. Ideally speaking, this would only happen once or twice, maybe three times, in a ministry lifetime. Otherwise one could remain rootless and end up having built nothing of real value. One can build on 'extras' that are desirable by extending the foundations. But that can go too far—you could end up losing the integrity of who you are and what you were called to.

The problem with the information highway, the explosion of knowledge and the idea that God is doing 'a new thing', is that we become insecure. We think that others have 'it' and we need 'it'—or much more of 'it'! Our focus becomes so diluted and eclectic, that in trying to become everything we become nothing. People who have accomplished meaningful things with and for God are always people who are deeply rooted and radically focused on just a few basic things that God has called them to. A clear philosophy of ministry will do that for us—if we keep focused and apply it long enough, without renegotiating the basics every time something 'better' or 'more' comes along.

So, the value of having a philosophy of ministry and a plan of how to implement it, is that it makes us rooted and at home. Then we can confidently and maturely engage with others, without feeling insecure or comparing 'us' with 'them'. We are freed to enjoy what God is doing with them, to imbibe something of their spirit and learn from them, without having to copy what they do. We don't have to buy the package, get the manual and attend the conference!

A philosophy of ministry functions as a filter

The philosophy of ministry will act like a filter, screening what comes across your path, helping you to decide what you should give time to. Is this way out of my vision and values or will it help me do better what I am already doing? Many pastors go to a conference and bring back the new method or the 'new thing that God is doing' believing the Church really needs it. Then, after a while, they wonder why it does not take root and transform their Church, but instead causes upheaval and tension, even to the point of division in the Church. Adding onto the building a new development for which the people do not have a value (i.e. is not in the foundation or the ethos of the Church) will bring the whole building into tension, sometimes causing it to collapse. Often it causes more harm than good. Pastors are generally poor agents and managers of change. You have to know your Church culture and know how to bring about foundational change. It requires time, patience, modelling, revisiting the vision and values, winning the key leaders, educating the Church and slowly changing structures.

A philosophy of ministry acts like the sign on a bus

On the other hand, a clear philosophy of ministry also acts like the sign on a bus—it helps others who meet you to know who you are, what the Church is about and where it is going, so as to neutralize any wrong or unrealistic expectations. People can the see the number on the bus and decide whether they want to travel with you—if they are going in the same direction as you. As John used to say, 'If you join our bus, don't try to change the bus or its direction—rather, find your place and make your contribution—because we already have the bus, the driver and the direction. Remember, you joined the bus, the bus didn't join you!' It does not mean we are inflexible or cannot be influenced. The question is how much influence, by whom, and for what purpose. If people discover that this is not for them, we can stop the bus and allow them to get off. It is not a matter of a better or worse, a right or wrong bus, just a different bus, a different vision and set of values that you humbly and confidently are up front and honest about. People need to know what your non-negotiables are. You should not make a big thing of them or be arrogant about the issues—which would say, 'something is wrong here'.

Now let us look at the Vineyard approach and plan to building the Church from the bottom up.

'BUILDING FROM THE BOTTOM UP'

When you set out to build a building, you go through a particular process, step by step, from the beginning until completion. This process is what John called 'building from the bottom up'—you certainly cannot build a building from the top down (mind you, these days anything is possible!).

John's phrase has been understood by some to refer to how Vineyard plants new Churches. Among the many ways of planting Churches, the basic idea is to start with relationships and evangelism and draw the people into a home group experience, then grow the home group and multiply it by raising up leaders. Once there is a minimum of three home groups, you 'go public' by starting a public worship service with the three home groups. This way of doing things will ensure a higher level of relationship, a deeper understanding of what this Church is all about—the vision, values, priorities and practices—and a broader sense of ownership among the people. It is laying a good foundation and then building on it. But this is more of a practical application of what John meant by 'building the Church from the bottom up'. Technically, he meant the process of working out your philosophy of ministry and then implementing it.

Applying the building image—begin with a dream

To construct a building, you begin with a dream, an idea of what kind of building you need to or want to build. This dream is converted into a process: a decision is made on what type of building for what purpose, e.g. a hospital or hotel or office block. Then the design and plans are drawn up and construction begins. The foundations are laid and slowly but surely the building emerges: the pillars, the walls, the windows, the roof, the electrics and plumbing, the furnishings, the staff and the departments of activities or work. And let us not forget the gardens to beautify the place!

Therefore, to 'build from the bottom', to develop a philosophy of ministry, you begin by dreaming of Church as you believe it should be. Then you embark on a six step process: you first define the purpose of the Church, then clarify the values, then establish the priorities, then model the practices, then choose the personnel and then you implement the programmes.

What is important to add is that this framework can be used for every major department of ministry in the Church. Each ministry leader or pastor can work out with their team their own particular purpose, values, priorities, practices, personnel and the programme. It should obviously fit into and reflect the overall philosophy of ministry of the local Church.

I need to introduce these steps, defining them and giving a brief explanation. The diagram at the end will summarise the key concepts. The following chapters will give a more detailed discussion on each of them.

Defining the purpose

Defining the purpose of the Church is like deciding what type of building we are going to build, whether a hospital or hotel or whatever. ('What type of Church are you building: a hospital for sinners or a hotel for saints?') This decision is fundamental, as it will affect the design of the building. What do you want to build, and how can you construct it so that you effectively achieve your purpose?

Defining the purpose answers the question *who* we are and *where* we are going (or another way of saying it, who we are becoming). This is not easy because many of us do not really know, or we have not yet decided, who we are and where we are going, let alone our Churches. That is why to my mind, a theology of belonging, of home, is so important—you begin where you are within the family. Tony Campolo always says to young people, 'You do not have to go to the Rocky Mountains to find yourself— your identity and purpose in life is a decision of whom you want to become, and then step by step by daily decisions you become.' So purpose gives *identity* and *direction* to the Church.

There is the purpose of the Church in a more general sense, which is theologically informed, and then there is the more specific purpose of a local Church—the particular calling that God has for each local Church. The general purpose forms and informs the particular local purpose, which has to do with leadership and context and other factors.

The purpose of the Church is often expressed in terms of a *mission* statement and a *vision* statement. You will notice that I have been using the phrase 'vision and values' because, besides the alliteration, it conveys the heart of any philosophy of ministry. A mission statement embodies who you are, your reason for existence. A vision statement points to whom you are becoming, your direction—it is a future oriented picture of what you see the Church becoming.

Clarifying the values

Clarifying the values is like making the big hole in the ground, and pouring the foundations of the building into it. The depth and dimensions of the excavation and the quality and integrity of the foundations will determine the size, stability and the limits of the building. You can only go as high as you go deep—like the high-rise office blocks in cities. So values are there, perhaps unseen, out of view and not consciously thought of. But they are absolutely crucial to the superstructure, which is what the people see. Values determine what you think and what you do.

Values answer the question *why?* They give the reasons for what you do. People do not often stop to examine their values, asking why they are doing what they are doing. To quote Socrates again, 'the unexamined life is not worth living'.

Values, strictly speaking, are defined as that which is of great worth, that to which you give your time, energy and money. They give you the *criteria* and the *principles* by which you make judgements, by which you evaluate things, your preferences and choices. They determine what is non-negotiable and important as opposed to what is urgent and flexible. Values guide and inform your decision-making.

The way the word 'values' is used in the Vineyard philosophy of ministry refers to the underlying non-negotiables in the form of a few core principles or beliefs that make us who we are. These beliefs are not Biblical doctrines per se, they are rather a mix of historical doctrine and current sociological factors, and that which God has quickened to us. In that sense they are both Biblically and contextually determined. They function as the criteria and principles by which we evaluate and measure what we do and say. Thus they determine what we do—our priorities—and they also affect the way we do things—our style, or what we call our practices.

There are two extremes we must avoid in regard to clarifying our values. The one is to make them absolutes—non-negotiables in the ultimate doctrinal sense. The other is to have so many values that there is no core, no centre of gravity. There are so many values in normal life that sociologists speak of a hierarchy of values—the few at the centre and then the many more flexible and peripheral values. The same applies to absolutes—there is a hierarchy of absolutes that puts values in their right place. Because values are so important and foundational, we will discuss their nature and role in more detail in chapter five.

Establishing the priorities

Establishing the priorities is like erecting the pillars firmly on the foundation of the building. They are the key structural columns set along the edge of the value boundary. They rise directly out of the foundation. The rest of the construction will hang on these pillars. Priorities grow directly out of the values. They are the visible and high profile extension of the unseen values. If you try to make something a priority that is not in your foundation it will be a non-starter, no matter how much energy you put into it.

Priorities answer the question *what*? They describe what we actually do. Note that it is not what we talk about but what we actually do. Pastors, Churches and people can deceive themselves, by talking about things that they believe in and that they want to do or even think that they are doing, but what is actually done on a regular basis reflects the real priorities.

Technically priorities mean that which is primary, important. So priorities give us our *goals* and *plans*—that which we continually work at and do together. They tell us where to channel most of our energy and effort. All the other things we do extend from these, but these are the most important—otherwise they would not be priorities.

Modelling the practices

Modelling the practices is like building in all the functional aspects of the building and then making them fully operative. Practices hang on the priorities, they are built around and out of the priorities. Practices are like the functional aspects of the building—the windows, lights, plumbing, electricity, air-conditioning and furnishings. They are sometimes in view and sometimes out of view. These functional practices are so assumed and common that they become almost invisible as they flow through the super-structure, but they become visible at the point at which they produce their intended effect.

Practices answer the question *how*? In other words, how to do what we do. Our priorities tell us what we must do and the practices tell us how we should do it. Practices function in a number of ways through individuals and groups with skills, gifts and disciplines.

Practices give us *skills* and *disciplines*. They have to do with our style and methods, our way of doing things. Although practices are more oriented towards individuals, in terms of skills and style, they definitely have a corporate effect; i.e. they directly impact how we do things together, our particular style—which we can change from time to time so as to more effectively embody our values and fulfil our priorities.

It is precisely here that the rubber meets the road. Generally speaking, the people in the Church do not mind too much what the leaders say, or even what they believe in terms of vision, values and priorities, but when the practices are affected or changed, then they feel it. When the personnel and programmes are changed, when things are restructured, when the way of doing things is altered, then people take note. It is partly because they are directly affected, and partly because they are used to leaders talking about changing ideas, but without much action. And more importantly, it is because only then, when things actually change, that they see the logical conclusion of what 'this vision, values and priorities stuff' is all about. Then they are faced with a choice: does it really express the values they bought into or are they in the wrong place?

As an example, you can talk about the Church being family till you are blue in the face. But it will only affect the people when you change things accordingly. For instance, re-arranging the chairs from a rectangle into a semi-circle will definitely upset some people—some will not be able to find their regular seats. They will be in crisis. What do they do; have a fit or yield to more communal interaction? The change makes them re-evaluate their own values—and that of the leaders—which is very healthy! Then the 'reason why' emerges. Hopefully the change embodies the values more meaningfully. If you think about it, it is not all that important, as long as the changes do not directly violate the stated values.

Choosing the personnel

Choosing the personnel is like filling the building with all the people who make it alive, workable, functional and efficient—the staff in the building. The personnel are the people who labour in the environment of the superstructure, fulfilling the purpose of the building, bonded by the basic values, guided and supported by the priorities and sustained by the practices.

The personnel answers the question *with whom?* In doing what we do, with whom are we going to do it? It would obviously be people who buy into our vision and values and become committed in a relational and functional belonging. But not all people in the building will feel at home in the environment and structure and some will not be able to contribute to the accomplishment of the Church's purpose.

The personnel give us our *workers* and *leaders*. The process of recruiting, training, deploying and monitoring workers will be looked at, as well as the criteria for appointing leaders.

Implementing the programmes

Implementing the programmes is like structuring the activities that happen within the superstructure—as well as that which happens from the building out into the world around it. Programmes are what are seen in the building—the activities and the work-departments with their various procedures.

For programmes to be effective and successful they must be part of the overall vision and purpose of the Church and must embody and express the basic values—or at least be consistent with them. Further, programmes must uphold and help to achieve the priorities, and they must be done through the common practices of personnel who are appropriately gifted and called. Programmes can be changed, adapted or transplanted, only as far as they operate out of the underlying philosophy, the values, priorities and practices.

Programmes answer the question *through what?* The programmes are the flexible and appropriate structures through which we carry out our ministries.

Therefore, programmes give us *structure* and *cohesion*. They make for effective and efficient ministry.

Summarised Overview of Philosophy of Ministry

Philosophy of Ministry	Building Image	Answers the Question	Gives the Following
Purpose	Design	Who & Where?	Identity & Direction
Values	Foundations	Why?	Criteria & Principles
Priorities	Pillars	What?	Goals & Plans
Practices	Functionality	How?	Skills & Style
Personnel	Staff	With whom?	Workers & Leaders
Programmes	Activities	Through what?	Structure & Cohesion

Putting it all together—practically, how does it work?

Following these six steps will help you to develop your philosophy of ministry. In fact, it can be used to develop your life philosophy, your approach to your marriage, your approach to your job or department of ministry.

As an example, what is the purpose of my life (or my job, or the Church)? Let's say that I decide my life-purpose—or at least one of my purposes—is to love God with all my heart. That is, among other things, who I believe I am or want to be, and it directs where I am going with my life. Then I clarify my values by asking why I want to love God with all my heart? It may be because I value faithfulness and obedience to God, or because I really believe in being like Jesus. What priority, among others, will grow out of and express that value and help me to achieve my stated purpose or vision? In other words, what is the most important thing I must now do? The answer will be different for different people, but let us say, 'relationship with God'.

Establishing this priority raises the question as to how I actually 'do' relationship with God? I might develop my own practices or join up with someone who models certain disciplines, skills and methods that will help me to relate to God, like prayer and meditation, among other things. If the latter is the case, I am looking at with whom I do my relating to God in prayer and meditation. Lastly I ask through what structure or programme do I do my relating to God—it can be early morning devotions, or a programme of daily readings, or a regular prayer meeting that I attend.

By going through this process I develop a clear approach to my life. I know exactly where, why, what, how, with whom and through what I am doing and becoming. I will grow progressively into fulfilling my dream and life-purpose to love God with all my heart. And the fundamental reason is that I value, above most other things, being like Jesus, and this is evident in all that I do.

In summary: some qualifications and warnings

However, there are some warnings here—it is not as simple as it may appear. We often do not know what we want or what we really value; nor do we know how to manage our time and resources to achieve our purpose. Generally speaking, people are not very disciplined. Often there is a contradiction between what we say we value and what is self-evidently and actually valued. What we give time, energy and money to is what we actually value. Values are so ingrained, over so many years, that they are changed or transformed slowly, not instantly. Real change occurs only through a process of osmosis in relationships, through meaningful exposure to an environment embodying the values one wants to grow into or adopt. They are not changed through teaching, through a manual or a conference. A frequent mistake is that people see something they like and immediately want to do it without taking the time to imbibe the values. There is just no substitute for time and relationship in value-transformation.

The other problem is that if we spend time and energy on things that are not our real priorities, because they do not reflect our actual lived values, then an inner conflict is created, leading to feelings of meaninglessness and frustration. Reality teaches us that what we routinely do comes from and reflects who we really are. Reality is something we run into when we are wrong! This works both ways: if we say we value something but do not routinely and naturally do it, we contradict ourselves; and if we actually value something and we do not routinely do it, for whatever reason, we are a contradiction. Both ways produce problems of 'cognitive-dissonance'—a fancy word for a contradiction between one's mind and actions. It leads to confusion, hypocrisy, burn out and meaninglessness.

We're now in a position to discuss each of the above steps in detail in developing a philosophy of ministry. In so doing we will be describing the Vineyard way of doing Church. It may be a good idea at this point to look at the summarised overview of the Vineyard Philosophy of Ministry in appendix 3—it will clarify the basic framework in your mind before you begin the next chapters.

CHAPTER 4

DEFINE THE PURPOSE

I remember being with John for four days (in 1982) at Fuller Theological Seminary in Pasadena, when he taught a Doctorate of Ministry class on 'Developing a Master Plan for Church Growth' (another phrase for philosophy of ministry). John began by talking about the concept and importance of a plan, and the various steps involved in developing such a plan. The second morning he stood up and began with the first step by asking, 'What is Church? Why did God make Church? What is the reason for the Church's existence? What is the essential purpose of Church?'

Various answers were proposed and jotted down. This went on for some time. The board was almost full. When it was finished I never knew there were so many descriptions of the Church and so many more reasons for its existence! I felt quite overwhelmed and confused! Then John responded by explaining the need for a focused purpose, the few bare essentials, if not the central element. Then he proposed his answer for the purpose of the Church by writing one phrase on the board—which I will come back to shortly! Can you guess it? No cheating!

What we will cover in this chapter

In the previous chapter we introduced the six steps in building the Church from the bottom up. We said that the first step is to define the purpose of the Church, deciding on what type of Church we are building. It answers the question of who we are as a Church and where we are going. This then gives the framework in which one can draw up the design and plans—everything flows out of this definition of purpose. The result is that there is a clear sense of identity and direction. We cannot emphasise enough the critical importance of this first step. Equally important is the second step of clarifying the values (detailed in the next chapter). That is why we speak of 'vision and values'—the rest flows from this.

However, defining the purpose has two main aspects:

> • *The general purpose of 'The Church'*—applicable to all Churches everywhere—which is theologically informed.

> • *The more specific purpose for any local Church*—which is influenced by a mix of theological and local contextual and leadership factors. This is the sense of calling, of specific purpose that the local Church believes God has placed on them. This sense of calling may be adjusted and redefined or even changed from time to time in the life of a Church—often when the leadership undergoes change. As we have said, this local Church purpose has to do with developing mission and vision statements.

In this chapter, we will first discuss the general sense of defining the purpose of the Church. We will follow it up with some comments on potential problems or things to be aware of as we seek to define the purpose of the Church. Then we will look at the process of defining the specific purpose of the local Church, and all that it entails.

 ## DEFINING THE GENERAL PURPOSE OF THE CHURCH

Back to our story. The class of about thirty was surprised at John's phrase because it had not been mentioned by any of them as the specific purpose of the Church. Did you guess it? John wrote, 'The Kingdom of God'. Then he circled 'God' and 'Kingdom', and said the Church is for the King and His Kingdom. It means that we are for His pleasure and then we are the instruments of His rule to fulfil His purposes in this world. It seemed so simple and it made such sense.

For the King

The 'God' part first. John loved to put things in terms of Jesus and the Kingdom. Starting at the end as it were, the Great Commission (Matt 28:17-20), we have a picture of the Church seeing the risen Christ and worshipping Him and hearing His words, 'I have been given all authority in the heavens and the earth ...' This is the King of the Kingdom—triumphant through His death and resurrection and having been given, by the Father, all the authority over everything in both the unseen and the seen world. This is the vision that the Church must live and die for—to see and worship Jesus in all His Kingly power and authority (and the Father, who is the source of Jesus' Kingship). We can identify this as the first aspect of the purpose of the Church.

For the Kingdom

The second is 'the Kingdom' part—to be the instrument of the Kingdom, 'to go' with the delegated authority of the King 'and make disciples of all nations, baptising them ... teaching them ... and I will be with you always, to the very end of the age'. This second aspect has to do with evangelism and power encounter, integrating and training, in order to continue the cycle with every new disciple, right till the end of the age. In other words, each new Christ-follower must keep seeing the King in all His Kingly authority, and keep going out and making more followers of Jesus, integrating and training them, and then sending them out again. They go out with the vision of the King and His Kingdom and 'do the stuff' to the ends of the earth, till the end of the age. This second aspect of the purpose of the Church can be interpreted or expanded to involve a number of sub-purposes or aspects, as we will see below.

Worship and compassion

John has always spoken of the above two aspects of the purpose of the Church, in regard to the Vineyard, as worship (the King) and compassion (the Kingdom). In a Pastoral letter in the early '90s (Appendix 4, the subheading 'Vineyard Reflections'), John summarised the Vineyard in terms of a picture of a person standing on a platform with two arms reaching out. The two-tier foundation that we are built on, is first the Word of God, and second, the Kingdom of God (we discussed this in chapter two). The person stands balanced on two legs—the right leg is worship and the left leg is compassion. The torso describes the main functions of 'being Church'. The two arms reaching up and outwards describe the overall calling of the Vineyard, Church Planting, through the Association of Vineyard Churches, and Church Renewal, through Vineyard Ministries International. This picture aptly conveys the identity and direction of the Vineyard, both the Association of Vineyard Churches and the local Vineyard Christian Fellowship.

John's picture of the Vineyard

Aspects of the Kingdom purpose

However, back to the Kingdom purpose of being Church—the 'compassion' part. There are a number of aspects to the Church's purpose in being the instrument of the Kingdom of God on the earth. We started at the end, the Great Commission, and saw that it had to do with making disciples for Jesus—involving evangelism, integrating and training. To catch the spirit of this Kingdom purpose, to get to the heart and to the specifics, we need to go back to the beginning.

Theologically speaking, when we talk about these specific aspects of Kingdom purpose and ministry, we are talking about the 'signs' of the Kingdom's presence. They are done in and through the Church just as Jesus did them. The Church is, or should be, Jesus to this world, nothing more, nothing less. If we really fulfil this purpose, yes, we too will end up being crucified with Him ('all who live godly lives in Christ Jesus will suffer persecution', 2Tim 3:12). We must do what Jesus did the way He did it. We must teach what Jesus taught the way He taught it. We must live what Jesus lived the way He lived it. We simply must be Jesus to this world if there is going to be any hope—because that is our reason for existence. John's terminology would be to live the life of the Kingdom, speak the words of the Kingdom, do the works of the Kingdom and see the wonders of the Kingdom.

What impacted me when I first detailed this with John in 1982, was his request that we simply list the key aspects by listing the elements that certain key Scriptures summarise. Some of these elemental purposes will be duplicated in different Scriptures, especially the New Testament ones that allude to the Old Testament. Then, without adding any commentary, the full weight of the Kingdom 'commission', or purpose of the Church, will be felt. I trust that you will read the following slowly, as if you are hearing it for the first time, and allow the accumulative impact to deeply challenge you. Ask yourself: 'Are these things part of my life? Are they part of my Church's life?'

The elemental purposes of the Kingdom

The Old Testament promises God's liberation from evil—first for His people, and then through His people into the world. This happens in and through His Messiah (the Hebrew *Meshiach* means God's anointed King). The Scriptures give us the picture of the coming Kingdom in Messiah, and what will be done through Messiah, and by implication, through the people of Messiah, the Church. The New Testament Scriptures confirm, fulfil and expand on the Old Testament. We chose texts that are both descriptive and prescriptive in listing the work of the Kingdom. I will italicise the verbs to emphasise the purposeful action of Messiah and His people.

Isaiah 35:3-6

Strengthen the feeble hands
Steady the weak knees
Say to the fearful of heart, 'God will come ... He will come to save you'
Open the eyes of the blind
Unstop the ears of the deaf
Cause the lame to leap like a deer
Cause the tongue of the mute to shout for joy

Isaiah 61:1-3

Preach good news to the poor
Bind up the broken-hearted
Bring freedom to the captives
Release the prisoners from darkness
Proclaim this time as God's mercy and favour
Proclaim this time as God's vengeance on and defeat of evil
Comfort all who mourn

Ezekiel 34:1-4,11-12

Care for the sheep (the shepherds cared only for themselves)
Feed the hungry

Clothe the naked
Strengthen the weak
Heal the sick
Bind up the injured
Bring back the strays (backsliders)
Search for the lost

Luke 4:18 (this is the fulfilment of Isaiah 61—the 'mandate' of Messiah)

Preach good news to the poor
Bind up the broken-hearted
Proclaim freedom for the prisoners
Bring recovery of sight to the blind
Release the oppressed
Proclaim the year of God's favour

Luke 7:22 (this is the fulfilment of Isaiah 35:3-6)

The blind *receive* their sight
The lame *walk*
The lepers are *cured*
The deaf *hear*
The dead are *raised*
The good news (gospel) is *preached* to the poor

Matthew 25:35-40 (this Scripture, with John 10:1-11, fulfils Ezekiel 34:1-4,11-12)

Feed the hungry with food
Give the thirsty something to drink
Invite the strangers in
Clothe the naked
Look after the sick
Visit the prisoners

Matthew 10:1-8 (the commissioning of the twelve and the seventy-two disciples)

Preach this message, 'the Kingdom of the Heavens is near'

Heal the sick

Raise the dead

Cleanse those who have leprosy

Drive out the demons

Freely you have received so *freely give*

The 'Great Commission' Scriptures

(the following are summary statements from the Church's mandate in Matt 28:19-20, Mk 16:15-21, Lk 24:46-49, Jn 20:21, Acts 1:8)

1. *Go*—as the Father sent Jesus, even so He has sent you
2. *Preach* the gospel to all creation
3. *Make* disciples of all nations
4. *Baptise* them in the Name of the Father and the Son and the Holy Spirit
5. *Teach/train* them to obey all that Jesus commanded
6. *Be witnesses* of Jesus where you are, then progressively further afield
7. *Drive out* demons
8. *Speak* in new tongues
9. If you pick up snakes or drink any poisonous thing it will not hurt you
10. *Lay hands* on the sick and they will recover

How does this make you feel? Hopefully it inspires you with faith in what God can do and what we are destined for. It should not leave you hopeless, condemned and confused with 'all' that you and the Church 'should' or 'has to' do. The central idea is that the Church is for the world. Just as God so loved the world that He gave His own Son, so God gives His Church to the world in love. This is His compassion and mercy, in and through us, to the world. This how we live the 'Great Commandment' in loving God with all our hearts and loving our neighbour, as we love ourselves (Matt 22:37-40).

The basic concept is that all the above are 'signs' of the Kingdom's presence, various ways in which the Kingdom affects the world. Although it is mandatory, it is more descriptive than prescriptive. As the community and instrument of the Kingdom, if we keep 'looking to Jesus' (as mentioned above in reference to Matt 28:17-20), we will naturally deepen our involvement in His enterprise on earth. Worship is the fountain of mission—as we see Jesus having all authority in the heavens and on earth, we see the Kingdom manifesting itself in and through us with supernatural power. The signs follow the Kingdom's proclamation, presence and activity, in and through the Church. The 'doing' (the compassion) flows out of the 'being' (the worship—seeing the King). In other words, it is really a matter of vision and focus and then faith-obedience, not a matter of performance, duty and long lists of 'things to do'! This is the difference between law and grace, which is at the heart of Vineyard theology and experience.

To summarise

If we examine the lists and rationalise them into one list, it would really come down to a few basic things that describe the purpose of the Church as the instrument of the Kingdom: to be Jesus to this world—that is, preaching the Kingdom and then demonstrating it by caring for the poor and oppressed, healing the sick, driving out demons, seeking the lost, and integrating, teaching and training new disciples to do the same. That's it!

John would say, 'Doin' the stuff of the Kingdom.' Some Vineyards have printed that on Tee shirts, but one hopes that it is a lived life and not just a slogan—'been there, done that, taken the picture, got the Tee shirt!'

A good summary picture is found in Acts 10:38, '—how God anointed Jesus of Nazareth with the Holy Spirit and power, and how he went around doing good and healing all those who were sick and oppressed by the devil, because God was with him.' It applies to the Church in exactly the same way. But remember, it is more descriptive than prescriptive. It all comes from the King of the Kingdom, from seeing Jesus, born in the womb of worship.

As part of my time with John Wimber in 1982 we worked on a document that had been 'in process' for some time, called, 'The Vineyard Vision—1st Draft'. The idea was to capture the key purposes and understandings of being and doing Church as Vineyard was seeking to be and do. The '1st Draft' was elaborated on by John in a brief series that he presented, called, 'The Church I would like to join'—which we documented as the last section of the manual, 'Building from the bottom up'. I have given this explanation so that those who want to have a summarised picture of Church—in terms of its overall vision and purposes as Vineyard sees it—can read chapter ten at this point.

SOME POTENTIAL PROBLEMS IN DEFINING THE PURPOSE OF THE CHURCH

Not many people are sufficiently in touch with what forms their perspectives so as to be aware of their own presuppositions. The underlying assumptions that form our perspectives are called presuppositions. Culture, class, historical teachings and our gift-cluster can determine them. In other words, they are various 'lenses' through which we see things—and they need to be exposed and balanced if there is any hope of being reasonably objective. If there is not enough self-awareness or team participation (to balance our 'lenses'), a subjective or one-sided decision on the purpose of the Church will be made. We need to examine why we see things the way we do in order to discover how we really ought to be seeing things—maybe how they really are! There are a number of tendencies and potential problems in this regard.

There is the tendency toward selective obedience

Each group or Church tends to develop its own specialisation in ministry— for which it becomes known—and tends to neglect other important aspects or even the whole picture. This is often the result of a strong leader whose particular calling or 'bent' dominates. We need a team to help us see the big picture. And we need to move away from 'either/or' thinking and develop a 'both/and' approach in which we learn to integrate all aspects into the whole. Obviously, the opposite can happen where 'the whole' is so big and detailed that we are trying to do too many things and then we are not effective in any of them. The issue is, defining the key essentials, and then integrating each aspect into achieving the whole.

A strong Western worldview can be a problem

Our attempt to discuss the Biblical theology behind the purpose of the Church reveals a Middle-Eastern worldview, which is essentially more spiritual and experiential. (After all, the Bible is a Middle-Eastern book, is it not?) The Western worldview is rational and scientific, and if left unchecked will lead to a conceptual and cerebral type of Christianity (which is very common in the West, although there are many signs of dissatisfaction with an overly rational Christianity). It deeply estranges us from the real purpose of the Church, which has to do with spiritual engagement. We need to rediscover the experiential, the power encounter of the Kingdom, if we are to live out the Biblical purpose of the Church.

The danger of an overly 'spiritual' paradigm

On the other hand, an overly other-worldly understanding of the gospel can lead to an exclusively 'vertical' purpose of the Church—just concerned with getting souls into heaven. The 'horizontal' aspects of social concern and involvement in political and economic affairs are equally valid and important. In fact, Biblically speaking, it is impossible to conceive of the 'vertical' and the 'horizontal' dimensions of the gospel in opposition to one another—'if anyone says, "I love God", yet hates his brother, he is a liar. For anyone who does not love his brother whom he has seen, cannot love God, whom he has not seen' (1Jn 4:20).

The influence of outdated and invalid models

Models that we have been exposed to subconsciously form our view of things, our understanding of what the Church is about. What type of Church experience were you exposed to from childhood, or through your teenage years? What has it told you about the purpose of Church? Take a moment and think about it. Generally the Church is living in the past. In other words, we have models that we have inherited which were good for the time, but are now, in the main, out of touch. To break out of our subconscious conditioning and frame of reference is not easy. We need exposure to other environments and different models that seek to be relevant to their world. This will free us, not to copy them, but to discover our own unique sense of purpose to reach our generation and be relevant to our particular context.

We need a fully self-aware, fresh and creative team-approach, which will hopefully result in a Biblical, comprehensive, integrated and relevant purpose for the Church. This can be achieved in the local Church through particular processes, which we must now look at.

DEFINING THE SPECIFIC PURPOSE OF THE LOCAL CHURCH

How does one take the above—if it indeed does describe the Biblical purpose of the Church—and interpret it for the local Church? How does one word it so that it really expresses what the local Church is all about?

Some leaders try to take the overall Biblical purposes of the Church just as they are and present those as the purpose of the local Church. That is too general and vague, and even too detailed. Inevitably it has to be localised according the specific context so that it can work in the local situation.

Having said that, I need to say that we must never underestimate the tremendous power of a penetrating theological understanding of the Church and its purpose. Although this theology cannot really be reduced to a short statement without doing an injustice to its profound richness, it does work in and through us at a subconscious level, constantly challenging and forming our thinking and our actions. We must value good Biblical theology —it will always produce a growing hunger for prayer, a greater depth of emotional refinement, and an increasingly incisive and godly mind.

How do we go about defining the purpose of our local Church, being fully aware of Biblical theology, our own presuppositions and the potential problems that we have discussed? What other factors influence the process of purpose definition?

The pastor, the leadership team and the influencing factors

It obviously begins with the pastor and the team of leaders in the Church. A wise pastor will know three things: firstly, you cannot impose an ideal, or your ideal, on the Church. Secondly, the leaders must participate in the process of defining the purpose of the Church; and thirdly, you have to hear God together.

Therefore, to decide on the purpose of the Church requires time and energy in seeking God, in discussion and research. It means going through a process until things gel on the inside of the leader's heart, and the team's heart. They must know that God has spoken and that it 'fits' with who they are and their context.

The way the process takes place can vary greatly, but the basic elements would be the same. There would be some preparatory reading and discussions. There would probably need to be research of the community context. There would definitely need to be quality time away with the key leaders, and possibly with the help of a facilitator. This would allow them to seek God, share their hearts together, analyse where the Church is at and brainstorm the possibilities. This would include taking into consideration the Church's make up and resources and the community context and needs. Then they would come to some clarity and focus in regard to an agreed calling, and seek to capture it in a purpose statement.

Thus, a good pastor will be aware of the basic factors that influence the process of defining the purpose of the local Church, and will wisely work with them. The central issue is hearing from God, but in and through the mix of four key factors that I have alluded to: being theologically informed, having self and team understanding, knowing the Church, and its social context (these factors should minimise subjective or one-sided 'hearing from God').

Hearing from God

This matter of hearing from God should not be assumed. The fact that we do hear from God is crucial. The importance of a vision is often spoken of in terms of Proverbs 29:18, 'if there is no vision, the people perish'. It can be understood to mean that where there is no revelatory purpose from God, the people cast off their sense of self-discipline and lose focus and meaning. There are two unusual Hebrew words used here: 'vision' means 'prophecy' or 'revelation from God', and 'perish' is 'throwing off restraint'. The latter is used one other time in the Old Testament in reference to Israel at Sinai. When Moses did not come down from the mountain the people 'cast off restraint' and 'were running wild ... out of control'—they had made themselves gods of gold and were having an orgy (Ex 32:25). Hearing from God in terms of God's purpose for the Church is crucial for focus, discipline, direction and progress in the Church.

The role of Biblical theology

We hear God, firstly, by allowing Biblical theology to form and inform the purpose of the Church. This should be self-evident by now—and non-negotiable. We have looked at this aspect in some detail above, and what I have written can be used for this very purpose. On the other hand, it is no use deciding on a purpose for the Church that is just handed down or prescribed or written in a book somewhere. It has to be, to some extent at least, a personal and team discovery, something that grips you, gives you faith and conviction. God's written word must become His living Word that fills the pastor and the team with vision and faith.

The role of self-understanding—of gifting and personality

Secondly, we also hear God and seek to define the purpose of the Church within the realistic orbit of the gifts and personality of the senior leader. There must at least be other complementing gifts within the leadership team that can give some realistic hope of achieving the stated purpose. Often an evaluation process within the team, dealing with 'life-calling', 'gift-discovery', 'temperament analysis' and 'social styles', is very helpful and enlightening in this regard. One does not want to be like David in Saul's armour—it has to 'fit' the pastor and the leadership team. Having said that, the purpose or vision of the Church has to challenge and stretch you to exercise real faith, and full reliance on God, or else it ceases to be a vision from God, and it becomes human technology.

The staying power of the leadership

Another critical factor comes into play here—the commitment of the pastor and leadership team to stay, grow together and work for the medium or long term in order to fulfil the purpose. Who do we plan the Church for? Ourselves or others? If it is not for ourselves, why do it—surely we have to 'carry the can'? We cannot define the purpose of the Church and then just move on. That would be irresponsible, and we'd miss the fun and the fruit. Many studies show that those who stay together for the long haul are the ones most likely to do something significant with God, achieve their dreams and enjoy the fruit of their hard work and lived lives. Remember, often the best wine is brought out only toward the end of the feast!

Analysing the strengths and weaknesses of the Church

Thirdly, it is helpful to know the potential, the strengths and weaknesses, and the available resources of the local Church. The present 'ethos' of the Church must also be taken into account. We can ask, 'Why would someone join our Church? What can our Church do? Why does our Church exist?' The existing purpose of the Church can then be refined or redefined. We must not despise what is already there. God speaks to us through what we have, and He uses it for His further purposes. 'Moses, what do you have in your hand?' 'My rod, Lord.' 'Throw it down Moses ... now pick it up and use it as I direct.' From that time it was called 'the Rod of the Lord' and was instrumental in doing God's wonderful works.

The role of the community

Lastly, and equally importantly, is the community the Church is ministering to. It is obviously no use deciding on a Church purpose that is irrelevant and unworkable in your community. You have to know your community to some extent. God can also speak to you through it. What is its socio-economic profile? Will it change significantly in the next few years? How? Some people do detailed research so as to 'position' themselves to meet the needs in the community. The twofold question that should guide the thinking and discussion is: what does the community need and what can the Church be and do in order to meet that need? At the end of the day the Church, as it lives out its stated purpose, has to engage and impact, if not transform, the surrounding community.

However, to make the above discussion practical and workable, one must come to the point of developing a specific mission and/or vision statement. Although there are various views and definitions of mission and vision statements (e.g. some people recommend just one—a statement of purpose), it is commonly accepted that both are helpful, if not needful, and that there is a complementing difference between the two.

The Mission Statement

To define the purpose of the local Church, one needs to ask, who are we? Or who would we like to be? What are we for? What is the fundamental reason for our existence? The answer to these questions has to do with developing a mission statement.

A mission statement is a short and sharp statement clearly communicating your particular reason for existence. It is usually one brief sentence, often one line. The ones that work best are slogans that are easily remembered. It should not be too catchy or forced. It must genuinely say who you are, or at least whom you believe you are or want to be (as a Church). In my opinion it should not be too general or philosophic; it should be specific, gutsy and filled with conviction. Here are some examples from both Church and business.

Our Valley VCF mission statement is, *To Embody the Love of Jesus: a Community of Home Churches in Mission.*

The Association of Vineyard Churches (AVC): *To participate in the advancement of the Kingdom of God through the work of local Vineyard Churches that communicate the gospel of Jesus Christ in word and deed.*

Willow Creek Community Church (Bill Hybels): *To turn irreligious people into fully devoted followers of Jesus Christ.*

National Panasonic: *The quest for zero defect.*

Samsung South Africa: *Leadership through products.*

What do these tell you about identity and reason for existence? Do they communicate clearly and concisely? Does your Church have a mission statement? What is it? Is it satisfactory, or does it need to be worked on?

Of course, you may have the most eloquent and amazing mission statement, but if it is not being lived out, or at least being conscientiously worked towards, then it is not worth the paper it is written on.

A mission statement will not change much, certainly while the same overall leader is at the helm. He or she may adjust it once or twice, together with the broader leadership in the Church, and give good reasons for it, but on the whole, it will basically remain the same. One does not change who you are too often or else you lose your identity. And this is the heart of the mission statement: it embodies your identity.

The Vision Statement

If a mission statement gives identity by stating who we are, then a vision statement gives direction by describing who we are becoming and where we are going. It gives legs to the mission statement; it expands and empowers it in terms of spelling out the future picture and the basic strategy to get there. Some vision statements are even presented in point form, to make the few important purposes very clear.

A vision statement can be defined as a future-oriented picture of who or what you are becoming. Some people say that vision is creating a preferred future. It is longer and more detailed than a mission statement. But it must embody and clearly communicate the basic purposes and priorities of the Church—that which the Church is aiming for. It should also give strategic pointers as to how the Church will reach that preferred future. Lastly, it should inspire the people with vision and faith, giving them focus and motivation.

Two extremes must be avoided: a too short and 'reductionist' vision statement—reducing things to an unworkable or illogical extreme. This would end up being too similar to the mission statement and would confuse things. On the other hand, if it is too inclusive and detailed, it will lose its impact and dilute the focus. One has to strike a balance between the two extremes.

As an example, the Valley VCF vision statement as at 1999: *To be a community, that through worship and compassion, draws people into intimacy with God, and through loving relationships, heals and equips every disciple to assertively advance God's Kingdom in Gauteng and beyond.*

The AVC vision statement lists six purposes—each being fairly long sentences. (If you want to view it see appendix 4: Theological and Philosophic Statements.)

The Willow Creek vision statement is: *To become a Biblically functioning community of believers so that Christ's redemptive purposes can be accomplished in the world.*

What do these vision statements tell you? What are the key words? Do they convey the purposes and priorities? Does it communicate effectively? What is your Church's vision statement? Do you think it is effective? Does it describe what the Church is working towards or becoming? Or does it need adjusting?

Vision statements are more time and context specific. They may change or be adjusted from time to time, in different seasons of the Church's life. It often depends on a change in the context and/or a reflection on how accurately and effectively it communicates the purpose and priorities of the Church.

Communicating the purpose of the Church

Once the purpose of the Church has been agreed upon and defined in the form of a mission and a vision statement, it must be effectively communicated to the Church, not just one communication. This is critical for the well-being of the Church—it must be kept before the people on a fairly regular basis. Vision must not only be owned by the leaders, but by the people themselves if it is going to be a viable force in the Church. This does not just happen by itself. We need to think carefully about how we do this, because it needs to influence, govern and direct all the people and every aspect of ministry in the life of the Church.

There are many creative and effective ways to communicate the purpose and vision of the Church—through meaningful slogans, on brochures and letterheads, in pamphlets, through stories, symbols, logos, pictures, drama and video, in regular sermons, motivational talks, members' and leaders' meetings, etc. In doing this, we need to be careful not to become superficial or gimmicky, but rather, to marry efficiency with integrity. Ultimately, if the vision is really from God, and the pastor and leaders are passionate about it and live it out in their own lives and ministry work, it will have an authority from God that communicates itself—with the help of the various gifts in the team and Church.

Testing the effectiveness of our communication

An obvious test in any congregation is to ask various people—the new-comers, the regular members and the workers—what the purpose or vision of the Church is. Their response will immediately tell you how effective or ineffective the communication has been. But again, what is the real issue here? We can be pedantic about this or even deceive ourselves: what is stated and what is heard is not necessarily what is being lived out or being systematically worked towards. The ideal is regular and clear 'vision casting' and 'vision reinforcement' (as they call it), but with Church 'body language' that backs it up and 'incarnates' it through the priorities, practices and programmes of the Church.

If the people do not know or are uncertain or confused about the vision, it could mean one of a few possibilities. Either the vision is not being communicated at all or not enough, or the way it is being communicated is ineffective. The vision statement itself could be too long or not clear enough. Sadly, the body language of the Church could be undermining or even contradicting the stated vision.

If the people are apathetic or disinterested in the vision, it could mean that it has been communicated to saturation point, or the pastor has been too 'hot-air' or 'gimmicky' about it. Perhaps the contradiction between the stated vision and body practice has become too great. There could be other reasons as well.

In summary, effectively communicating the vision is a work of art! It is a fine balance between enough but not too much; between future projection and present reality; between 'sloganeering' and genuine understanding; between dreaming and genuine faith; between God's possibilities and our impossibilities; and between prayer and hard work. The focus of hard work should be on expressing and incarnating the mission and vision in your own life and in the activities of the Church.

CHAPTER 5

CLARIFY THE VALUES

John always used to say, 'What you give your time, energy and money to reflects your actual lived values, no matter what you say your values are.' He was quite blunt: 'All our human resources are summarised in the way we spend our time, energy and money—and they do not lie about our values and priorities!'

Therefore the best way to clarify your values is to start with the ones you already have. Get someone to live with you for two to four weeks in your normal life and record everything you do from your waking hours to when you go to sleep. It will show you what you regularly do (your priorities) so that you can reflect on why you do it (your values). Some business executives pay a trained consultant to do this, often leading to a wholesale restructuring of things. Or you can keep a detailed journal if you are honest, objective and thorough enough (the poor person's option!).

What do you think of that exercise? Quite radical! But then you will know your real values and priorities—in terms of the way you spend your time, energy and money. If you are the senior leader, your values will be affecting the Church, whether you know it or not. If you have measles and you preach mumps to your people, they will catch measles, not mumps. Who you are communicates louder than what you say. However, knowing your values allows you to decide if you want to change them, and to what you want to change and how you can change. All this has to do with intentionally clarifying and embracing a basic value-set that determines who you want to become.

You can apply a similar exercise to the Church to assess its present actual values through its lived priorities, and not necessarily what is stated. Decisions can then be made as to whether they reflect what you (as pastor) and the leadership believe or whether the values must change. Then you consider how to change existing values. What do we change to? How do we 'adopt' them?

With this, we come to the core of all that we are saying—we are now at the heart of this book. To clarify and build in the basic values is to establish the centre-point by which everything else is defined. Therefore, this chapter will communicate at a deeper level with considerably more detail—I encourage you to work carefully through it.

In chapter three we introduced the basic understanding and the essential role of values in developing a philosophy of ministry. We will now expand on this understanding and definition of values, and consider how binding are they, how they function and how we 'adopt' or grow into them. We will look at the values themselves, as John understood them in the late 1970s and early '80s. The values discussed in this chapter represent what the Vineyard is all about.

THE NATURE AND ROLE OF VALUES

We said in chapter three that values are like the foundation of the building, the substructure on which everything else is built. As the foundation is critical and definitive to a building, so values are absolutely crucial to the development, the strength and well-being of the Church—they are unseen, but their effect is seen and felt throughout the whole structure. Values consider why we do things so that we can intentionally plan and do what we really believe in. Therefore, values must be consciously reflected on, clarified and spelt out, because they give us the principles undergirding the way we operate and the criteria by which we evaluate all that we do.

However, we need to go further in our examination of the nature and role of values. I will be drawing on some broader understandings from Derek Morphew (in his membership course for Kenilworth VCF, see Appendix 4) which I have found helpful as a complement to John Wimber's insights.

What are values? (Historical and contemporary)

Some people say that values are beliefs and doctrines. Not quite—both yes and no. Values must be distinguished from historic doctrines, although they may arise from, and are certainly informed by, historic doctrine. In saying this we are not undermining Biblical doctrine in any way—it is normative for all Christians. Those who do not adhere to historic beliefs as summarised and agreed to in the Church creeds (the Trinity, the humanity and deity of Christ, the atonement, etc., in the Apostolic, Nicene, Reformed and Evangelical creeds) put themselves outside of orthodox Christian faith.

But values are more relative, more contemporary. They are emphases, understandings, convictions and principles that have been quickened in us by the Holy Spirit at the interface of root doctrines and current issues. Certain cultural and sociological forces give rise to specific issues that form a generation in a given time and place. Just think of the history of the Church. Various issues and social forces have come and gone from generation to generation, both universally and locally in different nations, giving rise to particular emphases and values at different times in the Church, e.g. 'justification by faith' in the Reformation era, 'social justice and liberation' in recent decades.

The gospel seeks to interact with these factors and incarnate itself in society in a way that makes for effective witness. This raises the question regarding what is relevant to our context, what is important to us at this time in order for us to effectively reach our generation. We are not saying that we must adopt 'worldly' values. It is defining convictions and principles that are in touch with our contextual reality and thereby establishing values that will hopefully engage with, witness to and even transform the values and the world around us!

In seeking to do this for the Baby-Boomer generation, John believed that the values articulated below would lead to a way of doing Church that could effectively reach and transform them. The same will have to be done, in many different ways, for the next generation (e.g. the 'Buster generation', those presently under 30 years of age)—and this is already happening in some parts of the world with exciting results.

How non-negotiable are values? (A hierarchy of absolutes)

The use of this language of values, priorities and practices, is a value in itself. It reflects an approach, when 'doing Church', that avoids absolutes, either/or, right/wrong, black/white categories and thinking. This does not apply when it comes to the basics of our Christian faith, as well as to ethical and other matters.

Disclaimer language

However, in 'doing Church' John used to talk of using 'disclaimer' language as opposed to 'absolutist' language. This applies to a philosophy of ministry, giving prophecies or when ministering to people. As an example, one would say, 'I sense God is ...', 'I feel ...', 'My impression is ...'; as opposed to saying, 'God says you must ...', 'Thus says the Lord ...', etc. The idea is to remove the suggestion of infallibility and the possibility of human manipulation. Disclaimer language helps us to acknowledge that we all see in part, know in part, prophesy in part (1Cor 13:9).

The same applies to values. We avoid the suggestion that what we stand for is exclusively from God, and we refrain from making disparaging comparisons with other movements and their philosophy of ministry. The reason why we speak of values is that we can clearly state what is important to us while respecting and honouring other movements and Churches with different value systems that are legitimate and useful to God.

Absolutist language

Absolutist language does the opposite, and it has its own wrong logic:

'God has called us'

'Therefore, what we do comes from God'

'Therefore we are what God is doing'

'Therefore to join what God is doing you must join us'

The twofold implication is clear: 'What others are doing is not really what God is doing, so if you do not join us then you are out of God's will or you will be left out of the flow of the Spirit.' The language and logic is never that blatant or obvious, but if one listens carefully, one can quickly identify absolutist language—it always makes one feel inferior and invalid, as if something is wrong with oneself and one's Church.

The language of values

The language of values deprecates such messianic consciousness and goes something like this:

'Other movements or Churches have such and such values'

'Their testimony is one we respect and accept as part of God's Kingdom activity'

'We have these values, which differ thus and so'

'It is not that they are wrong and we are right, or vice versa, we are just different'

The implication is clear: 'This is us and that is them—we have our reasons for our values, and they have theirs, and we are both happy and mutually respectful of each other and of what God is doing through each of us.' The Kingdom is much, much bigger than we are!

A hierarchy of absolutes

We all live and work with a 'hierarchy of absolutes' as Christians, whether we are conscious of it or not. Absolutes and clear definitions meet the basic human need for security. We feel secure when we know where the line is. Unfortunately, we often major in minors and make minors out of majors. We end up with a warped perspective and create problems for others and ourselves. For example, in our current 'post-modern' world we are facing a very serious erosion of absolutes and the relativization of most things. Relativism means 'if it feels right for you, it is right—for you'. In other words, your viewpoint or belief or feeling is valid, but only for you, not everyone else. The irony is that people are becoming dogmatic about their relative views! We now have to deal with 'relative absolutes' and 'absolute relatives' at the same time! Our world no longer sees clearly, for we have lost the anchor of absolutes and are adrift in a sea of relativity.

However, to see clearly as Christians we need to understand the hierarchy of absolutes, because it qualifies the role and nature of values.

- *God*, revealed in Jesus Christ, is the ultimate absolute.

- *Scripture* is our primary authority for faith and life. This is a lesser absolute because it involves human mediation and interpretation.

- *Historic orthodox evangelical doctrine* embodied in the Apostolic, Nicene, Athenasian and Chalcedonian creeds, form the fundamentals of our faith, the basis of our unity as 'one holy catholic and apostolic Church'.

- Other *statements of faith*, from the Reformation, from various Churches (see Vineyard Statement of Faith, Appendix 2), have a relative absolute value in that they are derived from the early creeds and they communicate what Denominations or Churches consider to be the Biblical non-negotiables of their faith.

- Lastly *'values'*, as we have been defining and using the term, are bottom of the pile (or the crest on the triangle of absolutes— depending on how you picture it). Values are the least authoritative, but are still important. They are foundational, giving us our basic non-negotiables, not in terms of Christian faith, but in terms of how we do Church, how we live out and practise our faith in and through a particular community of faith, in a particular place, at a particular time in history.

Summarising the nature and role of values

In summary, values are contextual, generational and can evolve over time. Although they are not absolutes, they are absolutely crucial as to what we do and why, and how we do things. They give us a sense of being family, enabling us to do something together in the Kingdom. They give us a common sense of gravity, a centre around which we think and organise our lives and activities. They are dynamic, not static, although they may remain constant for years. Unlike legal constitutional systems that become fixed in time, only to imprison later generations, a set of values reflects what is true to life and is more organic. While they are very deep convictions, they do change and develop over the years, thus indicating that we never stop changing under the hand of God.

Furthermore, values are flexible and open to interpretation and contextualization within various localities. In this sense John made the point that there is no one type of Vineyard Church—each one is unique—especially when it comes to cross-cultural Church planting. John used to ask what a Vineyard Church would look like in a particular nation and then say that only those people could show us. In other words, the values are the same but the contextualization makes it look unique and different. This is a value in itself, allowing for discovery, growth, experimentation, non-imperialism, open and free debate. While making room for much diversity, a common set of values does create a sense of like-mindedness, a model, and a common feel in Churches that are widely set apart in place and culture. We do not do cloning with values. We do not have to have party-liners. Yet, we do have the same seed, or deposit, that makes us family.

It is necessary to spell out all of the above because, if human nature is what it is, some might talk of 'The Vineyard Values' as the gospel, or the 'Kingdom measurement' for all Churches. It could become the means of judging each other as to how 'pure' we are—especially in Vineyard. Imagine always checking on one another to see whether we measure up! God forbid! Commitment and loyalty are to people and relationships, not to a system or structure or philosophy. The former works through certain basic values that we journey towards, each at a different proximity to the centre. The latter works through the coercion of rules and principles that clearly define whether you are in or out—it really is institutionalism and denominationalism, not a family.

The danger is that, because of our own lack of wholeness—our need for definition and control, for security in absolutes—we use the Centred-set values in a Bounded-set way. This must be guarded against. The best antidote is relationships—honest, open, loving, adult relationships. The whole thing stands or falls on the quality of our relationships! Yes, it is really as vulnerable as that!

How many values are there; how many should we have? (a hierarchy of values)

The strict meaning of 'values' is choices, preferences, and the criteria by which we make evaluations and judgements. For example, I prefer filter coffee to instant coffee—that is a value. But is it an important one? Will it change my life? (You never know; it is a matter of perspective!)

There are so many values in normal life, let alone Church life, that sociologists speak of a 'hierarchy of values'. The issue concerns which are the more fundamental, important, even non-negotiable values, and which are the more derived, lesser, negotiable and flexible values? The matter of perspective again! When working with John on the document, 'Building from the bottom up', he repeatedly asked, 'What are our most basic, most crucial values in the Vineyard?' Then he would add, 'Only a few, not many— the fewer the better—the less chance for rules and regulations, for ideologies and systems, and the greater the potential for true relationships around a few basic values.' Real leadership gives perspective, knowing what is important versus urgent, what is major versus minor, what is balanced versus extreme, and in this regard John was a gifted leader.

There are extremes in regard to what and how many values you have. You can become too 'reductionist'—reducing values to so few that justice is not being done to what is really foundational. 'Squashing' everything into two or three values may lose critical aspects of who you really are or want to be. At the same time, you cannot be too 'spiritual' or idealistic and say 'Jesus' or 'the Bible' constitutes my core values. What does that actually mean? With all due respect to Jesus and the Bible, it is too vague. Neither should you have too many values, trying to incorporate and articulate every aspect and nuance of what you are or want to be. In trying to be everything you become nothing. More than a handful or so becomes too many to remember, too complex to explain, too numerous and diverse to be a point of common focus.

The core values of the Vineyard

Changing the 'hierarchy' metaphor, we can talk about a centre of gravity, like a magnet that draws iron filings to itself. In other words, what few basic values are at the centre, putting into perspective and into place, at varying levels of importance, other more derived and peripheral values? What values would be core, and what would be derived and implied? Through his Church and theological journey in the late '60s and '70s John came to answer that question with six core values:

- *The value of the Bible:* a particular approach to Scripture.

- *The value of Jesus and the Holy Spirit:* the particular place of Christ and of the Holy Spirit in the Church—the Headship of Jesus and the Administration of the Spirit.

- *The value of relationships:* the particular primacy of relationships and reality.

- *The value of the individual:* the particular importance of grace and mercy.

- *The value of healing:* the particular effect of an environment and practice of wholistic healing.

- *The value of the Kingdom of God:* the particular concern for changing the world through a wholistic approach in 'equipping the saints' for ministry and mission.

(By the way, I spell wholistic with a 'w' and not 'holistic' so as to avoid any confusion with the New Age connotations identified with the latter usage.)

John's particular understanding of each of these six core values will be discussed soon. He was very clear that these core values implied other complementary and derived values that are not specifically part of the centre. For example, the Centred-set approach, with its various characteristics listed in chapter two, are all values that makes Vineyard who and what we are, but they are not specified as part of the six above. Another example would be the fifteen values mentioned in the Vineyard booklet, Theological and Philosophical Statements, published in 1995 (see Appendix 4). These fifteen values (the pursuit of God, Christlikeness, being Spirit-led, prayer, discipleship, the Kingdom of God, mercy of God, integrity, servant leadership, the individual, unity, collegiate relationships, reality, simplicity, and cultural relevance) overlap with and are implied in the six values stated above. One could add many more, like love, justice, honour, fear of God, the poor, etc., but too many is not functional. For John and the Vineyard, they all find their place as defined by and derived from the six core values.

What is the role of values? (spirituality and style)

We have already said that the role of values is foundational, giving principles and criteria that govern our sense of being and doing. But we need to comment on the role of values in terms of the Church's 'spirituality' and 'style'.

What we mean by spirituality

It is the formation of the inner character, the heart content, the ethos and culture of a group. This is the work and fruit of its value system. The roots determine the fruits—it takes time and careful cultivation before the fruit emerges. Once the ethos and fruit is established, you know its roots, and consequently, what kind of tree it is. Any serious examination of a Church or family of Churches will give you a feel for its ethos, its spirituality, which is the work of its values.

For example, Pentecostal Churches have a certain feel about them, whereas

Evangelical Churches are different. Examining what elements make up the feel, the character and spirituality, will quickly lead one to the core values. In this sense, 'spirituality' should not be used in a judgemental or disparaging way, but rather as a challenge to examine what we are forming, or how we are being formed. One can refer to Jesus' letters to the seven Churches in Revelation as an example of a 'corporate spirituality' and the values that have formed it—and Jesus' evaluation and challenge to them.

What we mean by style—both general and specific style
Values also determine our style, the way we do things, which is similar, yet different to spirituality. In fact, the philosophy of ministry that we embrace, whatever it may be, will end up determining our style in a general sense—and values will be at the heart of it. However, style is also determined by personality, gifting, culture and context, and is only really seen at the point of practices. It is seen in how we do things, or the way we do things when we do them. Here we must distinguish between general style determined by a value-set (a particular philosophy of ministry) and a specific personal style that is a mix of values, personality, gifting, culture and context.

For example, general style means that I will not consciously condemn or 'hype' the people in the way that I preach because of my value of non-manipulation. But specific style means that I might raise my voice or be unpredictable when I preach. The issue is, why would I do that? Does it come from my personality or God's inspiration or is it a manipulative 'gimmick'? If it is the latter, my style is unacceptable and needs to be lovingly corrected. If it is the former, my style is acceptable, although some people may not relate to it. If it comes from God's inspiration, it will be self-evident by having the desired effect. There can, unfortunately, be spurious 'inspiration' that covers a multitude of 'style-sins'! A further example: general style says that I will avoid 'religiosity' and 'be real' when I pray. But specific style means that the way the prayer actually comes out is different for different people. The issue is whether I have integrity with my values, and at the same time, honest and free expression of my personality, gifting and culture.

Evaluating spirituality and style in the Vineyard

Values are more binding, style is more flexible—precisely because style is influenced by a mix of values, personality, gifting, culture and context. Spirituality says that our values should definitely determine, or at least strongly influence, our style and way of doing things. It also says that our style should not be the sole measure of our values, otherwise we become ideological and legalistic. So if or when we say, 'This or that is not Vineyard style—it is more Pentecostal or whatever,' we must be careful what we are pointing to or seeking to address—the underlying values or the personality, gifting and context. It is difficult, as it is mostly a mix of both. Therefore, we should be slow to judge.

In this regard, people need time to 'lay off baggage' (learned styles and patterns) from other environments and value systems, in order to undergo inner transformation of values in the new environment, before they are given prominence or leadership in the Church. It is not a matter of conformity to 'our style', but rather a process of unlearning 'old' styles, laying aside habitual patterns and responses, while undergoing a growing inner transformation of values. This will express itself accordingly. The process is especially important for people in leadership, because they model the values, priorities and practices.

To summarise, values are common and shared, but style is different and diverse. There is one exception. When style directly contradicts basic values, it must be confronted. In this sense, there is a common style and correction comes, not through conformity to style, but through a deeper exposure to basic values. Trying to change the outer style without inner transformation of values is 'religion', the legalism of the Pharisees. Thus, we can talk about a 'spirituality of style' that says the more we live out our stated values the more common our style becomes—in Christlikeness, compassion, and non-manipulation. This will lead to the paradox of greater diversity and uniqueness in our individual and Church styles—because personalities and giftings will mature through increasingly creative responses to different cultures and contexts.

How do we adopt or change or grow new values? ('better caught that taught')

Having clarified the existing values—as per the exercise mentioned at the opening of this chapter—you then have to decide what values you want and how they can be integrated. It is easier to identify what you do not want than to know what you want. Often you 'discover' what you want by seeing or experiencing it, or even reading about it. This leads to a 'gut-feel' that 'this is home for me', but then you still have to find out what values undergird this experience.

The idea is to look out for a model that embodies the values that you believe in, where you feel at home. Then 'hang out' in that environment and begin the process of change. The cost must be counted. You will pay a price—maybe small or maybe almost everything. Worthwhile and lasting change always costs.

Values are adopted or imbibed through a process of osmosis in relationships, exposure to an environment that embodies the values you are looking for. Information, or teaching, or a conference, or reading a book does not transfer values. It takes place through living tradition, through people—via relationships and personal engagement. It is 'caught, not taught'—a matter of impartation and transformation. Listening to a person's story is an effective way of communicating values. We need to recover and practise the art of story telling (technically called 'narrative theology') as a means of imparting values.

Written materials help to confirm, articulate and reinforce the values, but they certainly do not impart or transfer them. So much for possibly treating this book as the latest manual or method, to be read and then implemented in your environment—it just will not work! It does not, cannot, and never will, replace the principle of incarnation. Values are in people, and you need to take the time and effort to connect deep and long enough with the people for the values to 'rub off' on you. There is just no substitute for relationships. It is a process of hidden and inner transformation, not outward conformity—no matter what type of conformity, whether behavioural, structural, legal or constitutional.

Having a Values Statement

We need to point out that many groups and Churches find it helpful to develop a concise Values Statement. As mentioned in the previous chapter, the sense of purpose a particular Church decides upon is best expressed and communicated in the form of a Mission and Vision Statement. This can be followed with a Values Statement that embodies the heart of the Church—one brief sentence clearly communicating each basic value. The dynamics governing the development of a purpose statement, as discussed in chapter four, equally apply when developing a Values Statement. This can be put on the Church brochure or other means of public communication.

We are now in a position to talk about the values themselves. With each value I will refer to the historical roots and its contemporary relevance, and then what it means in terms of its implications. The following then constitutes our foundational thinking about the way we do Church.

 ## VALUE 1: THE BIBLE

This has to do with valuing a particular approach to the Scriptures.

The historical context

The authority and role of Scripture begins with the establishing of the New Testament canon (the books in the New Testament), a finalizing of 'the faith that was once for all entrusted to the saints' (Jude 3). The authority of Scripture—the written record of 'the faith' entrusted to the Church—became an issue again when the Protestants raised it above Church councils and traditions in the 1600s. It again became an issue in the 1800s, when liberalism and rationalism affected theological thinking to the point of a sharp division between 'Liberal Theology' and 'Conservative Evangelicals' (the latter does not mean conservative in the modern political or fundamentalist sense).

The issue more recently, in the 1900s, has been the Pentecostal tendency to subjective interpretation of Scripture with 'proof-texting' (finding verses to 'prove' any given position). This has led to a fundamentalist approach that holds to a dogmatic, literal and legalistic interpretation of Scripture. The Liberal approach reacted to this resulting in what has been called, 'The Battle for the Bible'. (There has also been the influence of Liberation and other Contextual theologies, which did not strongly affect John Wimber's context and definition of Scripture.) However, all of this necessitated an unequivocal and clear approach to the authority of Scripture.

The result was John's type of 'redefinition'—a particular approach to Scripture within the conservative evangelical tradition (introduced in chapter two). We believe Scripture is inspired by God and is our authority for faith and life. But we must spell out the ways in which this is meaningful for us.

The relevance to the contemporary context

The Baby-Boomers, and people in general, are tired of talk and information. They are disillusioned with dogmatism and double standards. Furthermore, the explanations we give no longer satisfy or answer the questions being asked. There is a deep need for emotional expression, for experience, for spiritual and ultimate reality. However, as absolutes are being forsaken, there is a growing insecurity in the sea of relativity. What do people turn to? They are looking for integrity of life and talk; they want knowledge and action, insight and experience, relationship and meaning.

Therefore we approach the Bible with these things in mind, seeking a dynamic connection with God and people through Scripture. What does this really mean and how does it work?

The meaning and implications

Firstly, the Bible is not a book of doctrines; it is alive with God's presence and wisdom as we seek to practise it.

We want to hear, know and experience God. Rational Christianity has run its course; we need a more balanced and wholistic experience of God and Scripture. The Bible has the best information on living life, as God wants us to live it. But we will only experience what it teaches when we apply or practise it in our daily lives. We read of other people's experience of God in the Bible, which helps us understand our own experience of God. Thus we have a dynamic, not only a rational, approach to Scripture. The living Word, which is powerful and active, sharper than any two-edged sword, comes to us in and through the written word (Heb 4:12). How do we encounter God through the Bible? By meditation and study, but also through encountering God in the experience of Scripture when we practise it and apply it in our daily lives.

For example, people would come to John Wimber after he had taught saying, 'That was a great meal John, you fed us on the meat of the Word today.' John would reply, 'No, I just described the menu, you have to go now and do it—the meat is in the street.' We do not expound or eat the menu. Nourishment and strength comes as you enjoy the meal, not as you study the menu! We are not fed on 'the meat of the Word' by doing deep typological and mental gymnastics, or by attending the next conference, but by obeying the Great Commission, by caring for the poor, by worshipping, praying and healing the sick. The meat is in the street! It is no use 'knowing' truth if you do not live it.

Secondly, there is a balance between 'doing and teaching' the Word, the 'words and works' of Jesus, and being 'formed and informed'.

This New Testament language implies an approach to Scripture that is neither theoretical and abstract, nor subjective and uninformed. We cannot stop short at the point of strong evangelical doctrine, which can be technical and 'dry'. Neither can we go with every latest buzz-word or charismatic fad unless it measures up to sound biblical theology.

Thirdly, we must avoid extremes and dangers in regard to the use of Scripture.

Some groups 'worship' the Bible as if it is God. It is used to establish fixed positions and doctrines, to argue our 'right' positions with one another. Some have even become self-appointed protectors of 'the truth' by going around Bible-bashing others. The Bible is not the domain of academics or professionals, a technical book understood only by a few. Neither should people use it for their own purposes, whether to justify sin or cultural norms and taboos, or to find subjective guidance—using it like a horoscope. We must avoid rationalizing, politicizing or spiritualizing Scripture.

Fourthly, we must allow the Bible to speak for itself.

When reading the Scriptures we must put aside, or at least acknowledge, our cultural, doctrinal, denominational and philosophic presuppositions. We must not read our own views into Scripture (that is why expository preaching is so helpful, as it disciplines us away from our own 'bent'). Scripture must be read in its own context, taking into account historical doctrine, responsible Biblical scholarship and accepted orthodox evangelical principles of Bible interpretation. In so doing we hear God and know His truth, and are transformed as we practise it.

Fifthly, we have an approach to the wholeness of truth that allows us to integrate Biblical and 'other' truth.

We draw from the Bible, and from the human sciences for the purpose of establishing truth. John had a saying: 'All that is in the Bible is true, but not all truth is in the Bible.' This is not an either/or approach. To contextualize the historic message of Scripture, we need to dialogue with our current world. This often requires an appreciation for scientific enquiry—for example, sociology and 'Church Growth'; medicine and healing; psychology and counselling, etc. We must neither compromise on the authority of revealed truth nor bury our heads in the sands of fundamentalism.

In summary, to be 'Biblical Christians' is not to quote the right verses or to necessarily believe the right doctrines, but rather to handle the word of truth responsibly and correctly, and become and do what the Bible really says.

VALUE 2: JESUS AND THE HOLY SPIRIT

This has to do with valuing the Headship of Christ and the Administration of the Holy Spirit.

The historical context

The central issue in this value concerns who owns and who leads the Church? It began with Israel under God's invisible government and her later desire to have a physical king. The issue was seen in the early Church, as described in Acts of the Apostles—governed and led by the ascended Christ through the fullness of the Holy Spirit. The Churches had leaders, pastors and elders, but they were, at their peak, evidently under the control of the Spirit. They were the actual and continuing body and ministry of Jesus to the world. We can safely say that the Headship of Christ through the Administration of the Holy Spirit was a dynamic experience far outshining any static or fixed position or pattern of Church government and leadership that we may want to identify in the Biblical text.

Through the history of the Church three basic models of Church government and leadership emerged: the Apostolic or Episcopalian system, the Presbyterian or Eldership model, and the Congregational or 'democratic' system. They have often led to a sense of ownership of the local or denominational Church by its leadership, resulting in division and control—a Bounded-set experience.

John Wimber wanted to allow Jesus and the Holy Spirit their rightful place in the Church, recovering the organic dynamic of God's government. The issue for John was not a specific form of Church government. He sought the Spirit's freedom and control through responsible Spirit-filled leadership. The classic 'Charismatic Renewal' in the 1960s and '70s emphasised, among other things, the freeing up of the Church from human control by allowing Jesus to do whatever He wanted through His Spirit, by the gifts of grace that He so generously distributes. John fully bought into that reality—experientially and conceptually. In this historic developmental sense, the Vineyard is positioned within the Charismatic renewal.

'Give Me back My Church!'

I will never forget the first time I heard John speak in a large conference setting—during his visit to South Africa in 1981 (mentioned in chapter one). He spoke to about two thousand people and said, 'I have come to South Africa with one message. Jesus told me to tell you, "I want My Church back!" So please give the Church back to its rightful owner.' He spoke very briefly, for only about twelve minutes, repeating and emphasising this basic call, 'Give the Church back to Jesus!' Then he prayed and apologised to Jesus and the Holy Spirit for the fact that we had not recognised and given them their rightful place in the Church. This was followed up with an invitation to the Holy Spirit to come and minister. Heaven broke loose among us with all kinds of healings and manifestations of power. It was glorious!

I was dumbstruck, not by the shortness of his talk (this would be a record for most preachers!), but by the truth of Revelation 3:20. John used this text to say that Jesus is knocking, not at the door of our hearts, but at the door of the local Church, wanting to come back in. Through our indifferent luke-warmness and our blinding self-indulgence and satisfaction, we have left Jesus out of the Church—His Church, which He bought with His own precious blood! We have assumed full control, rejecting His leadership. This humiliating insult nauseates Jesus. But instead of vomiting us out of His Body, He knocks on the door of the Church and cries out, 'Hey, can anyone in there hear me? Amidst all your noise, meetings, songs, programmes, prayers, committees and goings-on, can you hear me? It's My Church, not yours—I want it back! If you hear my voice, and open the door, and allow me back in with full control, then I will share my resources with you, and we will discuss and do everything together.'

Can you imagine it—Jesus left out in the cold, desperately crying out for someone to hear and let Him back in? It's all for our own sake! We are so deceived by our own self-confidence and 'rich' resources that we 'run' our Churches, doing our own thing, leading and controlling without any reference to its rightful owner. We cannot see how utterly wretched, pitiful, poor, blind and naked we are. Is this not an accurate and disturbing picture of the contemporary Church?

The relevance to the contemporary context

John connected with the Baby-Boomers' rejection of authoritarian leadership—they are tired of being parented and told what to do. He wanted to correct the abuses and excesses of authority and model a style of leadership that was much more open, relational, real and functional. The Boomers have been looking for this. John wanted to counter the human need for control, the tendency to be king or to make a king. He wanted no part in the superstar syndrome—playing the game of adulation, titles, position and power.

Instead, John sought to operate out of a spiritual authority that comes from servant leadership by the indwelling Spirit, with His character and gifts. As long as leadership is genuinely gift-based and accountable, allowing Jesus and the Spirit maximum freedom to own, lead and administrate His Church, then the particular system or model of Church government will not be an issue.

Therefore, in developing this value of the Headship of Jesus and the Administration of the Holy Spirit, we have to learn how to live under invisible government. It is honouring Jesus as Lord over the Church and the Holy Spirit as Lord in the Church.

The meaning and implications

Firstly, it implies a thoroughly Trinitarian experience of God and Church.

We must love the Father and seek His face by honouring Christ's Headship and by being fully dependent on the Holy Spirit. John spoke of various kinds of 'Trinities' that are being worshipped in the contemporary Church (his Trinitarian approach is found in his book, Power Points—see appendix 4). We need to be clear on what type of Trinity we are in fact worshipping:

- God the Father, God the Son, God the Holy Church—an overemphasis of the Church as the only real frame of reference, resulting in traditionalism.

- God the Father, God the Son, God the Holy Bible—using and

worshipping the Bible as the third Person of the Trinity, resulting in legalism and fundamentalism (in the ideological or fanatical sense).

- God the Father, God the Son, God the Holy Experience—seeking the supernatural and spiritual gifts as an end in itself, resulting in sensationalism.

- God the Father, God the Son, God the Holy Ministry—the ministry and mission of the Church becomes the only and all-consuming reason for its existence, resulting in performance and manipulation.

- God the Father, God the Son, God the Holy Man—perceiving the 'man of God' (very rarely a woman) as the holy anointed one, the be all and end all of everything, resulting in idolatry.

- God the Father, God the Son, God the Holy Spirit—receiving and honouring the Spirit by giving Him His correct place in the Church, resulting in incarnation: the presence, power and freedom of the Father and the Son. Jesus said, 'I and my Father will come and dwell in you' (Jn 14:23; see also Jn 16:13-15, Eph 2:21-22, Acts 1:8, 2Cor 3:17-18).

Secondly, it means learning to love His presence and worship His glory.

We are, and we must be, the 'People of His Presence'. Like Moses and Israel in the wilderness, the only thing that should distinguish us and make us any different from all other people on the earth, is the evident presence of Yahweh with us (Ex 33:14-16). Biblically speaking, what makes Church real Church—as God intended Church to be—is His manifest presence. This will lead to, and be dependent on, among other things, right relationships among His people (Matt 18:15-20). Jesus' presence brings rest, in which we are led, not driven (Matt 11:28-30). In this sense, we should be a million times more the 'Presence-led Church' than the 'Purpose-driven Church'.

John's deepest desire was for God's presence. The song he wrote—that I recorded in my tribute to him—captures this intense yearning. His greatest fears had to do with the loss of God's presence, the loss of intimacy with the Father. This goes to the heart of what it means to be a human being: we were made by Him and for Him. Our ultimate fear is to be rejected by

Him, cast into hell, into outer darkness beyond His presence. The crucified Christ experienced this hellish rejection on our behalf when He screamed, '*Eloi, Eloi, lama sabach-thani*—my God, my God, why have you forsaken me?' John frequently echoed David's prayer, 'Cast me not away from Your presence and take not your Holy Spirit from me' (Ps 51:11).

Church should be structured and done in such a way that the minute the presence of God is not there everything should collapse. If the Holy Spirit withdraws at any point because He is grieved for whatever reason everything should go wrong. We should be as vulnerable as that! The universe is. It would instantly implode if God withdrew His presence and His Word (Heb 1:3). It is my considered opinion that most Churches do not even know if God's presence is among them or not. Business continues as usual because what sustains them, what makes them 'tick', is their own programmes, personalities, power and control. Would we know it if God withdrew His presence and wrote '*Ichabod*' over our Churches because 'the glory had departed' (as in the Temple in Ezekiel ch. 10)? Would anything change in the Church to show us that in reality everything has changed that ever could change—because God is not there? John used to say that if the Lord did not 'show up' when we gathered we should have the courage to call it a day and go home because there is no other reason for meeting!

Thirdly, it means a healthy and fearful respect for the Lord's control and initiative in the Church.

Jesus is the origin, owner and goal of the Church. Everything that happens should be from Him, by Him and for Him, 'so that in everything He might have the supremacy' (Col 1:16-20). The Church does not belong to the Senior Pastor or the Board of Elders or whoever. God must be free to do His thing in and through His Church. When Yahweh was restoring His presence and glory to His Temple, Uzzah presumed he could stabilize or control what God was doing by reaching out his hand and touching the ark as the oxen stumbled (2Sam 6:6,7). God struck him dead! Why? He did not honour God's way. How many times do we presume to put our own fingerprints on God's work—especially when it is not going well or when we think that we can do a better job! Despite the apparent weaknesses, God is sovereignly at work and

His Kingdom is doing fine, thank you! Do we not try to make 'the new thing that God is doing'—as some call it—into our own thing? Do we not package and put our own label on it and then market and make money out of it?

God is manifesting His presence and glory in and through the Church more and more. Consequently, ministry and leadership will become a precarious vocation. We may have to introduce 'danger-pay'! To whom much is given, much will be required. We must learn the art of letting God be God, that He can be Himself, behave the way He wants to behave and do what He wants to do in our midst. He should not be limited or 'preprogrammed' by our own liturgy, teachings, rules, expectations and our prescribed sense of 'order'. We should dare to trust Him fully with the reins of the Church! By nature, we are 'the people of the wind', as those who are 'born from above' (Jn 3:5-8). Therefore we have to learn to live by the unpredictability and free flow of the Spirit to achieve whatever purpose He has in mind. The Holy Spirit is predictable only in His unpredictability!

Fourthly, we must hear His voice, and be truly filled and led by His Spirit.

As the leaders in the Antioch Church worshipped the Lord and fasted together, they heard the Spirit give directions for the next phase in the life of the Church—which proved to be absolutely crucial for 'world missions' (Acts 13:1-4). True worship always results in 'hearing God' together and births ministry and mission. The early Church 'team mission' continued to be directed by the Spirit (Acts 16:6-10). Jesus said, 'Although I am the Son, I do nothing on my own initiative. I do only what I see my Father doing' (Jn 5:17-20). John Wimber used to say, 'We must not ask God to bless what we are doing. We must see what God is doing and go and bless it, learn from it, and work with it.'

In short, the Holy Spirit must be allowed to fully direct the affairs of the Church through our worship of the Father and the Son; through various gifts within the Church (including supernatural revelation in visions, dreams and prophecies); through the Word of God; through the witness of inner guidance and ruling peace; and through the community of discernment within the leadership team.

Fifthly, this value defines leadership within the Church.

The above discussion does not negate nor undermine Church government and leadership. It rather births, empowers, qualifies and determines the way government and leadership operate. Jesus ascended to the Father's right hand and gave gifts to the Church—leadership gifts (as recorded in Eph 4:11-13). The Church is not an organisation, it is an organism, the living body of Christ, of which He is the head. It operates by life-giving gifts that function for the good of the Body and for God's mission in the world. The leaders are to use their own gifts to evoke the gifts in people, equip and free them to function, and then to recognise and respect their contribution. Gifts have nothing to do with position, power or title. Ministry is functional and leadership has to do with functional responsibility. We do not talk of Apostles or Evangelists, or Prophet so-and-so or 'Pastor Alexander'. They are merely functions of the Spirit in the Church, in and through people, who are persons with names by which they should be addressed. Imagine that every time I see my wife I call her, 'Housewife Gill!' I assure you, she would lay hands on me rather suddenly!

Sixthly, it means that leadership is spiritual, enabling people to live under the invisible government of the Spirit.

Fallen human nature demands the security of visible structures, programmes and strong, directive leadership. True leadership grows people beyond the dictates of their own needs into a mature security in God. When Israel asked Samuel to appoint a visible king, 'such as all the other nations have' (1Sam 8:5f), Yahweh took strong personal exception to it. Their request was, 'Give us a King to lead us.' God replied, 'You are rejecting Me as your King, as your Leader.' It is remarkable—and terrifying—that God often gives people the human hero that they so desire. What a painful compromise! It is God's sad acknowledgement of their immaturity and a judgement on their unredeemed ego needs—both in the people and their heroes. Ultimately only God can meet our needs—not people, not even leaders. We will do anything to avoid living by faith (the invisible) and continue living by sight (the visible).

Leadership is first and foremost spiritual—it should draw people to God and enable them to live more directly under His rule. Many leaders are not in touch with their own need for power, control, significance, recognition, adulation and popularity. They can unwittingly become part of God's compromise deal with the crowds. In so doing, they set up themselves and their followers for judgement. Jesus refused to entrust Himself to or receive glory from the crowds. What we see in the Church today, especially in its leaders, is often different to what God sees.

Lastly, it means balancing creative tensions in authority, leadership, ministry and structures.

The headship of Christ in 'the heavenlies' is in creative tension with the administration of the Spirit in and through the earthly Church. This sets up a series of tensions—various aspects that apparently oppose one another, but if held in balance, give life to the Body. When one aspect is set against or detached from the other, destructive tensions begin to rule and the body becomes spastic and uncoordinated. This is death. We must guard against one aspect dominating another. I will mention a few examples.

The sovereignty of the local Church must be balanced by its belonging to the broader Church (or its particular Church family). If one dominates the other—either denominational control or local autonomy—a fundamental aspect of health is lost. Both become vulnerable to imbalance and its consequences.

The same applies to the local pastor, or senior leader, who is responsible for and accountable to the local Church, but at the same time, accountable to and part of a broader team of pastors within the same family of Churches. This also implies that leadership is both individual and team— effective leadership works in and through a team, but every team needs a clear leader. There is a creative tension here, a balancing both ways, between the pastor and pastors, between the leader and the team.

There are many other creative tensions, but let me mention in closing the balance between the leadership teams and the people to whom they are ministering. God's voice and direction can come through the people via a spiritual gift or by a weakness or a need in the Body. It can also come through the leader and/or the team—in terms of revelation or vision or strategic planning. In this tension they both experience and should submit to God's leadership, mutually yielding to one another's callings, gifts and functions in a life-giving process. Living creatively in balancing the opposing tensions is living under God's invisible government.

 ## VALUE 3: RELATIONSHIPS

This has to do with valuing the particular primacy of relationships and reality.

The historical context

This value goes back to the nature of covenant and community in Israel between Yahweh and His people, and between the people themselves. It was fulfilled in Messiah Jesus and His community. Paul's whole idea of being 'in Christ' introduces a profoundly personal and intimate understanding of our relationship with Jesus and with one another. The 'vertical' relationship with God has its outworking in 'horizontal' relationships of love between people (1Jn 4:19-21). Christianity is not a system of religion. It is a way of life, a way of relating in love to God, people and the environment that God has placed us in.

The New Testament speaks of a series of relationships that constitutes the very fibre of the Christian life, of the Church itself—all drawn from our primary relationship with God. There are the relationships between leaders, between leaders and Church members, between the members themselves, between the Church and the world, between the Church and the state, between employers and employees, between parents and children, between husbands and wives, and our relationship with ourselves (our self-image) and our environment.

Through the history of the Church, at various times in various places, organisations and institutionalism have replaced relationships as the basic expression of the Kingdom. The result is a subtle withdrawal from reality and a creation of a 'Christian' subculture that becomes ingrown and unreal. Relational Christianity is focused on reality because that is what life is all about.

The relevance to the contemporary context

Looking at the Baby-Boomers and the broader society we find a yearning for honest engagement—because of a deep disillusionment with phony people, functional relationships and pretence. People are tired of being used and abused. There is a rejection of top-down relationships. People want more participation and ownership. They want community. The growing dissatisfaction with technology and the scientific revolution is becoming endemic. The profound effect that the Internet, the information highway and virtual reality is having on our world is only now beginning to be felt. Much is being written about how cyberspace is radically redefining human beings, the nature of our relationships, and the very world we live in. But deep down inside, in the core of our beings, we need and want reality, true community—meaningful, intimate and long-term relationships. Sadly, we are unskilled at precisely what we desperately need.

If we do not find a way to experience meaningful relationships, or create an environment where this can happen, we will all degenerate into functional animals. In a certain sense, that is the way the world is going. One of the most revolutionary things we can do in the world today is to build community. What do we really mean by this value for relationships and reality?

The meaning and implications

Firstly, relationships are about reality and reality is about relationships.

We will always have to engage with people, at one or other level, no matter how much we may want to withdraw or escape (e.g. through virtual 'relationships' in cyberspace). The pain of people's lives and the discipline of daily tactile relationships keep our feet firmly on the ground, in touch with reality. Honest relationships with others (and with ourselves) will, among other things, keep us from escaping into 'spiritualism' or religiosity. We must avoid religious pretence of all kinds, whether in our speech (Christian jargon), or our dress (particular Church expectations), or our attitude ('holier than thou'), or our behaviour (doing meaningless religious stuff). Jesus had serious confrontations with the Jewish religious leaders in regard to these things. He modelled and taught openness, honesty and being real and up-front about oneself, God, life and others. Jesus constantly warned against the 'hypocrisy' of the Pharisees—seeking attention, affirmation and approval through pretending, wearing masks and acting out roles. It also implies that we avoid 'hyping things up', promoting ourselves, exaggerating advertising, having titles, or even claiming big things from God that evidently are not true or do not happen. We must be committed to integrity—being real, consistent and honest at all times.

Secondly, it means that personhood is defined through community.

We are defined as persons, in our individual identity and calling, through loving and trusting relationships. Biblically speaking, who I am and what I stand for is not commonly discovered by myself as my own private project or revelation in isolation from others. The individualistic mentality, so common in warped western Christianity, is foreign to Scripture. The Biblical norm is that my identity comes from where and to whom I belong. Simon Peter was called, 'Simon bar Jonah' (son of Jonah), not 'Simon the fisherman'. In our world we are known for what we do, or do not do, and it is assumed that that is who we really are. We derive our identity and significance from our work—relationships and character hardly come into it. That is why people are so lost and insecure.

'Doing' should really come from our sense of 'being', and 'being' should come from our relatedness—to the Creator of the universe for starters! The disciples were with Jesus, then He sent them out to preach (Mk 3:14). Paul teaches 'being' and then 'doing' through the body metaphor (1Cor 12:12-31). For example, a finger finds out who it is and what it does by virtue of where it is joined and to whom it belongs. If I 'hang in' relationships long enough, and yield to those I am connected with I will discover who I really am (not what I have decided I am). I will then be free to be my real self and will be empowered to fulfil what I stand for—through the relationships. I have found very few people who have the faith for this, who take the time and trouble to entrust themselves to relationships long enough to allow themselves to be defined and empowered to reach their full potential in God. Church really is a community of birth, discovery, growth, equipping and empowerment—through the quality and longevity of our relationships. Think of how a baby is born, discovers itself and grows into functional maturity—in and through family relationships. This happens less and less in our world because family has fallen apart. No wonder we have increasing lawlessness and delinquency.

Thirdly, the Church, corporate personhood, is defined through relationships.

Church is a family, God's family. What characterises and sets us apart as God's family, is that we, the children, take after our Dad. God is love, and by our love for one another will all people recognise and know that we are Yahweh's people, Jesus' followers, the Christian family (Jn 13:34,35). John Wimber used to say, 'Church is the extent to which we relate—the depth of our experience of Church is determined by the quality of our relationships.' Furthermore, John would say, 'People will join a Church for various reasons, but will end up staying for one reason only, because of relationship—they have made some friends.'

Therefore, we build a relational environment and structure. We do worship and ministry in a relational way. We build community as opposed to having meetings. It is a matter of becoming friends, sharing our hearts, our resources and our very lives. This is done through an environment of 'love, acceptance and forgiveness' that we seek to create (the phrase from Jerry Cook's book which explains a philosophy of ministry akin to the Vineyard, see Appendix 4). Loving relationships can be a revolutionary force in a loveless society, drawing people to the Kingdom, like moths to the light. The Early Church presents an inspiring picture of God's family, loving one another, and thus changing the world around them (Acts 2:44-47, 4:32-37).

Fourthly, it means understanding relationships—their nature, purpose, how they work—to create the environment of love, acceptance and forgiveness.

The goal of relationship is community—defined as intimacy, oneness, wholeness and maturity. The means of relationship is communication. And the essence of communication is love. How do we love? Through self-disclosure—the gift of self, given to the other. By sharing your feelings you are self-disclosing who you really are. This gift of self is your greatest gift of love that you can give to the other person. It is ultimately the most costly and meaningful exchange in any relationship. It is precisely this element—self-disclosure—that creates intimacy and community, a profound force for healing and growth. Relationships take root in the soil of self-disclosure and accountability, creating a safe environment for people to be themselves, to try and to fail, to be open and honest, without the fear of being judged, labelled, gossiped about or psycho-analysed, but just accepted and loved for who they are.

We fear self-disclosure because we fear rejection. To be known is to be very vulnerable. It goes like this: 'I know me, and I don't like me. If I let you see the real me you will not like me either—you will reject me.' We hide, play games and project what we think others want to see—so that they will accept us. We come to know, and are fully known, only through learning to give of ourselves in relationships, through honest self-disclo-sure (sharing our feelings). This leads to transparency and accountability, acceptance and forgiveness, protection and wholeness. This is the way to 'grow up before you grow old'. This is reality. As relationships face us with our brokenness, our 'stuff', we have to decide—do we self-disclose and invite help, or do we cover-up, shut-down, hide, mask, project, suppress, rationalise or regress (the 'games' people play)? We take responsibility for our 'stuff' (not other people's 'stuff') through self-disclosure. Relationships have a power for healing and growth that far outweighs their potential for destruction. Therefore, we value self-disclosure, the freedom to fail, acceptance and honesty—they are essential factors for growing relation-ships. Real adult-to-adult relationships are the hothouse of personal growth, ministry and maturity.

Fifthly, our relationships are covenantal, based on God's love for us.

God's commitment to us, displayed in Christ, is the basis of our relationships. We are not talking about 'covenant relationships' based on our commitment to one another in a structured, discipling, authority-submission fashion. Where this has been practised there has been spiritual abuse through control and domination. We must never use, exploit and manipulate relationships for our own ends, even if it is for the sake of 'the pastor's vision'. We have to let people be—they must find their own level. Motivation should come from within them, from relationship, from God's love—not from guilt, performance or pressure from leadership. Ministry ('doing') should come from belonging and relationship ('being'). We must not parent people, but rather develop adult relationships. Obviously this does not negate the need to nurture new believers and others, and for leaders to exercise authority in terms of confronting and correcting people when necessary. But it should be done in a loving adult way, not in a scolding parental fashion— as in 'pulling rank' or 'putting down'.

VALUE 4: THE INDIVIDUAL

This has to do with valuing the individual through valuing the particular importance of grace and mercy—not law.

The historical context

The value of the individual, which revolves around personal worth and human dignity, relates Biblically to the creation of the human being, and the issue of law and grace. It comes down to the way we view and treat people, including ourselves.

In Jesus' day individuals were largely seen as objects to be used, whether for the Roman imperial system, or the Jewish religious system. People were categorized and related to by religion, race, social class and gender. Law and grace was an issue of frequent confrontation between Jesus and the Pharisees—the way of compassion and mercy versus the way of legalism, categorization and performance. Paul had the same battle with the circumcision party (the heresy of having to 'keep the law' to be a true believer). He fought for the freedom and identity of the individual in Christ. The Early Church baptismal confession said there was 'no longer Jew nor Gentile, slave nor free, male nor female, but one new humanity in Messiah' (Gal 3:28, 5:1,13, cf. Eph 2:15,16).

Law and grace was also the basic issue in the Reformation, between the Roman Catholic Church and those who broke away from it. The gospel of grace in the evangelical revivals resulted in raised awareness of human dignity, seeking freedom from all forms of oppression, e.g. the abolition of slavery. In this regard, the Vineyard is rooted in the triumph of the mercy of God in Jesus—that salvation is by grace alone, by faith alone, not of any works of our own, whether religious or otherwise. This radically redefines and liberates human beings made in the image of God.

Legalism, categorization and performance have been present throughout Church history in one form or another, and are still very evident in the contemporary Church. Over the years, many Vineyard pastors have had to deal with the effects of subtle forms of legalism in people from Pentecostal, Charismatic, Reformed and Evangelical circles. Some people cannot connect with Vineyard because they keep looking to perform. They want to be told what to do in order to feel that they belong, that they are good members. Others are relieved to be left alone—they can relax and take time to 'get healed up' and find their own level of belonging and participation. However, this issue deeply affects the way we see individuals in the world; how we see their place and function in the Body of Christ. Some aspects of the fruit of legalism have already been alluded to in the above values, especially in regard to relationship and reality—it results in manipulative and controlling relationships, categorizing people on the basis of externals, and a performance mentality in regard to life and ministry.

The relevance to the contemporary context

The post Second World War generation has championed the cause of freedom, in various ways, for itself, for various groups and for nations.

Their drive has been for the restoration of human dignity and personal recognition; to be treated with respect, not as functional objects or numbers in society. They've been concerned with self-worth, identity, liberation, justice and freedom. This is epitomized in the recent decades by the hippie and feminist movements, the music and sexual revolutions, the 'struggle for justice' in nations receiving independence from colonialism— and many other similar social movements.

There is an even greater need for dignity and self-worth in our post-modern world, especially in the face of increasing poverty and calamities of all kinds. The explosion of technology further 'automates' human functionality and categorization (black or white, rich or poor, successful or broken, and old or young). The sense of alienation from one another and meaninglessness within us has deepened. We address these needs by recovering the dignity and value of the individual through understanding and practising God's grace and mercy.

The meaning and implications

Firstly, we must have a clear understanding and practice of grace and mercy, and thus avoid any elements of legalism.

Those who knew John well knew him as a man of grace and mercy— although it cost him dearly. I once witnessed him storming up the aisle after a service to confront a man who persistently gave attention-seeking 'prophecies'. But just as he got to him, John turned aside and sat down with his head in his hands. I saw him crying. Later John told me that God spoke to him just before he got to the man saying, 'John, have mercy.' Because he could not trust his own heart to operate in mercy, he turned aside and wept before God. At times John 'got into trouble' from other Church leaders for associating with 'questionable' people, showing them the mercy and forgiveness that they did not deserve.

It reminds one of Jesus and His 'prodigal' Father in Luke 15. They associate with various 'sinners', mercifully seeking them out. They welcome home the stinking reprobates in such a partying and dancing manner that it's scandalous.

Their grace is over the top, unreasonable, out of all proportion—it's utterly 'prodigal' (lavish, reckless and wasteful, in human terms). Yes, this is who God really is! Blessed are those who are not scandalized by God's grace and mercy, for they shall experience it, and it will drive legalism far from them!

Grace is the Father's extravagant mercy and unmerited kindness toward us. God loved us so much that He personally came down to suffer with and for us, taking on Himself our sin, dying our death, and rising to give us His life. This is a pure gift—through Jesus Christ. Legalism says we get this gift or favour from God by doing something to warrant it. Or if we already have God's grace, then we must do certain things to be worthy of it, to keep it, not lose it, and get more of it. In essence, legalism has to do with earning God and other's favour, approval and belonging through good deeds, resulting in controlling relationships and poor self-worth. On the other hand, grace means enjoying God's and other's favour and approval, as a gift of love and mercy, resulting in mutually freeing relationships and rich self-worth.

In summary, legalism leads to and is characterized by the following: motivation by guilt, performance by obligation, measurement by effort, belonging by conformity, well-being by approval, success by externals, security by submission, self-image by comparisons, and immaturity by control. Living by these (worldly) values results in the loss of self-image and dignity—through comparison, categorization, condemnation and control.

However, grace leads to and is characterized by the following: motivation by gratitude, obedience by love, belonging by relationship, measurement by honesty, well-being by wholeness, fulfilment by inner contentment, security by acceptance, self-image by God's values, and maturity by taking responsibility and being accountable. Grace restores and celebrates our humanity in the image of God, resulting in a healthy self-image—because of the value that God places on us in creation and in Jesus Christ.

As Paul says, 'Think on these things.' Pause and reflect on these two lists.

THE ISSUE DESCRIBED	ENVIRONMENT OF LEGALISM	ENVIRONMENT OF GRACE
SALVATION	BY WORKS	BY FAITH
MOTIVATION	BY GUILT	BY GRATITUDE
GROWTH	BY PERFORMANCE	BY YIELDING
OPERATES	BY RULES	BY FREEDOM
LEADERSHIP	BY CONTROL	BY SERVING
ACHIEVEMENT	BY MANIPULATION	BY BEING RESPONSIBLE
EVALUATION	BY EXTERNALS	BY INNER REALITY
BELONGING	BY CONFORMITY	BY RELATIONSHIP
IDENTITY	BY DOING	BY BEING
WELL-BEING	BY APPROVAL	BY WHOLENESS
SELF-IMAGE	BY COMPARISON	BY ACCEPTANCE
SECURITY	BY SUBMISSION	BY TRUST
OBEDIENCE	BY OBLIGATION	BY LOVE
RELATIONSHIPS	BY PARENT/CHILD	BY ADULT
SUMMARY		
ATTITUDE	JUDGEMENTAL	MERCIFUL

Secondly, it means operating out of the grace of God from our own brokenness and need of Him.

Biblically speaking, the dignity of the human being is in tension with our utter depravity. The more we see what God's grace and mercy does for us, the more we become aware of the depths of our depravity and darkness. The result is a greater love of God, a clearer vision of human dignity and a passion for its full restoration. We are also left with deep humility, a realisation that ministry flows by God's grace out of our own brokenness. We learn that God's strength is actually made perfect in our weaknesses. Therefore we cannot claim great things for ourselves and do things in a spirit of triumphalism or arrogance. Often it is only when we have been broken before God that real ministry is entrusted to us, that we minister to others with a sense of mercy and compassion. Remember how after His resurrection Jesus confronted Peter about his denial. 'Do you really love me?' 'Yes Lord, you know me, I'm fond of you—I've really failed you.' 'Well then, now that you know how vulnerable you are, the depths of your own heart, look after my Church, feed my lambs' (my interpretation of Jn 21:15-17).

People who are not in touch with their own brokenness lack mercy, often ministering with harshness and treating people as objects of ministry. Even worse are those who believe in extreme 'success teachings'. They deny any sense of failure in their own lives and consequently they are often cruel, superficial and arrogant in their treatment of others.

Thirdly, it means upholding the freedom bought for us by Christ on the cross, and being free to enjoy the fullness of God.

We must not judge others or ourselves for that matter, in regard to external criteria. Paul constantly fought against the legalists for the freedom bought by Christ—from Jewish laws and religious 'requirements' regarding what one wears, eats, drinks, or which days are 'holy' (Gal 5:1f, Col 2:16, Rom 14:1f). We nullify the grace of God by 'laying heavies' on one another and 'playing God' (e.g. by being arbiters of people's conscience). I'm referring to personal convictions, opinions, and scruples—matters of conscience—not with matters of clear morality or Biblical ethics, which must be confronted and dealt with. Whereas legalists love to parent people, we must practise adult relationships, allowing God's grace to change others, rather than trying to manipulate them into change by our own norms and expectations.

But freedom must not become a licence to sin or for undisciplined living (Gal 5:13). Neither must it become a standard for a new 'in vogue spirituality'—to see how liberal or 'laid-back' we can get. Neither must it become a stumbling block to others who are weaker in their faith or more sensitive in their conscience (Rom 14:13-17). The freedom that grace brings is the freedom to obey God—from deep within we are enabled to live as God wants us to live, evidenced in the joy of routinely doing God's will. However, moralists emphasise outward behavioural conformity to detailed rights and wrongs (like 'no smoking') without the inner reality of God's grace and freedom. Although they always appear to be 'godly', they are often the ones who have deep inner struggles with demons and 'carnal' sins (as Paul records in Gal 5:19-21). This is a result of a legalistic view and suppression of their natural appetites. Enormous energy is spent on keeping 'it' in check while integrity is being eroded and guilt and shame continue to grow. It is only a matter of time before 'it' pops out into the open for all to see. Grace produces authentic holiness—legalism can only produce pseudo-holiness, which is outward conformity via gritted-teeth performance.

Therefore legalism in leadership profoundly influences the Church, the entire system, from the top down. Leaders who are not in touch with their own 'stuff', who have not rooted legalism out of their hearts and lives, will not be to able create, lead and maintain an environment of grace. For example, grace does not only mean the freedom to obey God. Paradoxically, it also means the freedom to fail. Grace says, 'It is okay to fail, you will not be judged or condemned—you can try, and fail, and try again.' We all blow it from time to time; each sheep has its 'dark and cloudy day' (Ezek 34:12). This does not mean we encourage moral compromise. It means we make space for one another. We forgive people when they fail and nurture them through their pain. We do not kill off our wounded! Leaders who do not personally and experientially know God's grace are unable to live in the rarefied atmosphere of 'love, acceptance and forgiveness'—which is the very breath of the Father, the natural source of life for His children and the smell of death for legalists.

Fourthly, grace means treating each person as a unique individual, made in the image of God, with great dignity and respect.

We treat people as persons, whole persons, not as objects to do something to or through. In our healing practice, we seek to minister to the whole person and not just 'fix his problem'. We want to leave every person feeling loved after each encounter with us. His sense of dignity and value must be enhanced. Jesus often left the crowds to have compassion on the one person, to seek the one lost sheep (Lk 15:3-7 cf. 8:40f). Compassion and mercy is the 'way of Jesus' because it is the very nature of the Father (Lk 6:36 cf. Matt 9:13, 'be compassionate as your Father in the heavens is compassionate', 'I desire mercy, not sacrifice'). This also means that we refuse to relate to people on the basis of stereotypes, labels and categories, or as a collective whole. We must take the time and trouble to discover each person for who he really is, not for what we think he is—or ought to be. This is how we celebrate the mystery and uniqueness of God's creation, profoundly enhancing human dignity and worth.

Fifthly, valuing the individual means respecting the unique place of each believer in the Body—honouring the priesthood of believers.

God places people in the Body as it pleases Him (1Cor 12:13-30). This is where they connect and discover who and what they are for. This is where their gifts come to the fore and begin to operate. Everyone must be recognised, encouraged and celebrated in their special place, in their unique calling and gifts. They must be given time, space and nurturing to learn to minister, to spread their wings and fly. This is practising 'the priesthood of all believers' (1Pet 2:4-9).

The implication is that a 'one-man show' is unacceptable. Ministry must be given away so that all people can experience the joy and dignity of serving the Body of Christ. It also means that the individual believer must take responsibility for his integration, growth, function and fulfilment in the Body—and not to hold the leadership responsible for this. Individuals must also learn not to draw their identity and value from their gifts and function. This always leads to problems.

Sixthly, it means having mercy on the marginalized, showing compassion to the oppressed poor, the broken, the divorced, the orphans and widows.

Jesus' younger brother called this 'true religion' (Js 1:27). John Wimber called it 'having a heart for the poor'. He used to go around, at times taking his grandchildren with him, and hand out food parcels to the hungry. He understood this to be at the heart of the gospel—having mercy on the marginalized because God had mercy on him. The Bible is full of this theology. Jesus had so conditioned His little community in this regard, that when Judas went out to betray Him, the others thought that Jesus had sent him out to give money to the poor (Jn 13:27-29). When Paul was sanctioned to take the gospel to the Gentiles, the leaders asked one thing of him, 'to remember the poor', 'The very thing I was eager to do,' says Paul (Gal 2:10).

The world is increasingly desperate, and ripe, for the lived gospel of God's mercy in and through the Church.

VALUE 5: HEALING

This has to do with valuing the particular effect of an environment and practice of wholistic healing.

The historical context

The values follow on logically from one another. Jesus and the Spirit, given their rightful place, create community. Then those relationships define the individual, and grace and mercy create an environment in which healing takes place. That brings us to wholistic healing, which is the work of the Kingdom of God in the Church and in the world (the sixth and last value). Much of what has been said in the above values anticipates the discussion of these last two values.

Healing has its roots in the Old Testament concept of *Shalom* (peace) and the New Testament understanding of *Soteria* (salvation). Both are wholistic ideas and experiences. They refer to God's intervention and acts of deliverance, salvation, liberation, healing and restoration—and the effects spiritually, emotionally, mentally, physically, socially, economically, politically and even ecologically. It is all the result of the life and work of Messiah Jesus.

In later Church history the concept of salvation was divorced from wholistic healing. For example, the divide between 'Liberal Theology' and 'Conservative Evangelicalism' led to two opposing gospels: the social gospel of liberation from societal sin, like injustice, and the private gospel of forgiveness from personal sin, like adultery. Both these extremes are reactionary, and they reduce the gospel from its wholistic nature to a particular need or cause.

John Wimber's approach was to recover the wholistic nature of healing as a work of God's full salvation for humanity, and in so doing, to tap into the growing need and search for wholistic healing in the world today.

The relevance to the contemporary context

Both grace and healing are relevant and contemporary ways of expressing the fullness of the gospel of Jesus Christ. The Baby-Boomers lived with parents who experienced the Second World War. The postwar disillusionment, with the realisation that humanity can now destroy itself—and planet earth—led to a period of purposelessness, and then a profound hunger for healing and meaning. We speak of the 'me generation', the all-consuming passion to understand ourselves, the quest for personal growth and fulfilment, for health and fitness, for experience and spiritual reality. 'Each person shall have their own shrink' is fast becoming 'each person shall have their own guru'. The New Age Movement has flowered with myriad beliefs and practices—the West is being saturated with philosophies and experiences of 'holistic healing'.

This presents a great challenge for the Church, an unparalleled opportunity for evangelism. One such opportunity is to address the need and the confusion in the area of healing—its philosophies and practices. The knife-edge potential for demonic deception or authentic salvation is unprecedented. People are more open and needy now than ever before—perhaps than in the entire history of humanity—for God's healing power. South Africa, for example, has been through deep waters (apartheid and transformation) and the need for healing, both individually and corporately, is overwhelming. Can the Church meet this challenge?

The meaning and implications

Firstly, healing, health and wholeness are God's desire for everyone, whereas sickness, oppression, demons and death are expressions of evil.

The former is God's Kingdom and the latter is ultimately a result of 'the fall' into sin (Satan's Kingdom). If we do not have this clear in our minds we will always be 'double-minded' and hesitant in regard to healing. We are in a war between good and evil. In Jesus we see God's willingness and ability to heal. Jesus said to the leper, 'I am willing ... be healed.' Immediately he was healed (Mk 1:41,42). Literally everywhere He went, He preached the good news of God's rule and healed the sick and drove out demons. This does not mean that God, on the rare occasion, cannot 'use' Satan as a 'servant' to inflict torment on people as a means of discipline or judgement (1Chron 21:1 cf. 2Sam 24:1, 1Cor 11:29-32). That's why sometimes, in ministering healing, we must check on the presence of unconfessed sin (Js 5:14-16). However, the point is that God heals and that He wants us to be whole by experiencing His shalom.

Secondly, healing is both an act and a process, an expression of God's compassion on victims of evil.

We practise healing by 'the laying on of hands' as an 'elementary principle' of Christian faith (Heb 6:1-3). The motivation should never be for self-glory ('my healing ministry'), for money, for drawing crowds, or for any reason other than compassion. This is what motivated Jesus when He saw the people as helpless victims of sin and sickness (Matt 9:35-36). Compassion is often born in our own struggles and weaknesses—the more we are in touch with them, the more we can have compassion on others, and not be harsh or abusive. In that sense we are all 'wounded healers'; we are all in process; none of us has arrived yet. Thus we view healing as a process requiring faith, love, patience and perseverance. It would be great if all healings were an 'act' of instant and miraculous intervention of God. This is certainly what we pray for! But reality teaches us that healing is both a process and a miraculous act—and the former is more common. Healing is really a process of recovery and growth out of the bondage of sin and the woundings of evil, into maturity and wholeness in the image of God. The fullness awaits the resurrection of the body at the coming of Christ.

Thirdly, because healing is more a process, we have an environmental and wholistic understanding and approach.

This goes back to our discussions on relationships and grace. We create a healing environment through self-disclosure, love, acceptance and forgiveness. Mercy is the spirit and attitude of healing, and if faithfully practised, will become the atmosphere of the Church. Healing is the place where righteousness and mercy kiss, where people are healed by being in that environment. I remember the first time I arrived at a Vineyard meeting at Canyon High School, Yorba Linda, in 1981. The very air was filled with healing and wholeness—through the intimate worship, the relational environment, the gentle teaching, the compassionate ministry—I felt tender and affirmed. It opened me up to God and communicated healing in conscious and unconscious ways.

This includes having a comprehensive and integrated model of healing. We must not be superficial or simplistic in our understanding and approach— the human being is a sophisticated creation (we are 'fearfully and wonderfully made', Ps 139). Our brokenness has profound depths and our journey toward wholeness is not a simple matter—it involves mystery and transformation. Therefore healing is for the whole person and it takes place in many ways, through various means. We identify various dimensions of healing: of our spirit (sin), of our mind and emotions (past and present hurts), of spiritual powers (demonization), of our bodies (sickness), of our relationships, of society and of ecology.

Fourthly, healing means expecting supernatural signs and wonders by exercising the gifts and power of the Holy Spirit.

These 'gifts of the Spirit' include healings, faith, working of miracles, discerning and expelling of spirits, supernatural words of knowledge and wisdom (1Cor 12:7-10). Jesus promises that the works (miracles) that He did, we can also do, by His Spirit (Jn 14:12 cf. Acts 1:8). We've been given power and authority to do the supernatural works of the Kingdom of God (Lk 9:1,2). This whole idea, and its experience, is still foreign to many Western Christians. It often requires a 'paradigm-shift' from a rational and materialistic worldview to a more spiritual and experiential way of seeing reality. This is important for us in the Vineyard because if we do not rely on and experience the supernatural power of God, what hope is there for the Church, let alone for a dying world? However, we must take into account the 'already' and the 'not yet' of the Kingdom in order to keep us from becoming either defeatist or triumphalistic.

Fifthly, healing means having a heart for the pain-filled world—especially focused in evangelism and social concern.

The type of compassion and healing that we are talking about goes beyond the Church into the world otherwise it is not the real thing. This reflects our previous discussion about having mercy on the marginalized and the dispossessed. Evangelism is the sharp-point of our involvement in the world. It is the beginning of all healing else we can end up with mere humanistic efforts in the form of social programmes or psychological techniques. The ultimate lostness of being damned forever must keep us confronting people with eternal issues. But, because we are whole beings, with multidimensional needs, we must engage in acts of social concern as an expression of this value of healing.

VALUE 6: THE KINGDOM OF GOD

This has to do with valuing a particular concern for changing the world through a wholistic approach in 'equipping the saints' for ministry and mission.

We have already discussed the theology of the Kingdom of God in chapter two, and in a sense, it is the undergirding summary of these core values— it is the centre of the centre—if that makes sense! The particular value of the Kingdom that we are discussing here has to do with the essence of God's rule, which is the mission to save and change the world, and to equip those who are changed to be the instruments of the Kingdom's mission in the world.

The historical context

It begins with God's calling on Israel to be a light to the Gentiles. This was fulfilled in Jesus the Messiah and His community, especially in His commission to the apostles, and through them to His Church, to take 'the gospel of the Kingdom to the ends of the earth as a witness to all nations, and then the end will come' (Matt 24:14).

We see how this has taken place through the history of Church missions. More recently it includes the great evangelical surge of the last few centuries, culminating in the Church growth and missions emphasis of the twentieth century. The 21ˢᵗ century poses the final challenge for the Church to complete the Great Commission. This great surge has coincided with the 'rediscovery' of the New Testament theology of the Kingdom, creating a fresh appreciation of the message and mission of Jesus in His own context. This is worked out in the Vineyard primarily in terms of mission and training.

The relevance to the contemporary context

The value of the Kingdom connects with the whole idea of living for 'a cause'. The Baby-Boomers were cause-people. The many social justice movements in the '60s and '70s bear witness to this. It also links into the sense of meaninglessness and disillusionment with the establishment, and consequently, the strong desire to live intentionally, to do something worthwhile with our lives. Many people do not want to end up being a statistic. They want to make their mark and personally participate in human destiny. That is why there is a growing search for ultimate meaning and purpose in spiritual pursuit—and for many it means serving humanity in some worthy cause.

What better cause to give your life to than the enterprise of God on earth? People are more and more willing to give their lives for something they believe in. We need to challenge and enlist them in the greatest cause ever—the Lamb's war—defeating evil in all its forms to the ends of the earth, and in so doing, freeing people into God's eternal Kingdom.

The meaning and implications

Firstly, it means having God's heart for the nations.

We must enter into God's passion for this lost world—'for God so loved the world that He gave ...' (Jn 3:16). We want to be driven by God's love to give our best—like Paul when he says, 'Woe is me if I do not preach the gospel'

(1Cor 9:16). John Wimber was born again in an atmosphere where winning people for Jesus was expected of every Christian, and he willingly obeyed, joyfully leading hundreds to Christ in his early years as a Christian. This passion led to a heart for the nations, to plant Churches in every major city around the globe. In the years before he died John increasingly emphasised evangelism and saving people from hell. Sadly, many Christians have lost a belief in hell—there seems to be no sense of reality associated with it. The passion of the Kingdom for this dying world is born and nurtured through worship in the presence of the King (Matt 18:17-20). Then we are thrust out into the joy, privilege and power of hands-on Kingdom mission. Mother Teresa would say, 'We find Jesus in the distressing disguise of the poor and needy.'

Secondly, it means more than evangelism, proclamation and witness.

Mission includes the whole vision of what it means to advance the Kingdom of God, to disciple individuals and nations, from personal conversion to the full social implications of the gospel. Mission must be wholistic and partnership oriented—that is, to respect and work with various types of mission activities and enterprises in all areas where they are present (e.g. Bible translators, relief and development workers, etc.). Our concern for not being imperialistic in any way, nor parenting others, would qualify our partnership with some mission initiatives, and would focus us on equipping and releasing indigenous Kingdom work. Further, the priority of the local Church means that we are committed to local Church mission, although we are open to working in partnership with para-church agencies.

Thirdly, the heart of missions is Church planting.

We believe the New Testament clearly teaches that the method sanctioned and empowered by God to extend the Kingdom is through Church planting—and mainly Church planting in virgin territory. Because we are like-minded, we seek to network as local Vineyard Churches in order to plant Churches more effectively. John always said that the primary reason for the Vineyard's existence is Church planting in fulfilment of the 'Great Commission' (Matt 28:18-20).

Fourthly, it means not only planting like-minded Churches, but to love the whole Church and give away through Church renewal what God has given us.

The second aspect of Vineyard's mission is to help bring renewal to the broader Church. If we cling to what we have been given, it may be removed from us. This means a ministry of renewal to the whole Church, no matter how 'institutional', without strings, without manipulation or judgement. We do not espouse the 'come out from among them' idea, or the 'God has finished with them' language. God loves the whole Church and often surprises those who have written off some part of it by choosing to bless just that part. In fact, by giving away the blessings that God has given to us, we ourselves experience renewal by embracing what God is doing in other parts of the Body.

Fifthly, it means 'equipping the saints' to do the work of ministry and mission.

Our understanding and practice of training will be discussed in detail in the next chapter, so my comments will be brief. Valuing the Kingdom implies an ongoing value for learning and training so as to be better equipped to cooperate with God's rule. It is basic to human nature that we never stop learning, growing and changing. That is why we continually dialogue with new perspectives and models in ministry and missions in order to keep the edge on our readiness to spread the gospel. Furthermore, as we learn, we teach and train others. The primary method of training or discipling is apprenticeship—watching and doing. Therefore, to fulfil the Great Commission of Jesus, we live in a continual cycle of worship and mission, learning and training, imparting and sending.

CHAPTER 6

ESTABLISH THE PRIORITIES

One of the things that struck me when I first came to the Vineyard in Yorba Linda was the simplicity of the Church experience. I could immediately see what was going on, what was important to these people. There did not appear to be anything that was very complicated. What they did was plain and easy, warm and personal, up-front and unapologetic, and evidently enjoyable.

In the first Sunday meeting that I attended they worshipped, they taught the Bible and they ministered to each other. Then they stood around having coffee and talking for quite some time after the meeting (I quickly found out, with great gastronomical delight, that this continued in various eating places near to Canyon High School!). The handouts and bulletins immediately connected me with a kinship (home group) and made me aware of the healing/equipping emphasis of the various courses and programmes that were being run. I also became aware of the buzz around people frequently 'going out' to do evangelism or to feed the poor or to do 'translocals' (team ministry) in other Churches or to help with a Church plant. Going to a mid-week kinship confirmed this simple and clear experience of Church—it seemed to embody these same basic ingredients.

This describes priorities very well—the things that are done on a regular basis, not only talked about. Priorities are the things that are immediately seen, not only advertised. I referred to John Wimber in the opening of the previous chapter describing values as that to which we give our time, energy and money. The same applies to priorities—they give visible form to what we value and believe. Priorities are the actual things we do in terms of investing our time, energy and money—they can be measured by these criteria.

We will look at the importance of priorities and how they are established in the local Church, and then we will list and discuss each of the Vineyard priorities.

 ## THE IMPORTANCE OF ESTABLISHING PRIORITIES

Priorities are like the pillars of the building that emerge directly from the foundation. The whole structure is built around these pillars. Therefore, establishing the priorities is absolutely crucial to the entire well-being and functioning of the Church—they are the superstructure on which everything else hangs. But this can only be done once the underlying values have been clarified and put in place. That is why the previous chapter is so crucial. Remember we are building from the bottom up, not from the top down!

Priorities are immediately seen; they are the first things you run into when you go to any Church or organisation. Like values, they are there whether they have been consciously thought through or not, whether they have been intentionally chosen or merely adopted by default. Most of us, I am sure, will have learnt that if you do not work out your own priorities on the basis of your purpose and your values, then you will almost certainly end up serving someone else's agenda, doing what is important to others or what is circumstantially expedient. Your life will be run by other priorities, which are not your own, and not consistent with your values. This leads to cognitive dissonance—a fancy way of saying real inner conflict! So, how do we determine our priorities?

Priorities help us do the right things

'Priority' means 'that which comes prior to, or before, other things', i.e. those things that are primary and must be done first. This is decided on the basis of our vision and values. Priorities should visibly reflect our unseen values. They describe what we do, which is determined by the where and the why. Once we have decided on our priorities, the rest flows from that—we work out our goals and plans to establish these basic 'doings' in the life of the Church. This focuses our effort and energy and gives clear guidelines to keep us on track.

The question we have to constantly ask ourselves is not 'are we doing things right?' but rather, 'are we doing the right (most important) things?' This will also help us in the eternal struggle between the urgent versus the important, between demands versus being proactive, and between doing the exotic versus doing the basics. Continually doing the important is directly connected to the levels of frustration or fulfilment in achieving the overall purpose in the Church. We really have to be radical about continually doing the basics and doing them well. John Wimber used to say, 'We must do and teach "the main and plain".' If we consistently pursue our basic priorities—do them long enough without distraction—we will achieve our overall purpose. We must not underestimate the faith, focus, vision, consistency and perseverance that are required.

Priorities make things clear and help us keep focus

The other advantage in having and doing basic priorities is that it makes things clear to the newcomer—they immediately see what is important and what they will have to 'get into' if they want to become part of the Church meaningfully. In a sense, priorities are the corporate disciplines in which the Church regularly engages. They provide stability and continuity in the face of all sorts of crosswinds of feelings, doctrines, circumstances and comings and goings. They are the much-needed staples—as opposed to the exotic and the unpredictable—of the Church's life and diet. In this way they help to form the ethos and culture of the Church.

Once decided on, the priorities are established in the life of the Church through a process of modelling (example), teaching, leading and equipping, and creating structures through which they are enacted. For example, if worship is a priority, it must be seen as such by the pastor and leaders not only modelling it, but teaching and training the people in the particular way it is done. This implies training worship leaders, setting up worship teams and equipment, teaching the Church how to worship by actually worshipping whenever they gather and by teaching the Biblical theology of worship. It is crucial that the structures (or programmes) that embody the priorities must be flexible so that they can be adjusted from time to time so as to better fulfil the particular priority.

There should only be a few priorities—as with values. Trying to do too many things, making them all priorities, dilutes the overall focus and dissipates the effort. However, this must not be confused with the fact that there can be a number of programmes built around one priority, e.g. if evangelism is a priority there can be any number of programmes or ministry structures facilitating evangelism. The point is a few key priorities that are clearly stated and enacted make for a united focus and effort within the Church.

THE PRIORITIES OF THE VINEYARD

Before we discuss each priority we need to establish their connection with the basic values (the diagram below) and give a background explanation. Initially, when I first worked on the document 'Building from the bottom up', John spoke of four priorities that reflected our underlying values: worship, fellowship, training, and evangelism. He asserted that love—the love of the Father—was the heart of it all, and that the priorities were the means of experiencing and expressing God's love. We had a saying at that time that went like this: through worship we give God's love back to Him; through fellowship we give God's love to one another; through training we give God's love back to ourselves in one another; and through evangelism we give God's love to the world. But we found that this list of priorities did not fully embody our basic values and did not fully state what the Vineyard was trying to do. So they were broadened into the present list of 'The Priorities of the Vineyard':

Worship

The Word

Fellowship

Ministry (the sick, the lost, the poor)

Training

Sending

One can immediately see that while some priorities are derived directly from a specific value, other priorities are derived from two or more values. There are some overlaps. We will explain this in more detail as each priority is discussed. This diagram shows the foundational links between the values and priorities.

The foundational links between values and priorities

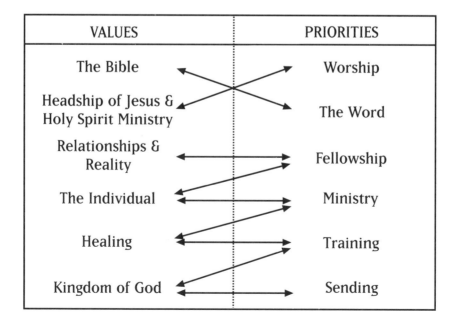

We need to make an important observation. The list of priorities is precisely that—a list in order of priority. If that is so, why the criss-cross lines with the first two? Why is Worship first and The Word second, whereas in terms of values, we put the Bible first and the Headship of Jesus and the Ministry of the Holy Spirit second? John was emphatic that worship is the first and highest priority in the Vineyard—and everything flows from that. This reveals a crucial balance and tension in the Vineyard between faith and experience. In terms of values and beliefs, our foundation and final authority is the Bible. But in terms of what we do, our experience of God is primary—hence worship is our highest priority. Through worship we recognise and honour Jesus in His rightful place as Head of the Church and the Holy Spirit is released to pour the love of the Father upon us. Through worship we experience God and He encounters us. Then the Word of God can enter hearts that have been opened and softened through God's presence in worship. Most Churches begin their meetings with worship, then they teach the Word of God (not the other way round).

The developmental nature of the Vineyard priorities

What we are talking about is an experiential development of the Father's love (which is still central). There is a logical progression in regard to the priorities in the life of the Church: through worship we directly experience the love of the Father and we give it back to Him. This leads to a receptivity of The Word, through which we instruct one another in the love of God. This naturally creates an intimate and safe environment for Fellowship, through which God's love is given to one another. This overflows into Ministry, through which God's love is given away in service to others (in and beyond the Church). This then raises the need to equip one another for more effective ministry to others. Therefore through Training we give the love of God back to ourselves in and through one another. Logically, this leads to the ultimate purpose: to send people out to advance the Kingdom of God. Thus through Sending we give the love of God directly to the world.

Having presented this overview, we can examine each priority in turn.

FIRST PRIORITY: WORSHIP

The birth of worship in the Vineyard

Perhaps one of the most well-known phrases associated with the Vineyard is the title of the Vineyard Music worship series, 'Touching the Father's Heart'. This phrase says it all. Its roots go right back to 1976 when a group of hurting people sat and worshipped God through simple love songs, tears and guitar music. Carol Wimber refers to the experience as a raw hunger for God that was birthed in their brokenness and simple worship. If they did not have Him, experience Him, know Him, and receive His mercy, they would have nothing at all and there would be nothing to live for. Brokenness and worship were both the seed and the soil out of which the Vineyard grew.

The intimate and warm worship did not satisfy them—it only served to deepen their desperation, their longing and hunger for God. It led to an increased awareness of their utter brokenness and the depths of the Father's unconditional love. True worship always has this dual effect. It is a paradox. When Isaiah saw Yahweh in His holy glory, he immediately became aware of his sinfulness and was cleansed while worshipping (Is 6). This is how the Vineyard was born. This is the stuff we are made of. This is the heart and fountain of the Vineyard—we must drink deeply from these waters every time we gather as a people.

Worship is our first and highest priority. We are called first, before anything else, to love and enjoy God forever—and ever! We better get some good practice before we enter the forever! John loved to preach from Revelation about the many times people fell down on their faces before the throne in the presence of Father and the Lamb. They are constantly laying down their lives and their crowns in worship—again and again. It seems that whenever something in heaven is said or moves or happens, the response is immediate and joyful worship—everyone prostrates himself or herself in fresh and adoring surrender before God. John and many others that we know are there doing just that! Maranatha! Yes, come quickly Lord Jesus!

Worship from God's point of view

Worship is what He enjoys most. John used to say, 'It's the only thing that God gets out of this deal.' Worship pleases and pleasures God. It is our ultimate gift to Him. It is giving Him our love by giving Him our lives—we cannot give Him anything more than our very lives, now and forever. We were created 'for His pleasure' (Rev 4:11 KJV), and worship directly fulfils this.

In some mysterious sense, only we can satisfy, through worship, something deep in the self-sufficient heart of the Triune God. Mind-blowing! Something of this mystery is felt in the haunting cry of God when He went hunting around the garden, looking and searching, 'Adam, Eve, where are you?' Even Jesus said, 'The Father seeks those who will worship Him in spirit and truth.' There is a sense of loneliness, of aching, of incompletion, almost of desperation—God cannot live without us (and yet He can!). And we cannot live without Him (and yet we can!). David captures something of this profound spiritual yearning for ultimate union when he cries out, 'Deep calls to deep at the sound of your waterspouts' (Ps 42:7). In our utter brokenness, our 'deep' and God's 'deep' call out and connect with each other to become one.

Worship from our human perspective

From the human perspective worship is the same. It is the only and complete connection between God and us, the fountain of fulfilment and pleasure. There is no other substitute for this ultimate reality. The substitutes cannot satisfy—they only give false intimacy and lead to enslavement and addictions. Whom or what we worship incarnates us. When we worship God, we become like Him and we fulfil the ultimate purpose for which we were created. There is nothing beyond it. It is the ultimate, because it is all about Him. That is why the opposite is so horrendous to God and hellish for human beings—the worship of any other god leads to the incarnation of evil in our bodies, in our lives, with all the death and destruction that it brings, both immediate and ultimate. Hence the first of the Ten Commandments. The worship of Yahweh and the adoration of Jesus make us complete. Our deepest needs and longings are satisfied in union with God.

Worship is not only an act or an event, it is also a lived life. The two Greek words for worship in the New Testament convey this: *proskyneo* (Jn 4:23-24) is the act of worship—it means to bow down and kiss the King (from Ps 2:12). This speaks of love and surrender in relational intimacy and adoration. We pay homage by placing all that we are and all that we have at His disposal, as an act of love. But *latreuo* (Rom 12:1) is the lifestyle of worship—to do every act of life, moment by moment, whether it is work, ministry, family time or recreation, as 'unto the Lord'. Every act of life becomes a service 'for the glory of God'. In fact, *latreuo* is often translated as 'service' in English bibles. In short, worship is whole-life and life-long service to God revealed in Jesus Christ.

Worship from the Vineyard perspective

We see worship as an absolute non-negotiable Trinitarian priority. It is all about giving and receiving love—the Love of the Father. It honours and gives tangible expression to the value of Jesus' Headship over the Church, anticipating His Headship over all things. As we worship, we 'build' His throne (Ps 22:3) and He takes His rightful place and rules among us, cleansing sin, healing sickness, driving out demons and defeating His enemies. Jesus does this by the Spirit. Through worship the Administration of the Holy Spirit is respected, received and released in the Church, and through the Church into the world.

Therefore, we describe worship in the following way (I encourage you to ponder each word): worship must be regular, real, non-religious, relevant, contemporary, simple, love-song-oriented, honest, free, warm, open, personal, tender, non-manipulative, non-hyped, and above all, sincere and intimate. The key is simple love-songs to Jesus, not complicated, nor sophisticated. The intensity of our 'loving God' in our Church or home group gatherings should naturally lead to a lifestyle of godly obedience and service. The more one worships the more one wants to please God. The more exquisite the worship experience, the greater the overflow into a lifestyle of worship. Worship changes us. We cannot encounter God's presence in worship without being transformed (as Moses was filled with light on the mountain). The quality of our worship will determine the quality of our lived life.

Our practice of worship and worship leading

The first thing that should happen when people come into Vineyard Churches is that God should assault them in worship! From the first song, God should be all over them! Worship should be in the very air that we breathe. Worship should be in our very bodies that we bring. The many different words used for worshipping Yahweh in the Hebrew Old Testament all describe body-postures, thus showing the mysterious and dynamic relationship between Spirit and body. What happens inwardly is expressed outwardly in our bodies. Conversely, by adopting certain body postures in worship we invoke certain attitudes and experiences. In worship people stand, or kneel, or sit, or lie prostrate. Their hands may be in a receiving posture in their laps or at their sides or raised to the heavens. People might look around or close their eyes. Faces may be expressionless or serene or shining with tears or simply bubbling with joy. Heads may be bowed or raised, with feet and legs moving or dancing or standing still. Bodies may be straight or swaying or bowed over. There may be no words. Or there may be tongues-speaking and songs and cries and sighs and shouts of joy—simply lost in God, lost in love, lost in worship. The only 'rule' is that you must not draw unnecessary attention to yourself, nor interfere with your neighbour. True worship is both profoundly personal and completely communal at the same time. They cannot be separated.

To 'enter into' this kind of worship, some people simply relax and yield to what is happening. I find that you have to come to worship with intention and focus and a willingness to be vulnerable. You have to let go of self-consciousness and forget about the person next to you (but not to their detriment!), forget about your fights and feelings, and give yourself to God through the attitude of your heart and body, and through the songs and the words that the worship team has chosen. However, our values tell us that everyone is free to 'enter into' worship at his own pace and in his own way—no pressure! We have found that some people need to sit and watch for months before they begin to engage. Others take to it like a duck to water. Others sit and quietly weep and get 'healed up'. Yet others find that it is too personal or too contemporary and loud—not really for them, so they move on. No problem!

Vineyard worship is 'led-worship'. We believe God gifts people to creatively lead worship according to our basic values and style. God gifts musicians and songwriters and together they form teams to facilitate the worship experience in the Church. Worship leading is therefore a great privilege and a serious responsibility. It is both a skill and an art form— being a Psalmist. The first requirement is to be a true worshipper oneself. The worship leader must have the ability to sense where the people are at and to know what to do when God is present (very few people have this sensitivity and skill). It is the art of sensing and moving with the wind of God's Spirit, as He, together with the worship leader, creatively draws the gathered community into ever new ways of coming near to bow down before the Father and to 'kiss the Son' (Ps 2:12).

A 'Vineyard theology' of worship and worship leading from Psalm 95

One of the all-time favourite Vineyard songs, 'Come, let us worship and bow down/let us kneel before the Lord Our God, our Maker ...' comes from this Psalm. Worship and worship leading in Psalm 95 has three movements.

- First, we come into God's presence with an active will of praise and thanksgiving for Who He is and what He has done (v 1-5, also Psalm 100, we 'enter His courts with thanksgiving ...'). This focuses our minds, disciplines our feelings and softens our hearts. It helps us to 'warm-up', to 'en-joy'—'enter into' His presence, to come before His throne.

- This moves us naturally into a place of true worship, which is a heart response to God's self-revelation (v 6-7). The only adequate response to God is surrender, to bow down, to kneel and worship—an act of intimacy and adoration. The Lord encounters us. We experience the numinous. We touch the Father's heart. This is the peak-point in worship, a cathartic release. A good worship leader is like a skilled and experienced lover, knowing how to draw us there. He or she will sense each moment, where the people are at and what the Spirit is doing, and will know what to do next to blend the people and the Spirit until we encounter His manifest presence. Each and every experience of intimate worship can be creatively different.

- Then the movement shifts to hearing His voice and entering His rest (v 8-11). When we have come to the centre-point, the cathartic release, we hear His whisperings of love and we experience profound peace and rest—a kind of spiritual jetlag or the afterglow of glory! In the stillness, God's words of love (and ours to Him) come both personally and corporately. At this time, often towards the end of worship, we receive prophetic words and revelations from the Lord that affirm, encourage, heal and empower us. Then we sit and absorb God's love. Sometimes we engage in ministry to people or we rise and celebrate with joy and dance. God is indeed our great Lover!

In summary, worship in essence is intimacy with God that flows over into a lifestyle of service. This does not exclude praise and celebration.

 ## SECOND PRIORITY: THE WORD

Intimacy with God opens us up to His Word, to warmly receive not only prophetic whispers, but also sound Biblical teaching. Our approach to the Word of God is explained in chapters two and five. But what does this mean in terms of the Bible as a priority in the Vineyard? How do we 'use' the Bible in our lives, in our Churches?

Because we value the Bible as God's Word—our final authority for life and faith—we seek to teach and train our people in the Scriptures. This is not a matter of Bible knowledge, but being formed by God's Word in our worldview, in our thinking, feeling and acting. Our primary goal is to hear God through His Word, and then obey and do what He says. This is how we become like Him.

Equipping the saints through preaching and teaching

We prioritize the Word of God by preaching and teaching in our corporate gatherings. Expository preaching (systematically teaching through a passage or a book in the Bible) is important, because it is the more responsible way of teaching God's Word. It takes into account the original context, the intention of the author, the language forms and the applied meaning for us today. It also keeps us from our own pet subjects or subjective views—expository preaching 'pushes' us to preach the full counsel of God. Once again, our goal is to hear what God is saying to us and then obey it. This is the 'deductive' way of using Scripture—to hear God in what He said then to those people to whom the text was originally written, and therefore what He is saying now to us in our context.

Topical or thematic preaching has its place as God may be emphasising certain things at different times. But all our preaching must be relevant, non-technical and life-related, with specific practical application for our ministries and our daily lives. In this sense Biblical teaching is central to discipleship—it is used to 'equip the saints for works of service', to grow people into 'faith and knowledge of the Son of God and become mature' (Eph 4:11-13). Paul encourages Timothy to work hard in 'correctly handling the word of truth', because 'all Scripture is inspired by God and is useful for teaching, rebuking, correcting and training in righteousness, so that the person of God may be thoroughly equipped for every good work' (2Tim 2:15, 3:16-17).

We will discuss 'equipping the saints' in more detail below, but I need to mention that we also prioritize God's Word through teaching and training in seminars, workshops, conferences and retreats. These events typically address particular themes and are aimed at the equipping process. They always lead into a clinic type experience where teaching is not only received, but also applied and practised in one or other form of ministry.

Here again, we try to balance the tension between Word and Spirit, between teaching and training, between hearing and doing, and between knowledge and application.

Using the Word in counselling, home groups and personal devotions

The use of Scripture in our counselling practice is important. This is part of our recognition that the Bible is our 'rule for life' and a means of equipping to live life the way God lives it. This applies to pastoral counselling, therapy and healing, and spiritual direction. We avoid the Biblicist or fundamentalist approach where the Bible is 'thrown' at anything and everything—by 'proof-texting' and applying verses too literally and out of context. We draw from helpful sources in the human sciences and from experience, and seek to integrate truth in our ministry to people. However, the Scriptures still remain the rule against which we measure everything, the ultimate truth that sets us free (Jn 8:31-32), the power that heals us (Ps 107:20), the light that guides our path (Ps 119:105), and the sword that exposes our inner being (Heb 4:12).

God's Word is also prioritized in personal discipleship. This takes many forms. For instance, in the kinships (home groups) the leader will sometimes facilitate sharing around God's Word—either he leads it or the people share what God has been saying to them through the Word. But this is not a 'Bible Study'. It is not debating technicalities or points of view. Rather, the Scripture becomes a means of sharing our hearts and lives, of disclosing where we are at, for the sake of being known and accountable, and with a view to receiving ministry. Paul says, 'let the Word of Christ dwell in you richly as you teach and admonish one another with all wisdom' (Col 3:16). This can be called an 'inductive' way of using Scripture—a type of devotional approach where the emphasis is on our heart response to Scripture. We are allowing Scripture to read us more than we read Scripture. It has to do with being vulnerable, with meeting God through the text, with self-disclosure and ministry (giving advice or correcting technicalities or debating issues in this environment is destructive).

This goes further, as we seek to train our people to be personally devoted to God's Word, to know how to encounter God in the Word, to know how to interpret Scripture and how to 'feed' themselves. This is fundamental to their growth, their relational apprenticeship to Jesus. God's Word has a profound effect upon us—it gives us guidance, keeps us from sin, instructs us, heals us—just to mention a few. Therefore we seek to equip our people to do regular personal devotions. This takes place through various programmes like workshops and seminars—some Vineyards do silent retreats and spiritual companioning. Our people must not only know how to read and study Scripture, but also how to meditate on it so that they can hear God and obey, and in so doing, become more like Him.

THIRD PRIORITY: FELLOWSHIP

Intimacy with God leads to intimacy with one another on the basis of the Word of God. In other words, our mutual belonging and relating is founded on God's presence and on God's Word. The priority of fellowship is all about the importance of relationships, actually 'doing' them, operating relationally, sharing a 'common life'. It means being family to one another in loving and caring relationships. Because we value relationships and reality (the why), we prioritize fellowship (what we do). What then is fellowship and how do we do it?

Our understanding of fellowship

The old English word 'fellowship' can be popularly understood as 'two fellows-in-a-ship' (sorry gals!). It originally meant participation or member-ship in a privileged association or body leading to mutual sharing and benefit. This is rather formal—a bit too British! In some contexts the word had more intimate connotations, like shared community or companionship, or even communion. But if we go to the Greek New Testament word *koinonia*, we immediately have the idea of 'common'—it means 'to share things in common', or as the New English Bible puts it, 'sharing the common life' (Acts 2:44-47). My understanding of the concept behind *koinonia* goes like this: fellowship is a sharing of life in true community, which comes from real companionship founded on quality communication and communion—originating in union. This oneness or kinship of heart and life is what Paul calls for in Phil 2:1-11, a quality of *koinonia* through an attitude and practice of *kenosis*—a self-humbling in service of others.

The Biblical John complements this understanding of *koinonia* (in Jn 17:20-24, 1Jn 1:3-7) by saying that the Father becomes one with us, through the Son, by the Spirit, in a 'shared life' (His life in us). Relational union with God (worship again!) leads to union and communion with one another. We share His life together—we are family, His family. These relationships are a tangible sharing of who we are and what we have with one another—loving not in word but in deed. 'By your love for one another all people will know you are my disciples' (Jn 13:34). The result is (God's) authentic community in each locality—'The Body of Christ' or 'The Fellowship of God's People'. The Hebrew reality would be 'Covenant Community'. Christianity and Church is basically an organic network of covenant relationships pulsating with God's shared eternal kind of life.

Fellowship is various levels of quality relationships

How do we 'do' this fellowship? We prioritize relationships and relationship building—with God and with one another. We seek to live and work and do Church in a relational way, learning to 'share the common life' through different activities and levels of relational belonging.

At its widest level, fellowship means that we build relationship with the broader Church (through 'Ministers' Fraternals' and other means) because we are one Body and we need the life of God in the other parts of the Body. God loves the whole Church—we dare not withdraw from fellowship with the broader Church.

The next level of *koinonia* is when the local Church gathers on Sundays (or whatever day). God's life flows in and through us as we share together in worship, the Word and ministry to one another. Although the relational intimacy and friendship building elements may be limited in this larger environment, it does provide a vital expression of fellowship in terms of celebration, festivity and feasting (food is an important part of fellowship in the Biblical context). This can happen in the form of love feasts, camps and conferences.

However, 'doing' kinships or home groups is the most important way of having real fellowship, being family—not just social interaction or 'hanging out' or having tea. Becoming true friends within a safe environment of love, acceptance and forgiveness is what it is all about. This type of connecting, through small groups of meaningful relationships, is the greatest means of healing and growth this side of heaven. An exaggeration? I think not. Obviously, when relationships go wrong, they can be the greatest source of pain and sickness this side of hell. God made reality to work like this. Marriage is the ultimate example—it can be wonder and oneness, or agony and disintegration.

The potential for pain in Christian relationships, let alone other relationships, should not deter us from building and committing to them. We should never give up on them. The quality of our relationships defines Church. Relationships and people come before projects. In fact ministry comes out of relationships. This is where the individual is restored and affirmed. The pain in relationship should motivate us to love even more. We should become skilled at resolving conflict, equipping each other to do it the Biblical way (Matt 5:23-24 cf. 18:15-20). I find very few Christians who take Jesus seriously and even fewer who try to obey Him. No wonder the Church is in such a relational mess. In Paul's words, we need to 'maintain the unity of the Spirit through the bond of peace' by being 'completely humble and gentle, patient and bearing with one another in love' (Eph 4:2-3).

Equipping home groups, the 'two's and three's' and marriages

Therefore we prioritize home groups, and equip the leaders, and make sure that they are functioning and healthy, because this is where the Church rubber hits the road of life. Dysfunctional groups, like dysfunctional families, lead to all sorts of problems. We also do seminars and support-group work and offer courses—through various programmes—to heal people from relational brokenness, to re-establish boundaries and to equip them to maintain healthy relationships. This is another important aspect of fostering real *koinonia* in the Church. Such courses and programmes operate as a complement to the kinships in most Vineyards.

At a smaller level we have the 'two's and three's' (Matt 18:20). These are the smallest 'units', often comprising the closest fellowship. These organic networks of 'prayer-partners' or 'buddies' constitute the smallest cells, the most vibrant connections of life in the Church. Here is where people share their deepest and darkest secrets, their dreams and aspirations, their fears and longings. We need to respect, nurture and work with these David-and-Jonathan type relationships, without allowing them to become narcissistic or incestuous.

Marriage and family is at the heart of all sharing of life. Fellowship also means that we foster real *koinonia* in our marriages and families through various courses and programmes. If our marriages or our children are not doing well, then we are not doing well, and the Church is not doing well. The Vineyard has always placed a priority on marriage and family above Church fellowship, ministry and mission. Not like the little ditty that says, 'Mary was given a little lamb to keep, but she gave it to the Church, and it died for lack of sleep!'

FOURTH PRIORITY: MINISTRY (THE SICK, THE LOST, THE POOR)

Fellowship, or intimacy in relationships, naturally leads to ministry. Where there is love and trust we can easily receive God in and through the other person. Relationships give a safe context for specific ministry—over and above the general healing dynamic inherent in healthy relationships. Ministry is built on, and gives visible expression to, the value of the individual (grace and mercy) and the value of healing (an environment and practice of healing).

You may have wondered why the priority of ministry comes before training—not the other way round. There is a natural progression. As people connect in relationships they begin to be healed. Then they begin to love. Then they minister to each other in one form or another. 'Loving', as the most basic form of 'ministry', needs to be developed and equipped, therefore training follows. John Wimber had a clear understanding of this. It came out of years of experience. He said that everyone should minister in one way or another, and that training is not there to motivate or get people to minister, but rather to equip the people who are already motivated and ministering, so that they can do their ministry more effectively.

John's understanding assumes that we are not in the business of motivating people, hyping them up or promoting a ministry. We treat people as adults and allow organic processes and motivation to 'happen' in relationships. We work with people who are taking responsibility and who are already trying to do something. It also assumes that there are no 'experts'. Ministry is for everyone even though we all have needs of our own—we are all 'wounded healers'. We take responsibility for our own brokenness while being available to minister to others in their brokenness.

Every believer is in fulltime ministry

We believe that everyone who is called to follow Jesus is called to minister to others. In Paul's language, it is 'the saints' that should 'do the work of ministry' (Eph 4:12). Peter's concept is the 'priesthood of all believers' (1Pet 2:4,5). Jesus says, 'Come, follow Me and I will make you fishers of people' (Matt 4:19). The images may differ but the message is the same. Every Christian is a fulltime minister or missionary no matter what your occupation is! We are all 'fishing' for God, bringing people to God and God to people, in one way or another. This is ministry. We have to live out this common vocation in and through our occupations, our families, our Churches.

Have you realised that you are already in 'fulltime ministry'? The next question is, which ministry? Your ministry? Many Christians say, 'This is my ministry, you have no right to interfere or tell me what to do!' The ministry we are talking about is not your ministry. In fact, strictly speaking, there is no such thing as 'my ministry'. John Wimber frequently said, 'There's only one ministry—HIS ministry!' We are all called to continue the ministry of Jesus in the world today. We cannot 'possess it', make it our own, privatise it, put our name all over it or franchise it. God forbid! John frequently said we are all 'small change' in His pocket to be spent the way He wants to spend us. We are for Him, for His ministry and service. It is all about HIM, not about us. It is not about our ministries, our egos and our success. Ours is the privilege of being in ministry with Him. We are called to do what Jesus did the way He did it. We are called to teach what Jesus taught the way He taught it, to love what Jesus loved the way He loved it and to live what Jesus lived the way He lived it. There is one calling! We are literally the Body of Jesus Christ to one another and to this world.

The Biblical understanding of His ministry

Specifically, what is His ministry? What is this one calling? What is your answer? Ministry is nothing more and nothing less than service. It presupposes an attitude and character that God seeks and delights in—that of a servant. The common New Testament Greek word for ministry, *diakonos*, means service or servanthood. This goes against any hint of pride or ownership in personal or private 'ministries'. Ours is the enormous privilege of being in His service, and hopefully we will one day hear those rewarding words, 'Well done my good and faithful servant, enter into the joy of your Lord.' True servants instinctively respond, 'Oh, it was nothing really, I am an unworthy servant, I've just done my duty' (Matt 25:21 cf. Lk 17:10). Therefore, the bottom line in the issue of ministry' is not position, power or greatness, but to be the servant of all—like 'The Son of Man' who 'did not come to be served, but to serve and to give His life in suffering love for others' (Matt 20:25-28). Doing His ministry presupposes having His heart and attitude.

What then is His ministry? Lk 4:18 is an adequate summary—it was the 'Ministry Mandate' or 'Mission Manifesto' of Jesus, and therefore it is ours as well. We can summarise the priority of ministry in terms of the sick, the lost and the poor (and not necessarily in this order). Obviously ministry is much more than this. It has to do with the whole of life, not just 'spiritual' ministry. However, for our purposes, we emphasise these three as being at the heart of Jesus' ministry.

We do not require high standards of qualification for people to minister. It obviously depends on what ministry we are talking about, but the general ministry of Jesus has only two 'qualifications': faith and compassion. Jesus ministered because He believed Father could and would help people and because He had compassion on them. In fact, He had such compassion that He could not but minister to people (Matt 9:35-36). Being in touch with our own wounds and weaknesses, and dealing with them, gives us compassion for others who are in need. Not being in touch with our own 'stuff' makes us hard, arrogant and 'professional'. We are all in process. None of us is perfect. Vineyard has been called 'the Church of the walking wounded'. We encourage all our people to minister, unless their brokenness gets in the way of ministry, i.e. negatively affects the person they are ministering to. In such a case we need to take responsibility and have 'time out' to receive healing ourselves. We dare not restrict ministry to the pure, the mature, the leaders and the 'anointed man of God'. Ministry is all about mercy, grace and compassion—it can be a little messy.

Ministry to the sick

Ministry to the sick is wholistic. In a sense 'the sick' include the poor and the lost. We start with each other and those God has given us by ministering healing and growth. Then, as we begin to be 'healed up', we are motivated to reach out beyond ourselves to help others—to minister to the poor and the lost. We practice healing ministry through various programmes, courses, support groups, home groups and Sunday meetings. Our primary practice is through the laying on of hands during 'ministry time'. Beyond frequent 'ministry times', we work at developing a lifestyle of ministry to the sick; in the office, in the home, in the mall, wherever people need healing and are open to receive ministry.

Laying on of hands happens in a non-manipulative, non-religious, non-hyped way. We see those who minister as midwives and those receiving ministry as having their experience of birth in God. We facilitate healing by working with God, listening to Him and exercising the gifts of His Spirit in a compassionate and affirming way. John's book, Power Healing, explains this 'ordinary believer' model of ministry (see appendix 4). It is aimed at loving and healing the whole person, not just solving the problem. Healing is both a process and an event. It involves signs and wonders, physical healing, healing from past hurts, emotional problems, psychological damage, relational brokenness, deliverance from demons and giving and receiving forgiveness.

Ministry to the lost

Ministry to the lost is naturally linked to healing the sick. Jesus ministered to many people who were far from God, and often their healing brought them into relationship with God. In the final analysis, evangelism is the centre of all healing. Coming into the forgiveness and life of God is the beginning of all healing, growth and ministry. Doing evangelism and reaching the lost is a priority in the Vineyard. It is not only for the specially gifted and the leaders—the rank and file must do evangelism. The role of the leaders and the gifted is to model 'fishing', and to equip the Church to do it so that 'everyone gets to play', as John Wimber used to say.

We see evangelism essentially as presence, proclamation, persuasion, and power. Power Evangelism (see appendix 4) explains John's approach to evangelism. It emphasises the power aspect, i.e. bringing people to Christ through ministry in the power of the Holy Spirit. This is where healing ministry overflows to non-believers—God using us in evangelism through supernatural words of knowledge and healing gifts. These incidents are often associated with 'divine appointments'. Once a person experiences God's supernatural presence and power, they are wide open to believe. The classic example of 'power evangelism' was when Jesus used supernatural knowledge to bring a 'questionable' woman to faith in the Messiah (Jn 4).

Power evangelism presupposes 'presence' in evangelism. Firstly, we need to be available and open to God to recognise the 'divine appointments' that

He sets up for us. It means being present to the opportunity to sow seed, to the moment of evangelism, being in the right place at the right time (as with Jesus in the above story). We need to cultivate friendship with non-believers so that we can be present to influence them and ready to share our faith in Jesus (1Pet 3:15). Many Christians have no relationships with unbelievers and therefore do little or no evangelism. Being present for evangelism means that we place a high priority on evangelism as a lifestyle, as opposed to programmed evangelism. We may use programmes to do evangelism, like Alpha Courses or Servant Evangelism, but the key is every believer doing natural evangelism, gossiping the gospel wherever we are (Acts 1:8 cf. 8:4). Secondly, 'presence' in evangelism has to do with involvement in the community or social concern, which I will discuss below.

Proclamation and persuasion is a vital part of reaching the lost. Jesus came 'to seek and to save those who are lost'. We seek to train our people to do this. John Wimber always said, 'tell your story' (how you became a Christian, what God has done for you) and then 'tell His story' (who Jesus is and what He has done for us in His life, death and resurrection). Proclaiming the good news includes persuading people to come to Jesus— not 'Bible-bashing', but really convincing them of their need for Jesus. Proverbs 11:30 says, 'He who wins souls is wise.' Jesus promises that His Spirit will give us 'words and wisdom' which people will not be able to 'resist or contradict' (Lk 21:15).

Ministry to the poor

Lastly, but by no means the least, we prioritize ministry to the poor. In many Vineyards it is one of the strongest aspects of ministry. Anaheim Vineyard at its peak was moving sixty tons of food every month in feeding the poor. God's concern for the poor and needy is well established in the Scriptures. To be a friend of Jesus (and of Yahweh) is to be a friend of the poor and the oppressed. It goes to the heart of the gospel and the integrity of our witness in the world. Real evangelism involves being present in the form of service to the community. The false dichotomy between evangelism ('saving souls') and materially helping the poor ('social concern') must be abandoned once and for all. Salvation is for the whole person, not just their souls. How can you preach to a hungry person and not give them food to eat? Jesus' younger brother would question whether such faith was really Christian! (Js 2:1-16). Ministry to the poor can take on as many forms as the people have a heart for and can creatively engage in. However it is done, it is a fundamental priority in the Vineyard.

 # FIFTH PRIORITY: TRAINING

Training is a natural follow-on from ministry because as people get into one or other type of ministry they quickly realise what they don't know. Then they naturally want to know more so as to do their ministry better. This creates both the need and the appetite for training. Have you ever tried to train someone who is not doing anything and has no desire for training?

The priority of training gives visible expression to the underlying value of the Kingdom of God and to the values of healing and relationships. We do training because we value the presence and ministry of the Kingdom in our midst. We are committed to 'equipping the saints to do the work of ministry' (Eph 4:12). John Wimber popularized Paul's phrase 'equipping the saints' to the point where it has become part of our Vineyard identity. John actually lived it. Wherever he was, wherever he went, he gave ministry away by equipping the rank and file to minister. I remember a morning in 1982, while walking with John in a park, when I asked him, 'What would you like to be known for? What would you like to have on your gravestone when you die?' He didn't hesitate; 'He equipped the saints.' Guess what is written on John's gravestone?

Training is whole-life apprenticeship to Jesus

What is our concept of training and how do we prioritize and do it? Training or equipping has to do with apprenticeship. The 'Bible word' is discipleship. The 'Great Commission' is key to understanding this idea (Matt 28:18-20). We are called on the basis of Jesus' authority to make disciples from people of all types. How? By initiating them into Christian faith and community, and by training them to do what Jesus did. The Greek word for discipleship, *mathetes*, really means apprenticeship: one who learns from someone by being with them, and doing what they do they become like them. This takes place within a disciplined relational context. Other words have been used: Christ-follower, pupil, student or understudy. John Wimber constantly said that it is Jesus who disciples us through His Word, His Spirit and His Body. We avoid the one-on-one type of discipleship model that stresses 'authority and submission'—it has led to spiritual abuse in some circles.

Our concept of discipleship is that we are being apprenticed by Jesus, learning directly from Him and through one another, how to do what He did—to live and love the way He lived and loved. In short, the purpose of training is to equip us to do 'the main and plain', the words, works and wonders of God's Kingdom.

Equipping or discipling is about the whole of life, not just 'spiritual' or Church training and ministry. It is about equipping in all aspects of life so that we can 'grow up into Him in all things' (Eph 4:12-16), that we can end up living the kind of life that God lives and become more like Jesus. We need to train our people to be skilled in relationships, marriage, the Word of God, employment, education, social service and ministry. It is all part of the life equipping process. Training is a process, not a once-off event like a course or conference, although they are helpful and have their place in the training process. Training as a process also means that we are committed to continual growth by being open to learning more effective and creative ways of doing things.

The Vineyard concept of training is apprenticeship, not education or teaching, although teaching is an important aspect of training. We confuse training with teaching in the West. If we have teaching on something and we understand it, then we think we know it. Biblically speaking you only really 'know' something when you experience it, do it and live it! The better you do it the more you know it and become it. In fact, only when you try to do it, do you realise how little you really know about it. You don't know what you don't know till you need to know it—when you try to do something! John Wimber emphasised information and training as on a 'need to know basis' for those already doing things. We need more relational 'on-the-job-training' than informational class teaching.

The 'show and tell' method of training

All this translates into a specific and practical method of training. John called it 'Show and Tell'. It has to do with the key concept of modelling. Discipleship and training comes through modelling (apprenticeship). What you see is what you become. We are deeply influenced by the models to which we have been exposed. Models impart, transfer and have a power to form and transform, both consciously and unconsciously. Real change comes about by changing the models that we expose ourselves to.

Who or what we model, as leaders, will influence our people and form our Church—for better or for worse! Therefore, care must be taken with who leads in what ministry and to whom we give recognition and public exposure. As John would say, the pastor should initially model the key ministries and practices within the Church. Or the pastor can point to others who are good models, who embody our basic values in the way they do their ministry. However, this does not mean that ministry is kept within an elite group of 'pure Vineyardites'! Our concept and practice of ministry and training means that we are committed to giving ministry away, to multiplying ministry by working ourselves out of a job as we continually train others to do what we are doing.

The other aspect to modelling is that we do not have to cajole or manipulate, or reinforce boundaries, in order to get things done or keep things in order. If we model our priorities and practices consistently enough people will imbibe them. Modelling is leadership by example. We do not need a lot of talk, explanation, persuasion and 'policing', just a lot of doing (modelling).

There are seven steps to the 'Show and Tell' method of training:

- You model it (do the ministry with others watching).

- Then talk about it (reflect on what happens, answer the questions that are raised because of what is seen and experienced).

- Get them to do it (to do it as you did it—while you watch them).

- Then talk about it (feed back to them your observations and discuss the questions that will arise from their doing it).

- Repeat the process (as often as is needed for them to 'catch it').

- Leave them doing it (monitor and encourage them).

- Get them to repeat the same process with others.

Contexts in which training happens

Such training happens primarily in the context of ongoing relationships—most practically through home groups and ministry groups. This is where people will experience worship, relational self-disclosure and prayer-healing ministry, and where they can interact and be 'coached'. It happens up to a point in our big gatherings. Through these basic structures people get exposure to who we are and what we do and they get to participate more and more—everyone gets to play! And 'coaching' makes you better at it! Training also takes place in various ministries 'in the field', like evangelism, ministry to the poor, translocal ministry trips and Church plants. To complement the above, we also do training in various ministry skills through courses, seminars, workshops and conferences. Most of these events would have a 'clinic' or 'ministry-time' in which 'practice' takes place. The safe environment makes for exciting learning experiences.

 ## SIXTH PRIORITY: SENDING

It all begins with God. Intimacy with God, through worship and the Word, leads to intimacy in fellowship with one another. This facilitates ministry, which creates the need for training for more effective ministry, which in turn overflows outwards to the broader Church and the world in Church planting and missions.

Sending comes from worship and leads to missions

It is a profound theological reality that all authentic mission is born in worship, and that true worship will lead to missions. Isaiah 'saw the Lord high and lifted up' and he heard Yahweh's sigh, 'Who will go for Us, whom shall We send?' and Isaiah answered, 'Here am I Lord, send me' (Is 6). The 'Great Commission' passage (Matt 28:17-20) says that 'when the disciples saw Him, they worshipped Him ... then Jesus said, "all authority in heaven and earth has been given to Me, therefore, you go and make disciples ..."' Seeing God in worship for who He really is causes us to have His heart for the nations. Then we cannot but go and do His bidding. The Pauline Church-planting team came out of 'worshipping the Lord and fasting' at Antioch. The mission to Asia, Europe and beyond originated here (Acts 13:1-5f). It has been said that a missionary is not a person who crosses the seas, but a person who sees the cross. When the early disciples saw the nail-pierced hands after the resurrection, they worshipped Jesus. They understood that He died for everyone and 'wants all people to be saved and to come to a knowledge of the truth' (1Tim 2:4).

The priority of sending gives tangible expression to the value of God's Kingdom. We use the word mission or missions in the broadest sense of advancing the Kingdom. Sending is visible evidence of having God's Kingdom heart, one that overflows with generous giving. God gave His best, His 'only begotten Son', because He loved the world (Jn 3:16). God's love, experienced through intimate worship, should cause us to give away our best in pursuit of His purposes in the world. John Wimber modelled incredible generosity. He gave of himself, and he gave his best away in terms of colleagues, ministry resources and money—all to advance the Kingdom of God. When we have spent years investing in a person, pouring in resources and training, only to give them away at the very point when their 'return' can now be maximized for our own set-up—that is what we're talking about! That is what John did, and God gave back to him more than he could handle! The old adage, 'you cannot out-give God' is true. The heart of sending is giving—giving sacrificially and generously.

We do sending in all sorts of ways

If something is a priority, you budget time, energy and money to make it happen. This applies to evangelism, ministry to the poor and any other form of ministry into society (strictly speaking, any ministry into the world is called 'mission'). Each local Church should budget and plan for 'sending' in the following ways. Remember that a priority is not only a plan, it is something you do regularly, something that is immediately visible in the life of the Church.

We do sending by giving away money, ministry resources, tapes, materials and books, to pastors and Churches needing help or seeking relationship and equipping. This can include giving trained personnel and pastors away as God calls people to serve in another Church or in the 'mission field' somewhere. It also includes giving away some of our people to other Churches or Church plants. This can be painful, but if it is correctly pre-pared and processed it can be an enormous blessing for both the sending and the receiving Churches. Some Vineyards have become 'Resource Churches' that help and empower other Churches, especially smaller and struggling Churches. Just think of what Anaheim Vineyard has done over the years—what a model it has been!

We also 'do sending' by training and releasing translocal teams for ministry trips to Churches, both Vineyard and others. These normally come out of invitations or need-identification among pastors. This is the renewal aspect of the calling God has put on the Vineyard. We must give away what God has given us or we can lose it (in terms of worship, healing ministry and Church planting skills). Translocal ministry trips take many forms—as creative as the Holy Spirit and the local needs are—doing seminars, conferences, Church camps, outreaches with the local Church, drama and concerts and training local leaders. Some trips are weekenders, some are short-term missions and others are for longer periods of time. The benefit of doing these translocals is the transforming effect that it has on the people who go, and the way they energise the home Church when they return. People come home overflowing with joy and wonderful stories of God's power—just like the disciples of Jesus in Lk 10:17-20. This is often how the Church is infused with vision, faith and power.

The same applies to the second calling of the Vineyard—that of Church planting. We train and send Church planters and teams to targeted areas or as the Holy Spirit leads (as in Acts 13). There are numerous ways to plant new Churches (see the Church Planting Course, appendix 4). We work in teams for the sake of support and protection, and to model community and ministry. Teamwork often plants a 'purer' seed that has a better chance of taking root and growing. We do not only plant Vineyard Churches. Our priority is to plant like-minded Churches, but if we can help Church planting in a broader sense we do so as well. Translocal teamwork reinforces our value for local Churches planting local Churches, rather than para-church agencies or centralized mission boards. (This does not mean that we despise them. Our policy is to work in partnership with them when we are able to do so.) Vineyard is a Church planting movement. It is in our blood. Each local Church should give birth to other plants as it grows in health and strength—all healthy cells multiply at some point, right? Vineyards in a local area should collaborate with one another to plant Churches.

 ## IN CLOSING

These six priorities should be the most visible things you run into when entering a Vineyard Church. They should be done in a way that reflects our basic values.

However, from time to time some priorities may be more prominent than others. One or two may even appear to be missing for a while! Or there may be some different priorities. We should not panic! This is part of the ebb and flow of Church life. The leadership team will have the overall picture as to the strategic timing, development and balancing of energy-input for this or that priority.

We must avoid being ideological and locked into a fixed type of 'Vineyard thinking' that boxes us in, that labels and categorizes people and things. Things are far more dynamic and 'in process' than we would ever realise. Neither must we hurry things—they take time if you know where you are going and how you plan to get there. We have to learn to ride the rhythms and interactions of organic life, God-given vision, planned development and Holy Spirit intervention. As an example, in 1982 John Wimber was asked why there was not much prophecy in his Church. I clearly remember his answer. His intention was to grow prophecy over a ten-year period so that it would not be under-present, or over-dominant, but would have its balanced place in a mature expression of its God-given function. Therefore, he would not be rushed. Neither was he insecure about the then lack of prophetic expression. He saw the big picture. He had a plan and felt that he was on track, trusting God and open to the Holy Spirit's intervention. Little did he know then that God would bring 'the prophetic' into the movement in the late 1980s (see Bill Jackson's account of this in 'The Quest for the Radical Middle', appendix 4).

CHAPTER 7

MODEL THE PRACTICES

We now come to the last of the three key elements that are definitive for our philosophy of ministry: values, priorities and practices.

By practices we mean the basic skills and disciplines that we believe all our people should have. As each individual in the Church regularly practises these skills, we feel the corporate effect. We establish our priorities and thereby achieve our purposes. In this sense practices make everything functional.

 ## THE VINEYARD PRACTICES

When developing the document, 'Building the Church from the Bottom Up', John Wimber asked the questions (as we got to this stage), 'What are the most basic practices that all Christians should be skilled in? Those that will directly embody our values and priorities? Those that will make the Church work as we want it to work?' He drew out a list of about fifteen 'spiritual disciplines' that he had brought from the Friends Church and said we should revise and develop this list into our own set of practices, i.e. reflecting our Vineyard values and priorities. I did this (as John's researcher/writer) and came up with the set of practices below—except for the marriage and family practices, which were added later.

The point of this story is that we conscientiously need to think through and decide on which particular practices are relevant for our Church. Having done that, we can confidently model them, knowing that they are a natural extension of our values and priorities. If we do not do this we end up, consciously or unconsciously, adopting by default certain practices that will undermine our stated values and priorities.

We instil practices by modelling them

We need to emphasise the importance and power of modelling. Practices are instilled in the Church by modelling, not by motivation through manipulation and cajoling—nor through teaching, for that matter. Adopting the 'motivational' approach often results in a fairly quick 'success' story, but sustaining it will require more and more motivational gimmicks, a sure sign of a 'Bounded-set' environment. The 'Centred-set' approach works by example and modelling. This is slower but surer growth, creating an adult, relational environment, and producing inter-dependence and maturity. The place of teaching then is to reinforce and explain what the leaders are already modelling.

One by one the various practices are faithfully modelled and one by one people acquire the skills and the disciplines that are modelled for them. They are caught, more than taught. This happens most effectively in kinships and ministry groups, and through other ministry and training relationships. If modelling is consistent enough, its effect will be exponential in the Church and beyond. It is not a process of cloning or making people into our image! On the contrary, it is being a conduit for Kingdom skills and disciplines, empowering people to live the Kingdom life in all its diversity. We dare not underestimate the power of modelling—for better or for worse. We are all modelling something all the time, whether we are conscious of it or not. It just depends on what we are modelling and how we model it, especially as leaders—which is why leaders incur a stricter judgement.

Values must determine the manner in which we do our practices

Modelling raises the issue of how we practise our practices. It has to with the idea of style and spirituality. The same set of practices in various Churches can be done in different ways, in a parenting and religious manner or in other ways reflecting other values. In this sense, values determine how we do our practices, and our practices should be done in keeping with our values. There is a 'Vineyard style' in the way things are done—this constitutes our spirituality.

What we are talking about is akin to Jesus' teachings to His disciples about three basic disciplines required in following Him: giving, prayer, and fasting (Matt 6:1-18). Notice how Jesus taught by shamelessly contrasting the way the Pharisees did their practices with what He wanted from His followers. Jesus had a 'style', based on certain values that clashed with the hypocritical Pharisees. He expects us to imitate and model His style. Every believer should do all the basic practices of the Kingdom of God in the Kingdom way.

If there is a 'Vineyard style', may it be that we do our practices in a manner not to be 'seen by people': neither to promote nor seek attention, neither to manipulate nor hype up, neither to be 'religious' nor phony, neither to be legalistic nor performance-driven. We should do our practices with honesty and reality, in love and compassion, being patient and kind, honouring human dignity, giving mutual respect, treating people as adults, with self-disclosure and vulnerability, creating a 'learning environment', with openness to explore and make mistakes and with acceptance and forgiveness in our hearts. Our practices should be without titles or offices or ego-trips or comparative judgements or any 'super-spiritual-stuff'. We should quietly go about our daily lives doing the 'main and plain' in an uncomplicated way. What would happen to our Churches and our world if we produce increasing numbers of disciples who daily do the basic practices of the Kingdom in the manner I have just described?

The basic practices of the Vineyard

The practices of the Vineyard cover three aspects: Prayer skills, Marriage and Family skills, and General Ministry skills (the third one has two aspects, namely communication and community skills. For a quick overview look at appendix 3). I will approach this discussion in point form with brief comments after each point. There are so many Scriptures one could refer to in elucidating each one of these practices, but we will restrict ourselves to only a few for each practice.

 PRAYER SKILLS

Prayer skills are first because they are fundamental to our relationship with God—from which all other relationship flows. These prayer skills also have to do, in one way or another, with spiritual warfare—overcoming the enemy in our lives and the evil in our world. We list five basic skills here.

The prayer of praise and adulation is a discipline that helps one to practise, moment by moment, the presence of God. It is more than a mental practice, because praise is actually a verbal expression (Ps 34:1), and it is our 'sacrifice' to God (Heb 13:15). Ongoing and ceaseless adulation trains the emotions and produces a spirit of joy and gratitude (Eph 5:18-21).

The prayer of petition refers to knowing how to ask and receive things from God (Lk 11:2-13). There is an emphasis on perseverance in this practice. Petition is about confessing our sins and our needs, about supplication for mercy and presenting our requests to God (Phil 4:6).

The prayer of intercession is a skill where one stands before God on behalf of someone else, to plead his cause. We are urged as a matter of priority to intercede for our leaders and for others in need (1Tim 2:1f). It involves learning how to co-operate with the Holy Spirit in intercessory prayer (Rom 8:26-27). We believe all Christians must practise intercession, although some are called to a particular ministry in this area.

The prayer of tongues or the 'gift of tongues' for the Church, the gathered community, is only for some (1Cor 12:28-30). But we believe that tongues as a private 'prayer language' is for all Christians—to 'edify' or to 'build oneself up' (1Cor 14:4 cf. Jude 20). This is prayer directed to God from one's spirit in praises, songs, mysteries, intercessions and thanksgiving (1Cor 14:2,14-18).

The prayer of faith (James 5:14-16) refers to this in the context of ministry to the sick. The prayer of faith is the skill to know how to use our God-given authority as we pray for the sick and demonised—as Jesus did when He 'commanded' sickness and demons to leave (Mk 1:25), and as He taught us how to pray in faith (Mk 11:22-24).

MARRIAGE AND FAMILY SKILLS

Marriage and family skills are next because they are the most important relationships outside of our relationship with God. If we are not doing well in our marriage and/or family, then we are not doing well, period! This is where the rubber meets the road. These relationships in the home give us the platform of credibility to minister in the Church and in the world. With the current breakdown in marriage and family, and our inability to sustain and develop ongoing relationships, the following five skills are desperately needed.

Intimacy in a broad sense, is about self-disclosure, vulnerability, closeness and affection in our relationships in the home. These are learned disciplines (Rom 12:10, Js 5:16). Specifically within marriage, it means the skill of loving in the sense of passion, romance and sexual intimacy (Song of Solomon 7:10-12—note that this book of the Bible is first and foremost a love-manual for marriage, and should be used as such).

Communication is knowing how to communicate effectively. Communication has different levels and is much more than words. Self-disclosure is the primary 'means to intimacy', both in the broad and specific senses. Besides this language of relationship (as in Song of Sol 7:6-9), there is also the language of information and motivation. We need be skilled in these forms of communication, 'speaking the truth in love'

(Eph 4:15); and our 'yes' must be 'yes' and our 'no' must be 'no' (Matt 5:37).

Child-rearing: acquiring the skill of parenting—learning how to be good and effective mothers and fathers so as not to 'exasperate one's children', but rather to 'bring them up in the training and instruction of the Lord' (Eph 6:4).

Financial planning has to do with viewing money correctly and handling it in a responsible way. We need to equip our people to budget well, in order to provide for their families and honour God financially. 'Dishonest money dwindles away, but he who gathers money little by little makes it grow' (Prov 13:11).

Life management: the skill of planning and managing our lives and families well does not come easily or automatically. We have to be trained to do this. Paul talks about 'managing our households well' (1Tim 3:12) and learning to 'put off your former way of life, corrupted by its deceitful desires, and be made new in the attitude of your mind; put on the new way of life ...' (Eph 4:22-24).

 ## GENERAL MINISTRY SKILLS

Communication skills

By this we mean the ability to speak in three areas of ministry. Often, although not always, the skill of communication or lack thereof determines how effective the ministry is. For some believers one or two of these aspects of communication-ministry may be a gifting and calling, and possibly their recognised ministry in the Body. The same would apply to all the other general ministry skills mentioned below. However, we believe that every Christian should be trained and have a basic level of skill in all the ministry practices below, whether it is their gifting or not, because we see them as intrinsic to the life of discipleship to Jesus.

The ability to witness: this is the skill of sharing your faith-experience in Jesus with others, particularly those who do not know Him. Peter says that we must always be ready to 'give a reason for the hope that is in us' (1Pet 3:15). Jesus promises power and wisdom for us to witness and to be witnesses (Acts 1:8 cf. Lk 21:15). Training our people in presenting the gospel is important.

The ability to counsel: this is the skill of healing and growing one another within our community relationships. We must learn to share God's wisdom and counsel in a life-related way with one another (Col 3:16). It is 'speaking the truth in love' so that we 'grow up in all things into Him who is the Head' (Eph 4:15).

The ability to teach: this is the skill of sharing God's Word with others and expounding its truths. We are not talking about teaching 'deep things' or 'Bible-bashing', but being able to simply teach the basics of the faith. The writer to the Hebrews expected anyone who was 'on the road' to be able to do this (Heb 5:11-6:1-3). Knowing how to use God's Word for mutual instruction and edification is basic to Christian discipleship (Col 3:16).

Community skills

This set of skills has to do with our ability to relate in three dimensions: in ministry to the Lord, in ministry to one another and in ministry to the world. Each of these dimensions has a set of skills that helps us to relate in the Kingdom. These relational ministry skills reinforce and live out our priorities and help us to achieve our overall purpose as a Church.

Ministry to the Lord

Worship: the ability to worship God from our hearts, both on our own as individuals and when we gather as a community of faith. This is the skill of satisfying the searching heart of the Father by knowing how to worship Him in spirit and truth (Jn 4: 23-24). The more we worship the more we learn how to worship. This basic discipline makes us skilful lovers of God.

Fellowship: the skill of fellowship with God leads to the skill of fellowship with one another. We must practise the discipline of 'abiding in Him' (Jn 15:4), which makes sharing His love with others a natural overflow, and this leads to warm, caring and cleansing relationships (1Jn 1:3-8). Fellowship with God is a summary of the prayer skills mentioned above.

Service: the discipline of obedient service in doing what pleases God. This skill is practised in two ways: in fellowship with Him we hear Him and learn to respond to His promptings like Jesus did—always doing what He sees the Father doing (Jn 5:19-20). It also means 'doing good deeds' (Matt 5:16) in serving the saints and other needy people, like the poor and the sick. Here too Jesus is the perfect example (Mk 10:45).

Giving: this is a natural outflow from the discipline of worship and service—to give of ourselves and our resources, which is symbolised in our financial giving. In the Old Testament, tithes are an acknowledgement of God's ownership of us (e.g. Gen 14:18-20 cf. Mal 3:8f), whereas 'freewill' offerings are an acknowledgement of God's blessing of us. The New Testament emphasis is on generous giving (Lk 6:38). We give to God by giving to the household of faith and the poor and needy (Gal 6:10, Matt 6:2f).

Personal Bible study: this is the skill of encountering God in His Word, of hearing God through His Word. It has been called 'reading the Bible responsively'. Here we learn how to study the Scriptures, to meditate and to 'correctly handle the word of truth' (2Tim 2:15) so that we may be fully equipped, not only to use the Scriptures in helping others, but also to live a godly life.

Ministry to the Body

Giving and receiving forgiveness: this is the practice of 'not letting the sun go down on your anger' (Eph 4:26). It is learning to receive forgiveness from God and one another, and to give forgiveness to those who offend us, or sin against us. Receiving forgiveness involves confession and repentance. Jesus' teachings are quite clear—we have to practise the discipline of forgiveness from the heart, even in worship, and in a way that secures the dignity of the other person, or else God will not forgive us our sins

(Matt 5:23,24 cf. 6:14 18:15-35).

Laying on of hands: this skill involves the practice of mutual ministry in the Body of Believers, both receiving laying on of hands and doing it to others. Laying on of hands is a foundational principle and practice for all Christians (Heb 6:1-3). It has to with receiving the Spirit (1Tim 4:14) and giving the Spirit in blessing, in recognition and affirmation, in healing and in other needs.

Exercising of spiritual gifts: here we are talking about discovering and exercising our gifts within the Family of Faith—especially in the small groups (1Cor 14:26). We need to be skilled in working with the Spirit in receiving other people's gifts, and in knowing and exercising our own gifts for the sake of others who may need what God has given us (Rom 12:3-8, 1Cor 12: 7-11).

Fellowship: this practice has already been referred to in a number of ways. This is the skill of fostering good relationships through humility and love, and 'maintaining the unity of the Spirit through the bond of peace' (Eph 4:2-3). Paul was always particularly concerned about fellowship and the need to maintain and practise it (Phil 2:1-11). It involves the discipline of regular gatherings for 'fellowship' in worship, teaching and breaking bread (Heb 10:25 cf. Acts 2:42f).

Healing the sick: healing is not only the provision of God for His Family through the leaders (James 5:13-16). It is also a basic skill for all Christians to learn and develop in accordance with Jesus' commission (Matt 10:1,8 cf. Mk 16:17-20). Sickness and healing is not just about physical illness, it is about 'dis-ease', or disharmony, in the person. We are talking about the skill of ministering healing spiritually, emotionally, mentally, physically and socially to the whole person.

Ministry to the World

Care for the poor: the discipline of some level of involvement with the poor is fundamental to Christian discipleship. Jesus made it mandatory. He said, 'When (not if) you give to the poor ...' (Matt 6:2-3). Ministry to the poor is not only giving finances or feeding the hungry; it takes on whatever form the needs may require in the context in which one lives (Matt 25:34-40).

Care for the lost: we have referred to this skill of sharing the gospel. It also involves exercising care for those unbelievers whom God may bring across our path. Every Christian needs the skill to develop some level of relationship and friendship with non-Churched people in order to be able to evangelise in a natural way. Sadly, most Christians have no friendships with non-believers.

Care for the sick: this too has been referred to. But it includes the deeper level of giving care to the sick—those who are not quickly healed, or those who are never healed. While Jesus said we should heal the sick, He also said we should care for the sick: 'When I was sick, you looked after me' (Matt 25:36). This can apply to many people, including the disabled and the terminally ill.

 CONCLUSION

These 'Vineyard practices' are drawn from an understanding of life in the Kingdom of God and what is important to us in the life of the Church. They are disciplines similar to what Peter talked about in his second letter to the early apprentices of Jesus. He says that if we 'make every effort' to add 'these things', these disciplines, to our faith-walk with Jesus, if we 'possess these qualities in increasing measure', then we will not be 'ineffective and unproductive in our knowledge of our Lord Jesus Christ'. Conversely, if we do not pursue these practices then we are 'nearsighted and blind, and have forgotten that we have been cleansed from our past sins'. 'Therefore,' Peter continues, 'be all the more eager to make our calling and election sure (because) if we do these things we will never fall, and we will receive a rich welcome into the eternal Kingdom of our Lord and Saviour Jesus Christ' (2Pet 1:3-11).

Strong words from Peter—some may think of it as guilt motivated performance. No, he is describing reality, saying what really happens if we do thus and so or if we do not do thus and so. The same applies to the practices that we have listed. The key is doing them and doing them regularly. This assumes of course, that they have been modelled to you in some way over a period of time and that you have developed them as basic disciplines in your life. Hopefully you are becoming a model of these practices, and equipping others to acquire them as well.

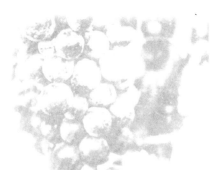

CHAPTER 8

CHOOSE THE PERSONNEL

Choosing the right personnel in terms of workers and leaders is absolutely crucial, because the well thought out 'philosophy' falls flat with wrong people working and leading in wrong ways. The ministries and departments of the Church are established through the recruiting, training and deploying of leaders and workers. This takes time and energy. The principles discussed below are absolutely crucial in worker and leadership selection and development. Anyone who has carried leadership responsibility for any length of time will know how important it is to recruit the right people for the right functions. Leaders make or break any ministry or Church. The 'making' is so wonderful and rewarding, but the 'breaking' is so hurtful and damaging. Leadership is critical. It is the key to healthy Church life and growth.

Character is more important than ability when it comes to choosing personnel. John Wimber emphasised this point and allowed things to go slowly and less efficiently, for the sake of honouring people with character above those who dazzled with their gifting. Paul instructed Timothy to entrust his life and teachings 'to faithful men who will also be able to teach others'—character first and ability second (2Tim 2:2). We are referring to a kind of 'spirituality of leadership' which is in major crisis in our day.

However, this obviously needs to be balanced with other factors that we will now discuss. This chapter is mainly about our understanding of leadership in the Vineyard and our criteria for choosing our personnel, especially potential leaders. We will also make some comments on women in leadership and the accountability and discipline of leaders.

 # A VINEYARD UNDERSTANDING OF LEADERSHIP

Our understanding of leadership anticipates some of the criteria for leadership mentioned below. To apply them without having caught the heart of leadership would invite institutionalism and legalism. John Wimber has covered much of this ground in two leadership letters (see appendix 4).

In examining our concept of leadership there will be a logical development and progression from the first to the seventh characteristic.

Firstly, workers and leaders emerge through the foundation and superstructure of the purpose, values, priorities and practices of the Church.

The best workers and leaders are those who have come up through the ranks. They bought into the philosophy of ministry, and grew in it, before they did anything or became anyone in the Church. This is crucial, because many people who join the Church—especially those who come from a performance environment—get their sense of worth and belonging from their need to do something or be someone in the Church. One has to watch out for this. Workers, and especially leaders, must embody and impart the basic values, priorities and practices. We seldom import leaders, unless it is clear to us over a period of time that they really do share our ethos.

Secondly, leadership, like ministry, is functional.

Leaders actually lead. They lead by example. When people no longer follow, leadership has effectively ceased. Leadership is essentially about responsibility and accountability—not about position or title. If leadership is based on the latter all sorts of problems emerge such as thinking too much in terms of honour and self-image, and not enough in terms of function and role.

It is unwise to recognise and release ministry and leadership publicly that has not already been functional for some time with a reasonable track record. Leadership must be tested before it is recognised. Some leaders are immediately seen for who they really are. With others, true character and ability emerge only later—often when it is too late to prevent damage being done to the people. Paul advised Timothy 'not to be hasty in the laying on of hands, and thus not share in the sins of others', because for some people 'their sins are obvious', but for others, 'their sins trail behind them' (1Tim 5:22-25). John Wimber warned us often, from his own experience, of the pain involved in 'laying off of hands'—removing leaders from leadership—we don't want too many of those!

Part of this functional understanding of leadership is the difference between leadership and management. Leaders break new ground. They go somewhere, they direct and develop people, structures and systems. Leadership creates vision, draws people together and works with and through them to achieve the vision. Managers or administrators maintain people and systems, they make everything work well and harmoniously. Obviously we need both leaders and managers, and there should be no difference in value between them.

Thirdly, leadership is not only functional, but also contextual.

Authentic leadership, like ministry, comes out of relationship and operates in a context. Paul 'ordained' elders in young Churches only about eighteen months after planting them (Acts 14:23). They were all relatively new believers. Leadership grew and apparently worked well. In another context, however, those same leaders would be not be leaders. Imposing leadership on people or on a particular situation does not work. A person who leads one group of people may not be able to lead another group. In addition, we should be careful not to assume leadership, unless the contextual relationships recognise and release it. We have to serve, starting from the bottom, and taking the lowest place at the table until the existing head of the table invites us to move up.

Context also affects the style a leader will adopt. Certain times or seasons, or particular socio-economic groups, require a more directive style of leadership, whereas other times or more sophisticated groups require a more consultative leadership style. A good leader can read the times, the context, and where the people 'are at', and then know what type or style of leadership is required to take things further.

Fourthly, leadership, like ministry, is servanthood.

It is all about heart attitude and hard work, not about position, power, privilege and control. If there is a privilege, then it is participation in the *kenosis* of Jesus, in His self-stripping for humble service—symbolically embodied in the washing of feet. Jesus said, 'You call me your Teacher and Lord, and you are right, for that is who I am. If your Teacher and Lord has washed your feet, how much more should you not wash one another's feet?' (Jn 13:13-17). Good leaders do not have the protective, proud or insecure mentality of 'my leadership, my ministry, my calling and my Church'. They have the 'kenotic' mentality of the Suffering Servant in Phil 2:6-11. As Paul says, it is often the authentic leaders who suffer most in their service to the Lord, the Church, and the world (1Cor 4:9f).

Although leadership is a gift in the Church (Rom 12:8), and should be respected and received as such, it functions as a humble service for the good of the Body, just like any other gift. Because leaders direct the whole congregation and form the people, their service has a higher level of accountability—a 'stricter judgement' (Js 3:1f cf. 1Tim 5:17-20—we will comment on this later).

But what about the Biblical 'office' of 'elders' and 'deacons' in the Vineyard? John Wimber was often asked this question. Again, it is a form of service, not a position of power. Real authority—spiritual authority—comes from service, from loving and laying down one's life, together with the operation of God's gifts of grace. This gives authentic substance to any 'position of authority'—which legitimately can be called 'structural authority'—whether in the home as husband and father, or in the Church as pastor or elder. That is why, in the final analysis, real leadership is spiritual leadership.

In the Vineyard, elders and deacons are functional roles in various expressions of service, as opposed to categories or positions. For example, most kinship leaders are functioning pastors or shepherds, the senior leadership team in the Church fulfils an eldership role and leaders of specific ministries or ministry groups would be deacons. Most Vineyards use practical job-describing 'labels' for ministry responsibilities, but some use the Biblical 'offices' or titles. Using the former is to counter the abuse and 'stuck connotations' people have in their minds through previous Church experience and Biblical teaching. This also applies to the increasingly vaunted 'five-fold' or 'four-fold' ministries (depending on how you interpret the Greek conjunction 'and') of Eph 4:11. We do not see them as offices or positions in the Church, but as functions. In fact, the Greek *dorea* (gift) in Eph 4 implies that the person is a gift to the Church, in the sense that his or her presence and function has a particular impact or effect—described as apostolic or prophetic or evangelistic. The person is important, not his function. We call the person by his or her personal name, not by a title. John Wimber did not allow people to call him an apostle, but it is evident that he functioned as one because we can all see the effect of his life and ministry. To quote John, 'You're only an elder as long as you're elding, you're only a deacon as long as you're deacing, you're only an apostle as long as you're apostolizing ...' (There's nothing like Americans for mutilating the English language!)

Fifthly, leadership facilitates and empowers.

Leaders get their hands dirty by equipping and empowering people, by including others and allowing them to participate. It is the art and skill of creating a safe environment in which people can discover, grow, be equipped and function. It is putting things together in a way that enables others to do what they are there for. This means facilitating other people's gifts and callings—getting things done through others in a way that makes them feel it was fully their own doing! It is facilitating what God is doing in and through people, in the Church and out into the world. This is an awesome privilege and fearful spiritual responsibility—to facilitate what the Father is doing, to be a partner and co-worker with the Holy Spirit. Here is spirituality again, the art of knowing where and what the Spirit is doing and how to enhance it in and through the people. This 'art of leadership' comes out of the discipline of being with and learning from the Spirit.

The point is that leaders, by facilitating what God is doing, equip and empower others. They delegate and deploy. A mark of true leadership is the ability to work oneself out of a job. That is why top leaders and staff appointments should not be for people who 'get the job done', but for people who can lead and develop others who get the job done. The function of leadership is to produce more leaders, not more followers.

John Wimber developed a seven-step process that describes this facilitating and empowering concept of leadership: you identify, recruit, train, deploy, monitor and nurture people, and then repeat the process. This is the tried and tested method of developing 'foot-soldiers'. Leaders then emerge from their ranks.

- The first step is to *identify* certain people who have potential in certain areas of ministry. The leader does this prayerfully, often identifying those that are taking responsibility and are motivated in an area of ministry. These people are willing and faithful and 'hang out' with the leader. God also shows the leader who He has drawn and given in relationship, as Jesus identified 'those whom the Father has given me' (Jn 6:44-70, 17:6). This selection process obviously takes into account any serious problems that may disqualify the prospective person—see our discussion on qualifications below.

- The next step is to *recruit* them into the vision of being equipped and serving in ministry. This is the ability of the leader to come alongside the person and win them into a relationship of trust and bring them to a commitment to some structure of empowering or training for ministry and/or leadership.

- The third step is to *train* them. We explained our concept of training through modelling—the 'show and tell' method—in chapter six. Training is not only for specific ministries, but also for life and character formation. Apprenticeship is crucial to the process of empowering and transfering leadership.

- Fourthly, the leader *deploys* those who are trained by matching skills and gifts with needs and opportunities; fitting round pegs in round holes. Deployment involves 'commissioning'—the laying on of hands and a giving of responsibility and authority. It is self-evident that to give responsibility without authority, or vice versa, is a recipe for frustration and failure.

- At this point, the leader must not 'let go', but rather *monitor* those he has deployed. Deployment and delegation without monitoring is a self-defeating exercise. This does not mean dominating or parenting or 'looking over their shoulder'. It means regular times of honest feed-back—both ways—as to how they're doing. This 'coaching' affirms them and raises their level of confidence, enabling them to do a better job.

- The sixth step is to *nurture* those who are being monitored. Leaders do not only facilitate a function, but also care for and nurture the person who functions in the function. After all, they are infinitely more important than their function! If they are not doing well, their ministry-function does not do well.

- Lastly, leaders *repeat this process* with others in other areas of ministry, encouraging new leaders to do the same in their spheres of ministry.

We need to be aware of the role-change that leaders go through as they give away leadership by empowering others—especially in regard to the senior pastor. John taught us how by constant training, delegation and developing of other leaders, the senior pastor goes through progressive role re-definition as the Church grows. I am not going to expand on this because it is well documented in John's Church Planning: the 1st five years (see appendix 4). However, the senior pastor can give away responsibility and some spheres of authority, but remain pastor to all at all levels of growth in the Church. He should never give away his God-given authority—unless another senior pastor is being appointed.

Sixthly, leaders produce leaders by operating primarily in and through team.

Leadership is participatory and inclusive. True leaders are team players.

They build teams and work in and through teams. We don't see leadership as holding on to power and knowledge, nor leading in a detached or arm's length fashion, nor being a 'lone ranger'. Being vulnerable and accountable, within a team, is crucial for responsible and godly leadership. This cannot be emphasised enough—there has been too much abuse by leaders who are insecure and unaccountable. We must not confuse this with 'team-leader-ship'. In any team there must be one recognised and respected leader, or else the team goes nowhere fast. Neither am I talking about leadership that has a token team being ordered around to do the leader's vision and work. Both autocracy and democracy are to be rejected as opposite extremes. There is a tension, a dynamic balance between the leader and his/her team, the fruit of which is realised in the quality of genuine vulnerability and community within the team. It creates mutual respect and releases the gifts within the team—especially the leadership gift of the leader. In this sense, leadership is recognised and given by others, from the bottom up. It is not to be taken by the leader and imposed from the top down. The result is authentic team-work, with both empowered and fulfilled follower-ship and leader-ship for the good of the Body and the glory of God!

Leadership is neither a solo effort nor an individualistic venture. Another angle on this understanding of leadership is the skill of getting 'buy-in' and 'common-ownership' within the team and among the people. Leaders are people who ask the right questions (it is not necessary to have all the answers) and know how to draw from others what is necessary. But more importantly, they are visionaries with a passion and calling to go somewhere or do something for the Kingdom. The effectiveness of their leadership will depend on their ability to communicate their vision and build a team to cre-ate the relevant structures to implement the vision. Leading through team takes skill and perseverance. It is so much quicker and easier to do it on your own—or so it seems. Here is the tension again, the leader can't go at the pace of the team, but neither can he run ahead and do his/her own thing! Team building is basic to integrity and success in leadership. John used to say that before a leader is able to keep and grow people medium to long-term in a team (or on staff), on average the leader will 'go through' or lose three to five team members. So be encouraged, it is a learned skill!

Lastly, our understanding of leadership in the Vineyard, or of potential leaders, includes some basic qualifications.

As John put it, when you are identifying or choosing potential leaders you must have 'a leadership shopping list' in mind. Obviously, the above understandings are part of this list, but we need to clearly and concisely detail the specific qualifications that are important for leadership—both for existing and potential leaders. Again there are some tensions that we must hold in balance. For instance, if the 'bar' is too high, then people have to jump through all sorts of hoops in order to qualify as a leader. The natural tendency as every movement develops, is that the bar goes higher and higher. The Vineyard will be no exception, unless we intentionally work against it. In the early days of the Vineyard people ministered and led with relatively little qualification, with all the raw successes and casualties that went with it. I experienced some of this first hand, and I wouldn't want it any other way. I would rather live with the 'mess' of untamed new life than the 'maturity' of clinical order.

On the other hand one has to be responsible before God and the people—one cannot have the bar so low that almost anything goes, otherwise most of our time will be spent tidying up the mess made by 'leaders'. We have to keep pioneering in order to maintain (and in many places to regain) that raw and radical ethos, that functional and 'missions' edge, or the growing professionalism that strangles most movements will overtake us. The minute we are led by maintenance, and no longer by missions (Church planting), then we decline and the bar goes higher and higher for ministry and leadership. We have to keep moving from maintenance to missions, or else we slowly die!

This tension relates to character versus ability (or gifting). One can be so radical on character qualifications in leadership that the organic basis of operation is undermined and replaced by an ideological correctness akin to the elder brother syndrome. Then organisation replaces organism. Conversely, ability, gifts, talents and skills are very important in leadership, but without (some) character qualifications, they can wreak havoc.

Another tension in qualifications for leadership is the availability of the person, versus their good intentions, gifts or skills in leadership—or even their great character for that matter. In our postmodern world this is a big one. People are busier than ever. The exploding pace of technological development, with its myriads of timesaving devices and gadgets, all promising us more efficiency, just makes us all busier and more stressed. Those that 'make it' in the world, in business, and emerge as leaders, often do not have the time and energy to serve and lead in the Church, although they seem to be the obvious choice. This is a trap! Often those who are available, consistent and faithful are a better choice than the skilled and experienced, but busy leader. However, there is a balance here: some people can juggle many balls at the same time while being effective in ministry and leadership, while others just can't.

There are many more tensions than the ones I have mentioned here. If you read Paul (in 1Timothy and Titus) in regard to his qualifications for elders and deacons—twenty-three of them (can you believe it?)—you will probably be overwhelmed with the feeling of the 'high bar'. But on close inspection, read within the historical context of those Churches, there are many balancing tensions between character and ability, between home and Church, between respect outside versus inside the Church, between spirituality and practicalities, between social and Biblical skills. Although John Wimber's list has just seven points, as opposed to Paul's twenty-three, it incorporates them all.

 ## SEVEN CRITERIA FOR LEADERSHIP SELECTION

An attitude of service and self-sacrifice

We look for people who genuinely want to serve and give of themselves, of their time, energy and money, for the good of the Church. Some of these people may not become leaders, but all of them will be good workers. We are looking for the right attitude. Those who want visibility or a platform to 'do their ministry', or who see leadership as a position, are to be avoided. Recruit those who are willing to get their hands dirty and be directed into whatever work needs to be done, no matter how small or menial.

Their attitude must be that their service (and at times their sacrifice—leadership involves sacrifice) is to the Lord and not to people, otherwise they will quickly be disillusioned and problems will follow. If self-image is too bound up in service, people will be looking for strokes and doing things for the wrong reasons. Leaders learn to receive their recognition from the Lord. As Paul says, 'Whatever you do, work at it with all your heart, as working for the Lord, not for men, since you know that you will receive an inheritance from the Lord as a reward. It is the Lord Christ you are serving' (Col 3:23-24).

A relational vitality with Jesus—a love for Jesus and for His people

In almost all the places where leadership requirements are mentioned in the Scriptures (e.g. Exodus 18 with Moses and Jethro; Acts 6 with the apostles and 'deacons'; Paul's discussions in 1Timothy and Titus), there is emphasis on being full of the Holy Spirit, full of wisdom and full of faith. This must not be viewed as describing a super Christian. It describes an honest disciple in vibrant daily relationship with Jesus. We must look for people who really walk with Jesus. A leader is first a disciple, then a leader. He/she will always remain a disciple. If leaders are not ongoing personal disciples of Jesus, things dry up from within, ministry and leadership becomes a job, and it is not long before others feel and know it. People must minister and lead from the life and love of God within them, from intimacy with Jesus. Once again, leadership is primarily spiritual leadership. One must not feel intimidated by the qualification 'full of the Spirit'. Are we not all supposed to be continually full of the Spirit? (Eph 5:18f).

The way we see these kinds of potential leaders is that they stand out as joyful people. They exercise faith, they keep personal spiritual disciplines (e.g. being faithful in prayer and financial giving), they are active in exercising gifts of the Spirit, they have insight and practical wisdom, and there's a spiritual authority about them. Vibrant disciples make the best leaders. Although one can often see in people particular gifts that are required for a specific job, people who are 'full of faith and the Spirit' (Acts 6:5) can give themselves to almost any job. They emerge as good servant leaders because the Spirit leads and teaches them, and people follow because they are being ministered to lovingly.

At the heart of this qualification is simple but passionate love for Jesus, and therefore, for His people. It is about loving. As Jesus asked Peter, 'Do you love me? Then feed my sheep!' Love is willing and joyful service. We cannot resent the people we're trying to lead, or feel obligated—we 'have to do this'. You don't have to do anything. No one is indispensable in God's Kingdom! Neither should there be any desire to benefit personally from being in ministry or leadership. We cannot 'feather our own nest' at the expense of the people—they are His sheep, not ours! Yahweh got really 'uptight' with the shepherds of Israel because they looked after themselves instead of loving and caring for His people. You should read Ezek 34:1-10— it's scary!

A loyal heart

Loyalty to Jesus implies loyalty to His family, and especially His leaders in the family. One cannot work with anyone who undermines leadership within the local Church. Paul often repeats the phrase 'selfish ambition' (e.g. Phil 2:3) as a cause for disunity. Division is caused by carnality, by wrong attitudes, very seldom by anything else. We call it being disloyal— Paul calls it selfish ambition. We have to be careful of people who will use us for their own ministry or calling. They want to be close to the leader, with an apparent loyalty to learn and serve, but underneath it is to enhance their own profile, for their own advantage. It can come in the guise of 'a calling' to personal loyalty to the leader or pastor. It's false flattery and dangerous. John Wimber responded to such people with, 'You're called to the wrong person, it's Jesus we're serving around here! You ought to go and serve Him for a while.' John made a big thing of con- stantly turning people to Jesus—we are His disciples. We must 'be with Him'

(Mk 3:14-15) through the regular practice of basic spiritual disciplines. Then loyalty to the whole Body emerges, not exclusively to the pastor!

We look for people who want to come along and play the game with us, who want to learn from the leaders and others. It is looking for people who are committed to work with, rather than against, the leader. As John repeatedly used to point out, this does not mean that we have to agree on everything, or 'toe the line'. Loyalty does mean that you speak your mind and are honest about your feelings and perceptions. One should do this in a loyal, not divisive, manner. Unity is not uniformity. If necessary we can agree to disagree and have no loss of unity or loyalty. The test is the attitude and the way it is done. Speaking to the wrong people about the wrong stuff is undermining and disloyal. If the leader, faced with all the reasons, still disagrees, then loyalty means joyful and genuine submission to him/her—not being sulky ('I'll just have to put up with it'). The leader is accountable to God, so joyfully leave God's problems to Him! God is well able to adjust His leaders.

Being trustworthy

This has to do with honesty, integrity and commitment to the light. We look for people we can trust or lean on without them letting us down. They do not have to be spiritual giants or sinless people, having everything 'together'. We are all wounded healers. We only ask for honesty and self-disclosure. We look for people who are in touch with their own brokenness, who disclose it and are working with it. They can be trusted with ministry and leadership—unless of course, their brokenness is such that it overwhelms them and will damage the people. Sadly, in most cases we only find out in what aspect of life or character a person is not trustworthy when they let us down.

Think of Peter around the fire after the resurrection (Jn 21:15-17). He had let Jesus down by denying Him three times. Then Jesus entrusts the Church to Peter after he discloses his sin, vulnerability and impoverished love, 'Lord, you know all things ... I *phileo* you.' Jesus did not break this bruised reed, nor snuff out this flickering candle. Instead He made Peter a leader! Jesus found him trustworthy—or He decided to take a chance! Would you have done the same?

The idea of trustworthiness in the Scriptures had to do with money—not being bribed or bought (Ex 18:21). It also had to do with not being seduced by glory, power and sexuality. Intimacy needs—and other needs—make us vulnerable if they are not legitimately satisfied. They can lead to addictive patterns and a loss of integrity. Leaders have to be trustworthy with money, sex and power—these are the 'biggies'! If leaders 'fall', it is generally because of vulnerability in one of these areas. Trustworthiness applies to all sorts of 'smaller' stuff as well. For example, can they be trusted with confidentialities, with another person's vision and ministry, or to complete a simple task on time? As Jesus said, 'If you are trustworthy in small things, you will be trustworthy in big things' (Lk 16:10-12).

A proven ministry ability

We have spoken about this in our understanding of leadership as a functional reality. We look for people who are motivated, who are already doing ministry and are well spoken of. This applies especially when considering people for weightier leadership roles. They need to be self-starters with a proven capability and a good track record. They must be relatively mature in the faith, not novices in the things of God. They must be respected in the sense that they have earned it—both in the home, at their place of employment and in the Church. Paul lists these things, and more, in his qualifications for an overseer (1Tim 3:2-7). Here is the blending of character and ability. A senior leader definitely must have a proven track record in both.

We need to strike a balance in regard to younger or potential leaders. To involve people from 'the bottom of the rung' and further up, we have to take risks and trust them. We do this within reason. Often the 'permission' that we give energises them into much more growth, service and faithfulness. If they fail, we help tidy up the mess! Proven ministry ability only comes from actually doing ministry—or being allowed to do it—and senior leaders only come from new or young leaders. Some senior leaders risked trusting them! Developing leaders is the essential challenge and task of existing leadership.

Being accountable—being a team player

We look for people who are open and make themselves accountable. This applies not only to ministry and leadership in the Church, but also to their 'private lives' in terms of marriage and family, and work and money. They are people who live a disclosed life, not a closed life (with various 'no-go' zones). It means being willing to receive correction—being humble when confronted and being quick to repent, as opposed to being defensive, evasive and self-justifying. Think of King David when Nathan, the Prophet of Yahweh, confronted him with his sin (2 Sam 12:1-13). Was David really accountable?

There are different levels of accountability for different levels of leadership. Senior leadership is judged by a stricter accountability because of the influence they have on people (Js 3:1f). Accountability should be more relational and organic than structured and organisational. Hence, we look for people who are 'naturally' accountable in relational ministry, which means being a team player. Team players are people who are not conceited nor filled with selfish ambition, but regard others as more important than themselves. They are willing to put their colleagues' interests before their own and to help them succeed (Phil 2:3-4). We look for interdependence in people and avoid the lone rangers or those who constantly pull in the opposite direction. We look for an attitude of relational submission and humility, a co-operative spirit. Accountability operates when one is a team player. We must have confidence to resist the proud, the arrogant and the independent—God does! (Js 4:6, 1Pet 5:5-6).

Having the support of one's spouse (and what about singles?)

If one is married, one must have the support of the one's spouse in ministry and/or leadership. One cannot have the situation where the spouse is indifferent or passively resisting, or even resenting and opposing one's ministry. That would undermine the person ministering and leading, as well as affect the people receiving the ministry. It would also undermine the integrity of the marriage. Paul talks of the critical importance of the marriage and family in the life of the leader (1 Tim 3:2-7). The leader must care enough for his/her marriage and family that the spouse and children truly know they come first, and the Church and ministry second.

Therefore we look for potential leaders whose spouses and children willingly accept their ministry involvement. At best they should sense a common calling to joyfully support and even be involved in their ministry. This does not mean that the spouse has to be gifted and carry responsibility with the leader as a co-leader (many spouses have been crushed under the guilt of the 'pastor's wife' syndrome). The least we can expect is that the spouse endorses the leader's calling to ministry and is willing to live with the implications it has for the marriage and family. Otherwise, when sacrifices are made and extra meetings are called for, the spouse will become resentful. We need balance here. There are rhythms and seasons in marriage and family that require understanding and flexibility. One can become too rigid and expect too much from the spouse, or too much from the leader in terms of his household needing to be in perfect order. The ideal is husband and wife teams. John (and Carol) Wimber always tried to model and aim for that—but within realistic personal and seasonal parameters. The next best is a leader whose spouse believes in and empowers the leader with home support, but is not actively involved in his/her ministry.

What about singles? There is obviously no value difference here, or else all leaders would have to be married before they can lead! We do recruit, train and deploy leaders who are single, but seek to do it with the safeguards that single leaders need. We must be aware of their special needs: loneliness and intimacy, team support, having a 'sounding board' or being 'debriefed'. The differences between the needs and freedoms of single versus married leaders need to be taken into account. Paul is a classic example of being single and leading. If you are single you can give your full focus and energy to the work of the Kingdom, because you are free from the concerns (Paul calls them 'troubles'!) that marriage and children bring (1Cor 7:26-35). The Catholics have a long tradition of wrestling deeply with the issues involved in being single and leading. We in the Vineyard can learn a lot from them.

WOMEN IN LEADERSHIP

Although this is not central to the process of 'building from the bottom up', it is appropriate and needful at this point to make a few comments on women in leadership. John Wimber wrote a leadership letter on this issue (see appendix 4). My intention here is not to go into the Biblical or theological arguments for or against women in leadership, but merely to summarise the 'feel' in the Vineyard in regard to this issue.

John's position was clear and simple. Women can and should lead at all levels of ministry and leadership in and beyond the Church: to teach (yes, teach), evangelise, prophesy, heal, counsel, administrate and shepherd people. There is one exception: governmental authority as in eldership or senior pastor. That is a God-ordained gender-specific headship role. It applies to the home, the Church and societal government. This was John's understanding of Scripture. Headship is not dominance. Male headship is taking responsibility under God to lead and govern from his 'created order' in the form of vulnerable servanthood. It is the rule of love—not exclusive and independent, but inclusive and interdependent. That is why John always encouraged husband and wife teams, to functionally balance and enrich one another without undermining any 'ordered' authority.

Although John maintained that eldership is a function in the Body, and in that sense open to both genders, when a Church reaches the point of maturity when elders are 'ordained' as 'overseers', then it should be male. However, the emphasis on the function of eldership has been such that, in practice, husbands and wives (and at times single men and women) have been in consistent dialogue together in elders and board meetings right throughout the journey of the Vineyard. This is the tension and balance that John (and Carol) sought to uphold and embody. Governmental decisions would be made by consensus within the mixed gender team as the norm and the overall leader would take responsibility for them. The exception would be when the overall (male) leader would need to make his own decision because of a lack of consensus, or take the senior male elders aside to finalize a particularly weighty or sensitive matter so that they take corporate responsibility in 'headship' under God.

In summary, it means mixed gender teams at all levels of ministry and leadership, with both men and women as team leaders, except for the overall governmental team leader, which should be male. The exception to this would be in a pioneering situation where a woman plants a Church and is the senior pastor. The point at which she hands over to a male senior pastor would be determined by the situation. I believe that this, in broad strokes, represents what John taught and practised. But then, he always said we do not have to agree with him to be Vineyard! We are free to adopt a more inclusive theology and practice: that governmental leadership is not gender-specific. To my knowledge, there are a number of Vineyard pastors and Churches that do adopt this position. They ordain woman elders and would feel free to recognise a woman senior pastor.

Where we agree to disagree on aspects of doctrine and practice (except for the basics of the faith embodied in the historical creeds), we should do it without being divisive. Being loyal means we honour one another, and the movement, by publicly acknowledging what is generally held in the Vineyard (or what John taught) and then stating our particular position, but not in a way that says this is the Biblical truth, and by implication, any other position is heresy!

THE ACCOUNTABILITY AND DISCIPLINE OF LEADERS

I will make some comments on the accountability and discipline of leaders by summarising what we learnt from John over the years and by adding some of my own thoughts. This will be more detailed because it has become an extremely serious issue in our current context of decay and compromise.

As previously noted, leaders, and especially senior leaders, are judged by a stricter standard. They are to be respected and honoured because of the position of trust and influence they hold in the Church. The idea of honour includes remuneration for some in view of their services (1Tim 5:17). We are called upon to pray especially for leaders (1Tim 2:1f), primarily for wisdom, protection and faith, because they stand at the forefront of the Kingdom's advance and the enemy's attack. They are at the vortex of opposing cosmic powers! Therefore, they need to be more accountable than most, for their own sake and that of the Church. The best form of protection and accountability is maintaining quality personal and team disciplines.

What to do when a leader 'falls'

It is a serious matter when a leader sins or 'falls' in a way that damages the Body of Christ, that effectively breaks the trust that people have placed in them (through moral failure or ethical wrongdoing). The person's integrity is called into question and the leadership or pastoral calling falls into disrepute. However, one cannot entertain an accusation against a leader in isolation. Only on the basis of clear corroborating evidence can one act (1Tim 5:19). It should first follow the 'normal' procedure laid down for all believers: one-on-one confrontation with the leader by the one who is sinned against or sees him/her sinning. If there is no repentance, then there must be disclosure to two or three other leaders so that they can intervene (Matt 18:15f). Because of the 'power relationships' between leaders and Church members, step one, let alone step two, is intimidating, and is often not followed. 1Tim 5:19 is there to protect the dignity of the office or calling, to protect the leader from false accusation, and to make sure that when one intervenes, there is a reasonable case not built on hearsay.

Once the 'two or three witnesses' (corroborating evidence) have come forward, then the leader must be confronted. A critical stage has now been reached (between v 19 and 20 of 1Tim 5). The way the leader responds to this confrontation reveals his or her heart and character, and it will determine the way the other leaders respond, who in turn will determine the future leadership of the person in question. If the leader responds with humility and grace, no matter if they are guilty or not, then they could possibly lead again. If they respond defensively and aggressively, whether they are guilty or not, their future leadership is in question. If they are guilty and admit to it with immediate sorrow and repentance, then they could possibly lead again. If they are guilty and do not admit to it, or partially admit to it, or justify and rationalise it, but basically refuse to humble themselves and 'come clean' in the face of clear evidence, then their future leadership is definitely questionable. It depends on the nature and the extent of the sin and their response to it.

There are further nuances to this. If the leader comes to his/her colleagues of his own accord, and discloses his brokenness, he could possibly lead again. Even here, his attitude is key: is it real sorrow at grieving the Lord and His people and a willingness to face whatever, or fear of being found out and the consequences for self and family? Paul warns us to distinguish between 'worldly sorrow' that is a false repentance that 'brings death', and 'godly sorrow' that is a true repentance that 'produces life' (2Cor 7:8-13). If the leader comes to, or is confronted by, his/her colleagues, because he has been 'caught', either by someone who 'reports' him or by the other leaders themselves, his future leadership is in question. It also depends on the individual's response when faced with the evidence.

The character issue and the judgement call

The basic issue at stake is the leader's character. The above responses all reveal levels of character flaws. Some are easily healed, but the deeper flaws can take years of diligent work to rehabilitate. The intervening leaders have to make the judgement call. Although this is a great responsibility, it should not be that difficult. In most cases the 'judgement' is self-evident. Paul says that even people 'of little account' in the Church could judge some of these matters (1Cor 6:1-6).

There are further criteria for making this judgement call. A once-off sin incident means a character flaw that can be forgiven. With some counsel and protective measures in place, the leader could probably continue to lead. But did he/she confess, or was he/she 'caught out'? A periodic lapse into sin may mean that the leader's character is flawed, but after a period of discipline and ministry to heal the brokenness, the person can be restored to leadership. One should consider as to whether he blew the whistle on himself, or whether someone reported him? If the latter, what was his response? Lastly, a history of sustained and regular sinning, a secret dark life, that is probably an addiction and/or demonization of sorts, can only be rehabilitated after years of healing. Then years are required to rebuild broken trust. Here we are talking about a seriously flawed character with all sorts of deeply ingrained patterns of wilful disobedience, deception and escape mechanisms. In some cases the person should never be restored to leadership.

The motivation of love and the goal of restoration

The confronting leaders, those 'tidying up the mess', must carefully examine their own hearts and tremble before God in dealing with matters of this nature, lest they are tempted with pride, with the misuse of power, or the temptation to gloat over or shame the fallen leader (Gal 6:1). They too are vulnerable sinners saved only by grace. Their motivation must be to really love the person and the Body, and their goal must be to 'gently restore' the fallen person and to secure the well-being of the affected Body of people. We cannot and must not kill off our wounded, or leave them to die. Neither must we be superficial and do a 'cover-up', and by our silence, or even our excuses, end up lying to the people. The sheep are not as stupid as we may think! And of course, the grapevine is alive and well— even in the Vineyard! The loving pain of cutting cleanly and deeply to remove all the cancer, so that the Body does not fester and the person is saved, is the unenviable, but profoundly spiritual task of the fellow leaders.

We must apply the blood of Jesus in dealing with the sin and the fallen leader. The cross covers all sin for all people, even leaders! We give forgiveness and extend reconciliation to all who put their trust in Jesus. Be aware of the fact that confession is not necessarily repentance, let alone restitution and reconciliation. Jeremiah says (17:9) that the heart is deceitful and desperately wicked, and Proverbs (28:13) says that 'whoever confesses and renounces their sin is forgiven'. Surgery again! However, once the fallen leader has 'come clean' the restoration process begins. Repentance and forgiveness are prerequisites for entering the restoration process, not qualifications for completing the process.

Six steps in the restoration process

- The first step would be to face the spouse of the leader (if they are married) with all the facts, and then process the consequent 'fallout'. The person must also be faced with those they have sinned against, acknowledge their sin and ask for forgiveness (if this is the case).

- The second step is to decide on the discipline needed to restore the leader—the 'judgement call' based on all the responses involved and the character evaluations. What period of time is needed, within what structures of counselling and rehabilitation, etc?

- The third step is to inform the Church. Paul says that they should be rebuked publicly (1Tim 5:20). This is not to shame them, but to save them and the Body. The level of previous leadership and the effect of their sin in the Body will determine the level of public exposure and rebuke (either the home group, or ministry team, or the whole Church). What went wrong, and what the leaders have decided to do about it, must be explained. The fallen leader must then take responsibility and ask for forgiveness and be publicly forgiven. This assumes they have committed to the discipline and restoration process laid out by the other leaders.

- The fourth step is to implement the agreed restoration process. The leader either remains in leadership with some measures in place, or is out of leadership for a while with some rehabilitative structures in place, or the leader is removed from leadership indefinitely and begins to pursue the course laid out for him/her.

- The fifth step is to monitor the progress periodically and at the appointed time to evaluate how things have gone, and then to decide whether, when and how to restore the person to leadership. Considerations like 'fruits of repentance' must be taken into account: was this true or false repentance? How has the person changed? Fruit takes time, sometimes years, to emerge and be seen for what it really is. We must give the necessary time. One of the greatest temptations is to relax the process and even shorten the time in the name of being compassionate and understanding. If the recovering person initiates any move in this direction, it should be a warning light! The time includes the process of rebuilding trust and becoming accountable once again through ongoing personal and team disciplines.

- The sixth step is, at the appropriate time, to bring the process formally to an end (although we will be 'recovering' all the way into heaven!). We do this by either restoring the person to leadership or blessing them in ongoing healthy Christian service.

In conclusion—two important questions and a warning

What happens if the fallen leader feels unfairly treated and disputes the process, or questions the integrity of the presiding leaders, or the local leaders are negligent in dealing with the matter? There is always recourse to outside arbitration through leaders in the broader team of pastors. In fact, it is advisable to bring in one or two outside leaders from the beginning when dealing with a senior leader in a local Church. Outside recourse should be an established principle and the agreed authority to finally settle these matters.

What happens if the fallen leader resists the whole thing, never comes clean, withdraws and fails to submit to the process? If they reject repeated attempts by the other leaders to resolve the issue, then the only recourse is to withdraw fellowship from the fallen leader. This would involve a public announcement and warning that people should have nothing to do with him/her.

If the Church were one Body in the town, city or nation, then the Churches would need to be informed of the 'withdrawal of fellowship'. They would uphold the discipline of the local Church and reject the fallen leader until he/she puts things right with the local Church. This reality seldom exists in our compromised and fragmented Church context. If it did, it would constitute genuine excommunication as described in Matt 18:17-18—the person is rejected with their sin 'bound' to them until they repent. Paul describes it as the raw spiritual reality of being 'handed over to Satan so that the sinful nature may be destroyed and the spirit saved on the day of the Lord' (1Cor 5:1-5 NIV). The 'sinful nature' can mean the physical body— it is handed over to Satan for destruction so that the person is hopefully brought to their senses and repents.

Let me sound a warning here. Because of our seriously compromised and spiritually impoverished state, we must be very careful not to be legalistic and abuse spiritual power. We may find ourselves judging or even excommunicating ourselves! Who among us can stand when the Kingdom is present in pure power? Remember the days of Ananias and Sapphira (Acts 5:1-11)? What was that? Divine or demonic, or both? Was it excommunication or expulsion or execution? We must be very careful. As Annie Dillard says, we should not wear hats to Church, rather crash helmets, because we don't know the power we're playing with! On second thoughts, Annie, crash helmets would not have helped Ananias and Sapphira very much.

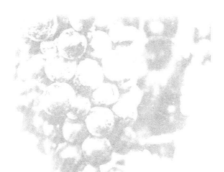

CHAPTER 9

IMPLEMENT
THE PROGRAMMES

Can you imagine a human body without a skeleton—trying to go somewhere? Impossible! Programmes provide the basic structure and give cohesive mobility to the Body. They are critical in the functionality of the Church, and without them it all falls apart. Developing and implementing the essential programmes in the life of the Church brings us to the last step in building from the bottom up.

Reverting to the building image, programmes are the things that happen within the superstructure; the organisational departments and activities within the building. They are the things that are done, that are immediately visible in the Church. For programmes to be really successful they must grow out of, or emerge directly from the undergirding values. They must embody the stated priorities and give expression to the practices of the Church. In this sense, programmes reflect the nature and needs of the Church. Equally importantly, they are directly dependent on the type of personnel available.

One of the most common mistakes among Church leaders is that they see a successful ministry programme and then get so excited that they attend the conference, buy the manual, and come back to implement it in their Church. But do they stop to consider whether their people have a real value for it? Is it their priority? Is there a leader in the Church who burns with the same vision that the programme represents? Later they wonder why it was not a success, why it didn't do what it promised, and why their Church hasn't 'taken off'. They are desperate to make their Church grow and be successful, but often they don't want to do the hard work of building from the bottom up.

Importing or transplanting programmes only works if you have taken the time and trouble to build in a value for it. It must be established as a priority in the Church through being contextualized into your local set up with the particular personnel available to model and implement it. If this is not the case, the leader will have to strive and struggle to keep the programme going. It is exhausting! Programmes should generate their own type of momentum, then they are working. People vote with their feet—if the programme isn't working, it will be self-evident. Never underestimate the extent to which programmes should reflect the underlying values and embody the stated priorities of the Church if they are going to be effective.

We will discuss some of the factors involved in developing and implementing the programmes and structures of ministry. Then we will look at a few of the basic programmes in Vineyard Churches.

 ## SOME CONSIDERATIONS IN DEVELOPING AND IMPLEMENTING THE PROGRAMMES

The flexibility of structures and programmes

There are two extremes when it comes to structures. They are either non-existent, an overly 'spiritual' approach, or they are too rigid and stifling, an overly traditional view. One has to have a 'philosophy' of structures that says they are essential to facilitate and enhance life. They must, however, be subservient to the life that they facilitate or they will hinder and restrict the very life that they are designed to serve. Jesus spoke of this in terms of the new wine of the Kingdom and the old wineskin of Judaism (Lk 5:37-39).

The more the Kingdom breaks through among us and the more our society changes, the more flexible and creative our ministry structures have to become.

That is why programmes must be seen as flexible, temporary and changeable. Here is where traditionalism becomes a problem. Programmes and structures are never holy. They are very human creations—even if they are for God's purposes (they most certainly never should be worshipped). We must regularly reflect on their effectiveness in achieving their stated reason for existence, and if and when necessary we should adapt, change or bury them.

Therefore structures and programmes can take on as many forms as are creatively needed to give full and effective expression to the life of the Kingdom flowing in the Church. There is no such thing as the true or the only Vineyard structure or programme. What appears to be common among Vineyards is quite different on closer inspection. For example, the worship or Children's Church programme in each Vineyard will have creative and unique differences that make it workable in that local context. Although the values are the same, the people and the programmes differ. Thus, at the level of values, we should have most in common, but at the level of programmes we should be diverse.

People before programmes

When dealing with structures, we must remember that we are in the people business, not the programme business. We must be people and relationship driven, not programme or organisation driven. People, through their vision and values, create programmes; programmes do not create people! People are more important than programmes. We must never 'use' people in our programmes, but must rather use programmes to grow and equip our people in their calling and gifts. We must love people and use things, not love things and use people. How many times have people been 'crunched by the system' or 'burned out by the programme'? Do we lead the programme or does the programme lead us? When the programme starts to dictate, then we must re-evaluate. We should only proceed at the pace of the people who have a heart for, and carry responsibility in the particular ministry.

Programmes depend largely on the vision, values and priorities of the Church and the personnel available to develop and implement them. First identify the essential programmes that are needed by the priorities of the Church. Leadership then becomes absolutely crucial. You need the right leader to develop the right programme. The particular ministry is then modelled, the team is created and the programme through which it is established in the Church is developed. This does not happen through committees or 'democratic' processes. It requires faith, leadership and gifting. Either the senior pastor pioneers the programme until a leader is raised up who can take over, or they find the right leader—one who is already doing it—to pioneer and implement the desired programme. As a general rule, if you do not have the right leader, the programme will fail. The process of identifying, recruiting, training and deploying leaders is an absolute priority.

Implementing and monitoring the programme

The leader of the programme must clarify the vision, values and priorities of the particular ministry programme within the overall vision and values of the Church. The leader then communicates the vision to the Church both by modelling the particular ministry and teaching it. Then he/she sees who responds or joins in, as God calls and prompts various people. The next step is to draw a team together from those who respond, identify the various gifts and functions within the team, and create the structure through which the programme can be implemented. The programme should develop organically and run at the pace of the workers and resources available. It must be life-giving, not life-sapping or stressful. We should be realistic and not run ahead of ourselves.

There is the monitoring of both the people and the programme. Generally speaking, if the workers are cared for the programme goes well, but if the workers are not doing well, then the programme struggles. The one exception is if the leader and/or workers are wrongly placed—round pegs in square holes—then things always struggle! One also has to ask the right questions and reflect on whether the programme is fulfilling its stated purpose or if it needs to be adjusted. A good leader will then over time work himself out of a job and hand the programme over to another leader. Thus we use programmes to love and grow people.

Part of the monitoring and evaluation process is to maintain the effectiveness of the programme by resolving the problems that arise. This includes resolving relational conflict and conflict within the programme itself. Most of us shy away from confrontation and trust that things will resolve themselves. But conflict is seldom genuinely resolved without confrontation and/or intervention. Unless one does this, we do not love the people, and it certainly is not healthy for the project.

Steps in resolving relational conflict

Jesus clearly spells out three steps involved in resolving this type of conflict (in Matt 5:23-24 and 18:15-20). Rigorous application of these steps will ensure healthy and harmonious relationships.

- First the private and exclusive one-on-one to resolve any conflict that may arise. The onus to initiate contact and seek resolution is always on both parties ('if you remember that your brother has something against you ... go and be reconciled', and 'if your brother sins against you, go and be reconciled ...'). There should be no talk to anyone else before this step is taken. It prevents gossip and gives dignity to both parties.

- Then if the issue is not resolved, two others must be invited in to help mediate a resolution to the conflict. Mediation is the process of helping the two parties to come to agreement—to be reconciled.

- Thirdly, if this is not successful, it must be brought to the senior leadership, who on behalf of the Church, arbitrate and 'judge' the issue, and decide on certain disciplines and a course of action. This is different to mediation. The parties are bound by the ruling of the arbitration. We should seldom, if ever, reach this step if we are faithful and diligent in applying steps one and two.

Steps in resolving conflict within the programme

This has to do with problem-solving in the programme itself, although it is never really divorced from the personnel involved. This type of problem-solving, or rather 'programme administration', has to do with the purpose, structures and systems of the programme. It always leads to a re-evaluation of the programme and often results in having to work smarter and not harder. John Wimber always used the Biblical paradigm in Exodus 18:13-27 and Acts 6:1-7 to solve problems in programme administration. Moses and the Apostles used certain basic principles:

- First was problem identification and clarification. If the people involved do not agree on the nature of the problem, they certainly will not agree on the solution. This first step is crucial.

- Then, if necessary, an outside consultant can be called in. They often see more clearly and are dispassionate and objective in their analysis and proposed solutions.

- Thirdly, redefine and establish the priorities that are in question.

- Fourthly, decide on the solution in the light of the real problem and the reasserted priorities.

- Fifthly, clarify the roles and job descriptions, or redirect them, or if necessary recruit new personnel.

- Lastly, train and authorize the personnel, both new and old, to implement the solution—the new or the adjusted programme.

These comments are of a more general nature. When we come to the specifics, there is so much one can say and so many resources available (from business and other circles) that it is not necessary for me to go into detail. John Wimber's Church Planning, the 1st five years, is helpful in this regard (appendix 4).

Some other aspects to programme administration

The programme must specifically detail its purpose, values and priorities. Its target group should be researched and defined if this is applicable, and the personnel involved in the programme should be listed, with their various levels of responsibilities and job descriptions. The long-range objectives or goals, as well as the specific goals for the particular year, and the strategies to achieve those goals should be listed. Such strategic planning is important. There should be clearly defined criteria for evaluating how the project is doing, with time-spans and meetings agreed to. What the programme does and how it is run, must also be defined. One has to consider the facility, furniture, equipment and other 'things' required to effectively administrate the programme. Do not forget the money! It is crucial that there is an adequate budget. What about the training needs for the staff and plans to recruit other workers? What about future dreams and plans for expansion or multiplication of the programme? These are some of the specifics one needs to take into account.

We learnt from John Wimber that each department of ministry and programme in the life of the Church should have its own document (a few pages) explaining its vision and structure—with the headings that would be applicable from the above paragraph. When I was in Anaheim in 1982, I went with John to Fuller Seminary for a few days where he lectured a Doctorate of Ministry class on developing a 'Master Plan' for the local Church. I later looked at the Master Plan document of the Yorba Linda Vineyard detailing the overall vision, values and priorities and then each ministry programme in the Church with its own vision and goals and strategies for the year. The idea is to have a five-year plan in broad strokes and then every year to reflect, evaluate, revise and update the overall planning, as well as the specific planning for each programme with its new goals, strategies and budget for the next year. This is how one moves through the years towards the fulfilment of the five year plan.

THE BASIC PROGRAMMES IN THE LIFE OF A VINEYARD

If programmes are primarily derived from the priorities of the Church, then what would the basic programmes of a typical Vineyard Church be? In answering this question, we should remember that programmes are diverse in personnel, context and expression.

Reading chapter six on the priorities of the Vineyard will have given you an idea of how they are embodied in certain structures or programmes in the life of the Church. Each of the six priorities: worship, the Word, fellowship, ministry, training and sending, are lived out in and through various programmes, not just one. The most common and 'comprehensive' programmes would be the Sunday meeting and the kinships (home groups).

The home group programme

Kinships are a foundational programme for all Vineyards. They serve the purpose of belonging, of integrating and of mobilizing the people in the Body. Although there are different kinds of small groups, they generally facilitate worship, prayer, fellowship, ministry, equipping and sending. Some small groups have an emphasis on teaching. The kinship ministry or programme would have an overall pastor/leader to oversee and train the group leaders. The kinship leader would facilitate the actual meeting, and most small groups would have a worship leader. There are many different, unique and creative angles to the kinship programme in each Church and in each local kinship, all aimed at meeting the needs of the people and equipping them to serve.

The Sunday meetings

The Sunday meetings serve the purpose of gathering the whole Body for identity and celebration. They facilitate the worship, the teaching of the Word and the prayer-healing ministry to the sick and needy. The Children's Church programme would normally be part of the Sunday programme, and possibly some other priorities would be served as well, such as training in an adult education class, fellowship around refreshments, or eating together after the meeting. One needs to look at the programmes within the Sunday programme and make sure that they are effectively led and working well. For example, the worship programme will have a worship leader and a band with its particular approach or ethos, with its own needs in terms of instruments and budget. Likewise the Children's Church and the adult education programme. The youth programme, which is equally important, is often on another night with its own structure.

Some other programmes

There are other basic programmes such as training. One has to decide how you are going to train the people in the Church, and for what ministries. Various structures can emerge out of this programme to meet the various needs—through courses or seminars, conferences, translocal team ministry and kinships.

'Sending' programmes have taken on many forms in the Vineyard, such as servant evangelism, various Church Planting programmes, different types of ministry to the poor and missions involvement. Many ministry programmes for healing and recovery have been birthed in the Vineyard. Some Vineyards have an in-depth counselling programme. Others are strong in marriage and family ministries. Some programmes have begun to impact Churches around the world, e.g. CAIR (Christian Adults in Recovery) and Living Waters (a programme for the sexually and relationally broken).

The key is first to do the basic programmes that fully express the values and priorities of the Church. The kinships, the Sunday meetings, the training and some outward (evangelism or sending) programmes would be the essentials for any Vineyard. Then one can grow other programmes that God brings about in the people that He raises up. This can be as creative and diverse as is the mix of needs, dreams, available leaders and resources.

Care should be taken when multiplying programmes so as to avoid spreading resources too thinly. We should operate organically and out of strength, rather than out of weakness. We must never be afraid to close a programme down if it is not working—people are more important than programmes! John always used to say that we should do the basics and do them well; do the 'main and the plain'. The more 'exotic stuff' can come later, if and when God provides the people and resources.

Each local pastor should list or detail, in one form or another (at the information table or in a welcome brochure), the various ministry programmes of his Church. It helps new comers to get an idea of what is going on and it helps the members to find their place at their point of gifting or need.

 ## CONCLUSION

The six-step process we have described in developing and implementing a philosophy of ministry should now be clear. You can see an outline overview of this process in appendix 3. I certainly trust that it has given you a challenging and helpful frame of reference, no matter if you are a leader or a worker or a new member in the Church. If it helps you to contribute more effectively in building up of the whole Body of Christ, then this book has achieved its purpose.

For those of us in the Vineyard, I hope that our discussions have clarified and communicated the essentials that have made us who we are today— and that these essentials will definitely be part of whom we become tomorrow. May we indeed take the best from John and the early leaders in the Vineyard and go on with the mission of the Kingdom to the ends of the earth, and so hasten the coming of our Lord and Saviour, Jesus Christ.

All that remains is to give an overall picture of general characteristics of a Vineyard Christian Fellowship as John Wimber saw it.

CHAPTER 10

"THE CHURCH THAT
I WOULD JOIN"

This last chapter summarises the key characteristics of a Vineyard Church, which have been communicated in one form or another over the years.

The first exposure that I had to a written overview of key Vineyard characteristics was in 1982 when I saw a document called, Vineyard Vision: 1st Draft. It was a 'document in process' that had been worked on and revised once or twice before that time. When John Wimber asked me to develop the document Building from the Bottom Up, I reworked the Vineyard Vision: 1st Draft. It became the last chapter called 'The Church that I would join'. John then did a series of talks in 1982 on 'The Church that I would join'.

A year later it was reworked by Winn Griffin and became part of the workbook, Church Planning: the 1st five years (appendix 4). Then in the late '80s John reframed the basic characteristics of the Vineyard in the form of 'The Vineyard Genetic Code' (appendix 1). That is the radically reduced version, but what follows is the older and more detailed version.

The original chapter on 'The Church that I would join', is now what follows. In some places it is more detailed and different, and in other places it overlaps with the later version of the Vineyard Vision: 1st Draft (which I am using with permission from 'Doin' the Stuff'):

The superstructure of the Church has certain characteristics that make it unique. Each building is different. None of them is perfect in the sense of being the ultimate in buildings. The perfect Church is the combined Church of Jesus Christ at His coming. Therefore, to speak of the Church that I would join is only a pointer to the type of superstructure that I would like to be a part of. This does not in any way imply a 'better' or 'more Biblical' Church. It is a matter of being at home.

Although there is no one Vineyard, for us it is home. We meet in gymnasiums, rented churches and converted industrial buildings all over the world. Each is unique. Yet, all of the Vineyards are like-minded in their approach to God and therefore we would all feel at home in each other's fellowship.

It is not always easy to define who you are, but it is sometimes necessary. The following characteristics describe the Church that I would join (not necessarily in order of priority).

A Bible teaching Church

Our desire is to do and teach just what the Bible says. Consequently, we have a particular approach to the Scriptures. We like to read and believe the Bible as it is, without imposing our own presuppositions and precon-ceptions onto the text. The basic issue for us is experiencing the Bible—not only knowing it. The Bible is the menu that describes living, which is the real meal we ought to eat. Therefore we highly value expository teaching, with an emphasis on doing and experiencing. This also means that we integrate all truth, both Biblical and other, into our experience of living ('all that is in the Bible is true, but not all truth is in the Bible').

A worshipping Church

Our first priority as a people of God, is to worship Him. It is an expression of our love for God. It is why we are alive. Our commitment to a lifestyle of relationship with God flows from our worship. Our worship therefore must be self-disclosing. It must express our thoughts and feelings in our own language, in a manner we understand. After all, worship is the place where we are most truthful with God—it allows us to say in public and in our own quiet places, 'We love you.' It is a time of repentance and the language of our love. And in this disclosure to God, we find ourselves able to disclose to others.

A fellowshipping Church

There is a release that happens in worship that opens us up and makes it possible for us to love and embrace people we wouldn't otherwise love. In this sense, worship leads to fellowship. The goal of our fellowship is wholeness, which raises the need for community. Therefore we place great emphasis on meeting together in small groups. This is where we become known and accountable to each other. We gather to worship, to learn, to explore and share our gifts, and to be healed. In effect, we're saying, 'I'm never more whole than someone else in the fellowship.' We are whole, mature and complete insofar we all are whole, mature and complete. It's all interrelated: worship leads to community, which leads to wholeness. Our fellowship is not just social activity, but something much deeper—something that heals. This fellowship should not create barriers, for even though we have a name, there should be no 'we are we' and 'they are they' to us. We belong to the whole Body of Christ, and as such we must learn to love all the people God loves.

A healing Church

Fellowship and self-disclosure lead to healing one another, and also those beyond our fellowship. God gives different emphases to different groups within the Body, yet all fit together to produce spiritual results. In that regard, we have a compassion to heal. We seek to extend the ministry of Jesus with signs and wonders and the preaching of the gospel by bringing healing to the sick, lame, and hurting. Jesus has granted authority to His Body to heal and preach the entire good news—healing, freedom and salvation. It's really nothing less than the restoration of the fullness of the

Church. Healing speaks of health and wholeness—mental health, spiritual health, social and emotional health, etc. Does wholeness not begin with relationship to Jesus, and then deepen as He works to complete perfection in us? As a fellowship, we want to bring healing to hurting people through the ministry of the Holy Spirit in the compassion of Jesus.

A training Church

In our society training has been viewed as education, but telling is not teaching and seeing is not learning ... we must do. Therefore we must all learn to pray for the sick, minister to the poor, witness, or do any other activity according to the course of Scripture. We have formal occasions for education, a place to receive the teaching behind what we are doing, but we place a higher priority on the New Testament model of relational apprenticeship. This is 'on-the-job-training'. We call it the 'show and tell' method. It is the process of equipping people for life and ministry, and must be open to the whole Body for all to learn so that we end up doing the whole ministry of the Kingdom. This training happens most effectively through the kinships.

A ministering to the poor Church

Healing, wholeness, intimacy, worship and salvation are all a part of our experience. As we gain health as a Body, it becomes of major importance that we reach out to the oppressed poor. It is our commission to minister to them, as an expression of our health and understanding of what God has done for us. The poor are the victims of racial prejudice, the working class, young marrieds, housewives, singles, teens, and the elderly. They can appear to be normal, but they live close to the edge, or in some cases, on the precipice of ruin. They are troubled and desperate, broken by sin in many ways: unemployed, addicted, dropouts, sexually broken, rejects, street people, etc.—commonly known as the 'fourth world'. We are God's extended hands and we must learn to minister to them with our time, energy and money. We must be compelled to operate in love, to clean up a yard for an invalid widow, to secure a job for someone, to bring a food parcel. Ours must be a fellowship with a wide-open front door for all to come, and a love-compelling heart to go and minister to all types of poor and broken people.

An evangelical Church

Evangelism is part of the ministry to the poor. As James says, we cannot try to evangelise a hungry person without feeding them, but to only do good works without proclaiming the good news of Jesus is also short-changing people. We must be truly evangelical and bring people to salvation. We must live in the light of eternity—people are going to heaven or hell. To have a heart for the lost is to have the heart of Jesus. All our people should seek the lost as a natural part of their discipleship, of their belonging in the Vineyard. A regular inflow of unchurched people, of new babes in Christ, will constantly keep things fresh, alive, challenging and healthily untidy.

A discipling Church

Evangelism is the first step in making disciples of Jesus in fulfilment of the Great Commission. Discipleship means radical commitment. Every Christian is called to unconditional surrender of his total life to Christ. Our desire is to have intimate relationship with the Father, free of legalistic, judgemental or comparative attitudes, free to seek God's will for our lives in our every-day activities and associations, as well as our life goals and aspirations. Discipling means that we pursue God together, learning from Him how to live our lives, not scrutinizing and 'discipling' one another into a performance mentality and a guilt motivation. We must create an environment with a merciful ethos that motivates a desire to please Him and organise our lives around Him. He is the discipler and we are a community of fellow disciples, stimulating one another in our common journey of passionate and radical love for Jesus.

A merciful Church

We are called to be merciful to one another and those in need. We neither want to make names for ourselves, nor build lasting institutions, but rather desire to meet the needs of broken people through a ministry of mercy. There is a place where righteousness and mercy kiss. We seek to be that place for people who come to us looking for a safe harbour. They are worn out, often anti-institutional. They may have crossed the line of what is permissible, and have come up against an unrelenting, legalistic interpretation of Scripture which expelled them from the Church. Or worse, they may have become rejects of society. They are like refugees, people without a country—because of their own sin or because they have been victims of other people's sin. Ultimately, they need a safe place where righteousness and mercy come together.

A giving Church

Being merciful means being generous in giving, firstly of ourselves and then of our resources. We seek to be generous, and even sacrificial, in our giving, in our tithes and offerings, so that we may empower and fulfil God's purposes. Regular and generous giving should be our regular practice, both as individual members, and corporately as a Church. Our giving is to God, out of a willing heart, as our act of worship, because it all belongs to Him in the first place (all we have is really His stuff entrusted to us—and it is always 'on call'). We avoid any hype, pressure, manipulation or exploitation from the pulpit around money matters. Resources, money and giving is a Church family matter, where the members must be free to carry their financial responsibilities before God and help meet the needs of the family and empower its ministry in the needy world.

A growing Church

We are convinced that healthy, Spirit-directed Churches grow. And we believe that God grows the Church. If we feel we have to grow the Church, we will fall into humanism—it ceases to be God's Church and becomes our Church. So our approach is to do the basics and do them well, and thereby seek to build healthy Churches. We want to be constantly worshipping God, healing and equipping one another and reaching out into the world in whichever way we can. There should be no dualistic thinking in regard to Church growth—spiritual and structural, qualitative and quantitative growth is all tied up together, the one dynamically affecting the other. We must not get into the numbers and performance game, but neither must we be 'only pure quality' oriented. We must be health and growth oriented.

A relevant Church

Vineyard is a current and contemporary expression of Church. Our commitment is to be relevant in meeting the needs of people and re-packaging Church to be effective in our radically changing world. We cannot become obsolete. People must have easy access by not feeling alienated by a strong Christian or Church subculture. Thus we seek to create a home within our contemporary culture for hurting and lost people without compromising the non-negotiables of the gospel or of Church life. This affects the way we dress, our music style, the way we communicate and do things. It also means that we will have to seek ways of constantly breaking into new cultures, especially the younger generation.

A kingdom Church

(Note that this was originally called 'A Risk-taking Church'. I have adapted it to the heading used in the Vineyard Vision: 1st Draft.) We are in a war in which we have to take risks. We seek to be a Church that really hears God, operates under His direction, is full of vision and faith (faith is spelt r-i-s-k), and is prepared to launch out in obedience to God. Where there is no risk-taking, nothing happens. Like the vanguard of an army returning to claim lost territory, we see ourselves as bringing the Kingdom of God to bear in this life while we look for Jesus to come and win the final battle. We are committed to establishing beachheads in Satan's territory. We are committed to raiding his camp of darkness to free the men and women he is holding captive. Yet we cannot do this alone, or think we are the only ones doing it. Being a Kingdom Church means that we fight side by side, not against, other Churches. We are part of the whole Church—our common enemy is Satan and his works of evil that we are called to destroy.

A mission Church

(Note as above, this was originally called 'A Serving and Sending Church'.) We have a mission from God in the Vineyard, a strong conviction and calling, without which we will die. It has to do with being a serving and sending Church, which is tied up with our understanding of missions. We see the local Church as a mission base to train and send translocal teams out for ministry and mission. For us in the Vineyard, it all comes down to God loving the whole world and the whole Church, and our desire is to do the same. This gives two aspects to our sense of mission and our understanding of missions.

Firstly, our primary calling is to Church planting, which is best done through evangelism. We want to find people like ourselves and love and help them. All around the world, especially in the big urban centres, there are 'Baby-Boomers' who are looking for a cause. They have a need for stability and a need to explore, and they are willing to leave all and devote themselves to a worthy cause. We want to ignite them with the love of Jesus so that they will save their generation and change the world. We want to mobilise a massive missionary force to plant churches wherever the Holy Spirit calls us. He knows the right time and the proper place. He draws the unsaved and joins them to what He is doing in and through us.

Secondly, we see Church renewal as part of our mission. God loves the whole Church and we see ourselves as fully part of that whole. Therefore we must be lovers of the things God loves—people of differing views, theologies, practices, etc. We want to be part of God's work of renewal in the Church to help equip the Church to do more effectively the works of the Kingdom and thus hasten the day of Jesus' return. So our desire is to bring renewal to the whole Body of Christ wherever God takes us and in so doing, we ourselves will be continually renewed.

APPENDIX 1

THE VINEYARD
GENETIC CODE

The first time I heard John Wimber teach the 'Vineyard Genetic Code' was at an International Vineyard Pastor's Conference in 1991. Shortly before this time he had begun to use this way of summarising what the Vineyard stood for. It arose out of a context of disturbance and the need for clarity within the Vineyard. 1987 to 1990 saw the 'Kansas City Prophets' enter the Vineyard and exercise their ministries with considerable impact, both with blessing and controversy. But in 1990 John said, 'The Vineyard has met the prophets, it is now the time for the prophets to meet the Vineyard.' So he actively began to give perspective and direction to the prophetic and 'cut the vine back', as he put it. John gave biblical correction, disciplined a number of the prophets, and reasserted what the Vineyard was basically all about.

John's approach was that the prophetic emphasis and ministry, and any other, both past and yet to come, must fit into and find its place in 'the main and the plain' of who we are and what we do as Vineyard. And what is that? It is contained in the 'genetic code' that was in the original 'Vineyard seed' when it was first planted. It is this genetic code that makes us who we are as Vineyard. John used it often in formal services, when adopting a Church into the Vineyard, or when ordaining a new pastor, or when commissioning a new Vineyard that had been planted and was now a fully-fledged Church.

The following ten hallmarks should characterise any local Vineyard. Although John did not put them in any particular order when he first presented them, I have taken the liberty of putting them in an order that logically reflects our values, priorities and practices. John purposefully did not give Scripture references. His intention was that it would stand alone as a ten-point summary of the basics of the Vineyard.

The Bible is central to our teaching, faith and life. This has to do with simple life-oriented teaching and Biblical exposition.

Worship is our highest priority—not just singing, but not less than that. It has to do with regular corporate worship that is personal, intimate and non-manipulative.

Small groups are the basic structure of the Church; the place of belonging, relationships, self-disclosure, growth, discipleship and practice of ministry.

Spiritual gifts are in every believer—they are to be identified, evoked and exercised for the common good. We must be more gift-based than organisational-based.

Training is fundamental to our being Church—to 'equip the saints' for the work of ministry in all its aspects, and also for life itself.

Signs and wonders are a normal and regular part of Church life—to practise the ministry of compassion and power in terms of healing the sick and broken, driving out the demons and doing the supernatural works of God.

Ministry to the poor is very important to God and to the Vineyard—it should be a regular practice of mercy in terms of feeding, clothing, helping, serving, etc.

Evangelism is the call of every believer—to bring others to Christ through friendships, power encounter, and other programmes of outreach. Real Church growth means reaching out into the world and advancing the Kingdom of God.

Other Churches must be loved, respected and worked with, because we are part of the one Body of Christ. We must seek to have good relationships with the broader Church.

Church planting and missions are at the heart of the Vineyard calling. Every Church must have a vision to grow and multiply and to touch other parts of the world. John always said that the best form of evangelism is planting a new Church.

APPENDIX 2

THE VINEYARD
STATEMENT OF FAITH

Foreword

This document is the result of approximately ten years of work. The need for a statement of faith arose shortly after the beginning of the Vineyard movement in 1983. On one hand, we felt obliged to set forth our biblical and historically orthodox beliefs; on the other hand, we wanted to describe the values and priorities that make the Vineyard unique within the context of Evangelicalism.

While many people have worked on this project, special thanks go to John Wimber out of whose calling and vision the Vineyard movement has emerged and matured. Also, to John McClure, senior pastor of Vineyard Christian Fellowship Newport Beach, California, who has shepherded the process along over this decade, and to Dr Don Williams, senior pastor of Coast Vineyard in La Jolla, California, who rewrote our original statements into the cogent, biblical kingdom framework that follows.

As evangelicals, the Bible is our final authority for faith and practice. Therefore, the statements that follow reflect our best attempt to understand and live our biblical precepts. Upon further reflection, greater biblical insight, or increased wisdom through experience, these statements could be revised. Until such a time, the Association of Vineyard Churches Board of Directors formally adopts this document as our official statement of faith as of the board meeting in November 1994.

We now commend this for use by all our pastors in all our churches with the prayer that God will bless our sincere desire and humble attempt to be ambassadors of the rule and reign of His Kingdom through our lives, that His will may be done on earth as it is in heaven.

Todd Hunter, National Coordinator,
Association of Vineyard Churches, Anaheim, California
December 1994

 ## VINEYARD STATEMENT OF FAITH

WE BELIEVE that God is the Eternal King. He is an infinite, unchangeable Spirit, perfect in holiness, wisdom, goodness, justice, power and love. From all eternity He exists as the One Living and True God in three persons of one substance, the Father, the Son, and the Holy Spirit, equal in power and glory.

WE BELIEVE that God's Kingdom is everlasting. From His throne, through His Son, His eternal Work, God created, upholds and governs all that exists: the earth, every living thing and mankind. God created all things very good.

WE BELIEVE that God created mankind in His image, male and female, for relationship with Himself and to govern the earth. Under the temptation of Satan, our original parents fell from grace, bringing sin, sickness and God's judgement of death to the earth. Through the fall, Satan and his demonic hosts gained access to God's good creation. Creation now experiences the consequences and effects of Adam's original sin. Human beings are born in sin, subject to God's judgement of death and captive to Satan's kingdom of darkness.

WE BELIEVE that God did not abandon His rule over the earth which He continues to uphold by His providence. In order to bring redemption, God established covenants which revealed His grace to sinful people. In the covenant with Abraham, God bound Himself to His people Israel, promising to deliver them from bondage to sin and Satan and to bless all the nations through them.

WE BELIEVE that as King, God later redeemed His people by His mighty acts from bondage in Egypt and established His covenant through Moses, revealing His perfect will and our obligation to fulfil it. The law's purpose is to order our fallen race and to make us conscious of our moral responsibility. By the work of God's Spirit, it convicts us of our sin and God's righteous judgement against us and brings us to Christ alone for salvation.

WE BELIEVE that when Israel rejected God's rule over her as King, God established the monarchy in Israel and made an unconditional covenant with David, promising that his heir would restore God's kingdom reign over His people as Messiah forever.

WE BELIEVE that in the fullness of time, God honoured His covenants with Israel and His prophetic promises of salvation by sending His only Son, Jesus, into the world. Conceived by the Holy Spirit and born of the Virgin Mary, as fully God and fully man in one person, He is humanity as God intended us to be. Jesus was anointed as God's Messiah and empowered by the Holy spirit, inaugurating God's kingdom reign on earth, overpowering the reign of Satan by resisting temptation, preaching the good news of salvation, healing the sick, casting out demons and raising the dead. Gathering His disciples, He reconstituted God's people as His Church to be the instrument of His kingdom. After dying for the sins of the world, Jesus was raised from the dead on the third day, fulfilling the covenant of blessing given to Abraham. In His sinless, perfect life Jesus met the demands of the law and in His atoning death on the cross He took God's judgement for sin which we deserve as law-breakers. By His death on the cross He also disarmed the demonic powers. The covenant with David was fulfilled in Jesus' birth from David's house, His Messianic ministry, His glorious resurrection from the dead, His ascent into heaven and His present rule at the right hand of the Father. As God's Son and David's heir, He is the eternal Messiah-King, advancing God's reign throughout every generation and throughout the whole earth today.

WE BELIEVE that the Holy Spirit was poured out on the Church at Pentecost in power, baptising believers into the Body of Christ and releasing the gifts of the Spirit to them. The Spirit brings the permanent indwelling presence of God to us for spiritual worship, personal sanctification, building up the Church, gifting us for ministry, and driving back the kingdom of Satan by the evangelization of the world through proclaiming the word of Jesus and doing the works of Jesus.

WE BELIEVE that the Holy Spirit indwells every believer in Jesus Christ and that He is our abiding Helper, teacher, and Guide. We believe in the filling or empowering of the Holy Spirit, often a conscious experience, for ministry today. We believe in the present ministry of the Spirit and in the exercise of all of the biblical gifts of the Spirit. We practise the laying on of hands for the empowering of the Spirit, for healing, and for recognition and empowering of those whom God has ordained to lead and serve the Church.

WE BELIEVE that the Holy Spirit inspired the human authors of Holy Scripture so that the Bible is without error in the original manuscripts. We receive the sixty-six books of the old and New Testaments as our final, absolute authority, the only infallible rule of faith and practice.

WE BELIEVE that the whole world is under the domination of Satan and that all people are sinners by nature and choice. All people therefore are under God's just judgement. Through the preaching of the Good News of Jesus and the Kingdom of God and the work of the Holy Spirit, God regenerates, justifies, adopts and sanctifies through Jesus by the Spirit all who repent of their sins and trust in Jesus Christ as Lord and Saviour. By this they are released from Satan's domain and enter into God's kingdom reign.

WE BELIEVE in the one, holy, universal Church. All who repent of their sins and confess Jesus as Lord and Saviour are regenerated by the Holy Spirit and form the living Body of Christ, of which He is the head and of which we are all members.

WE BELIEVE that Jesus Christ committed two ordinances to the Church: water baptism and the Lord's Supper. Both are available to all believers.

WE BELIEVE that God's kingdom has come in the ministry of our Lord Jesus Christ, that it continues to come in the ministry of the Spirit through the Church, and that it will be consummated in the glorious, visible and triumphant appearing of Christ — His return to the earth as King. After Christ returns to reign, He will bring about the final defeat of Satan and all of his minions and works, the resurrection of the dead, the final judgement and the eternal blessing of the righteous and eternal conscious punishment of the wicked. Finally, God will be all in all and His kingdom, His rule and reign, will be fulfilled in the new heavens and the new earth, recreated by His mighty power, in which righteousness dwells and in which He will forever be worshipped.

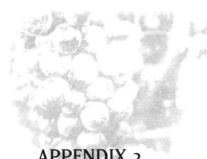

APPENDIX 3

AN OVERVIEW OF THE VINEYARD PHILOSOPHY OF MINISTRY

(As I have presented it in this book)

1. DEFINING THE *PURPOSE*

To be a contemporary expression of the Evangelical Church

To plant new Churches

To bring renewal to the existing Church

2. CLARIFYING THE *VALUES*

The Bible

The Headship of Jesus and Administration of the Holy Spirit

Relationships (and Reality)

The Individual (Grace and Mercy)

Healing

The Kingdom of God

3. ESTABLISHING THE *PRIORITIES*

Worship

The Word of God

Fellowship

Ministry (the sick, the poor, the lost)

Training

Sending

4. MODELLING THE *PRACTICES*

Prayer skills

1. Praise

2. Petition

3. Intercession

4. Speaking in tongues

5. Prayer of faith

Marriage and Family skills

1. Intimacy

2. Communication

3. Child rearing

4. Financial planning

5. Life management

General Ministry skills

1. Communication skills

a. to witness

b. to counsel

    c. to teach

  2. Community skills

    a. Ministry to the Lord in ...

      1. worship

      2. fellowship

      3. service

      4. giving

      5. personal Bible study

    b. Ministry to the Body

      1. giving and receiving forgiveness

      2. laying on of hands

      3. exercising gifts of the Spirit

      4. fellowship

      5. healing the sick

    c. Ministry to the world

      1. the poor

      2. the lost

      3. the sick

5. CHOOSING THE *PERSONNEL*

An attitude of service and self-sacrifice

A relational vitality with Jesus—a love for Jesus and for His people

A loyal heart

Being trustworthy

A proven ministry ability

Being accountable—being a team player

Having the support of one's spouse

6. IMPLEMENTING THE *PROGRAMMES*

Small Groups

Public Worship Gatherings

(the above two are common to all Vineyards—but the context will determine the many other diverse programmes that will emerge in each local Vineyard)

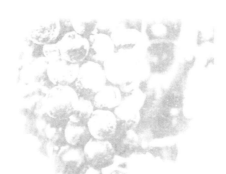

APPENDIX 4

SELECTED AND RECOMMENDED VINEYARD RESOURCES

Many of the resources below will be available through
'Doin'-the-stuff' at www.sales@doin-the-stuff.com
Fax: USA (714) 777-8119

Alternatively try the USA AVC,
PO Box 17580, Anaheim, CA 92817-0825, USA
Email: 102100.2657@compuserve.com
Fax: USA (714) 777-8841

Key audiocassettes by John Wimber:

I am a fool for Jesus—whose fool are you?

Church Planning: the 1st five years

Church Planting: God's heart for expansion

The Kingdom of God

Healing, volumes 1 to 4

The Cross

Spiritual Gifts 1 & 2

Signs, Wonders and Church Growth 1 & 2

Spiritual Warfare 1 to 3

Teach Us to Pray

Wimber on Wagner—Church Growth

Church Growth Leadership

Prophecy—God speaks in and through the Church

Key videocassette:

John Wimber's funeral—Carol Wimber's talk

Books on John Wimber's life and the history of the Vineyard

Carol Wimber, *John Wimber—the way it was,* Hodder & Stoughton 1999

David Pytches, *John Wimber,* Eagle Publishing House 1998

Bill Jackson, *The Quest for the Radical Middle—A History of the Vineyard,* Vineyard International Publishing 1999

Theological and Philosophical Statements

Beliefs and formal documents: (from AVC)

Vineyard Statement of Faith (see Appendix 2)

Vineyard Policy Hand Book — Policies & Procedures

John Wimber Leadership Letters— *'Vineyard Reflections'* (from AVC)

Who are we and where are we going? (Vol. 1 Issue 1, April/May, 1993)

Who are we and where are we going? Part II (Vol 1 Issue 2, June/July 1993)

Leading and developing foot soldiers (Vol 1 Issue 3, August/September 1993)

The Vineyard Movement: steering a course between chaos and traditional denominationalism (Vol 1 Issue 4, October/November/December 1993)

A leadership shopping list (Vol 2 Issue 1, January/February 1994)

Liberating women for ministry and leadership (Vol 2 Issue 2, March/April 1994)

Season of new beginnings (Vol 2 Issue 3, May/June 1994)

Refreshing, Renewal, and Revival (Vol 2 Issue 4 1994)

An Unchanging Destination (Vol 2 Issue 5, September/October 1994)

Learning from our elders (Vol 2 Issue 6, Winter 1994/95)

Calling the Church to a loving and accepting attitude (Vol 3 Issue 1, March/April 1995)

Calling the Church to a loving and accepting attitude, Part II (Vol 3 Issue 2, May/June 1995)

Staying focused: the Vineyard as a centered set (Vol 3 Issue 3, July 1995 - February 1996)

Unity and the withdrawal of endorsement from the Toronto blessing (Vol 3 Issue 4, July 1996)

The five-fold ministry (Vol 4 Issue 1, August 1997)

Apologetic papers: (from AVC)

John Wimber, *Why I respond to criticism, Vineyard Position Paper #1*, May 1992 (AVC)

Jack Deere, *The Vineyard's Response to 'The Briefing', Vineyard Position Paper #2*, May 1992 (AVC)

Wayne Grudem, *The Vineyard's response to 'The Standard', Vineyard Position Paper #3*, June 1992 (AVC)

Wayne Grudem, *Power & Truth—a response to 'Power Religion', Vineyard Position Paper #4*, March 1993 (AVC)

Rich Nathan, *A Response to 'Charismatic Chaos', Vineyard Position Paper #5*, April 1993 (AVC)

Derek Morphew, *Renewal Apologetics*, (Vineyard International Publishing, 1995)

Books written by John Wimber:

Power Evangelism, Hodder and Stoughton, 1985

Power Healing, Hodder and Stoughton, 1986

Power Points, Hodder and Stoughton, 1990

Vineyard Membership Courses (referred to in this book)

'Integration Course' for Kenilworth VCF written by Derek Morphew, PO Box 53286, Kenilworth 7745, South Africa

'Exploring Membership' for Valley VCF written by Alexander Venter, PO Box 67390, Bryanston 2021, South Africa (email: valleyvcf@global.co.za)

Other books closely related to Vineyard and its philosophy of ministry

Kevin Springer, *Power Encounters,* Harper and Row, 1988

Christian Schwarz, *Natural Church Development,* Church Smart Resources, 1996

Jerry Cook, *Love, Acceptance and Forgiveness,* Regal Books, 1979

Books on the Kingdom of God:

G. E. Ladd, *The Gospel of the Kingdom,* Eerdmans, 1959

The Presence of the Future, Eerdmans, 1974

A Theology of the New Testament, Eerdmans, 1974

James Kallas, *The Satanward View—A Study in Pauline Theology,* Westminister Press, 1966

Jesus and the Power of Satan, The Westminister Press, 1968

The Real Satan, Augsburg Publishing House, 1975

Derek Morphew, *Breakthrough,* (Vineyard International Publishing, 1998)

BOOK ORDERS

Name   ....

Address   ....

              ....

Tel/Fax   ....

Title   ....

Author   .... Quantity ....

Vineyard International Publishing
Books can be ordered from the following offices:

Australia
P.O.Box 440, Sans Souci,
Sydney, NSW 2219
Fax: +61-2-95295436
Tel: +61-2-95298811
vineyard@ssvcf.org.au

Benelux Nations
P.O.Box 1557,
3500 BN Utrecht,
the Netherlands
Fax: + 31-30-2340958
Jan_Bernard_Struik@compuserve.com

Canada
VMG Canada
9089 Glover Road
Fort Langley B.C. V1M 2S1
Tel: (1-800) 224-6891
worshipmusic@vineyardmusic.ca

England
Ed & Clare Evans
22 Park Street
Salisbury, SP1 3AU
Tel: + 44 1722 326885
edevans@talk21.com

New Zealand
VMG Aotearoa NZ
116 Wairere Rd
Waitakere, Auckland, NZ
vmg-anz@vineyard.co.nz

Norway
Gregg Shaw, Oslo Vineyard
Moldegata 1
0468, Oslo, Norway
vineyard@online.no

South Africa
P.O. Box 53286,
Kenilworth, 7745.
Fax +27-21-6832283
Tel: +27-21-6712633
vip@vineyardbi.org
www.vineyardbi.org/vip

Sweden
Patrick Engh
Stockholm VCF
Nybodagatan 6C
171 41 Solna
patrik.engh@stockholm.vineyard.se

Switzerland/Austria/Germany
Yvonne Briotti
Mühlebuck 2c
5424 Unterehrendingen
Tel & Fax: +41-562211187
briottolo@cris.ch

USA
AVC USA, Lucie Rosser
5015 Grove West Blvd.
Stafford, Texas, 77477
lucierosser@vineyardusa.org

Copies of this publication are also available from the author on:
www.kingdomtreasures.co.za